Happy as the Grass was Green

© Copyright 2004 Catherine McColl. All rights reserved.

No part of this publication may be reproduced, stored in a retrieval system, or transmitted, in any form or by any means, electronic, mechanical, photocopying, recording, or otherwise, without the written prior permission of the author.

Printed in Victoria, Canada

```
National Library of Canada Cataloguing in Publication

McColl, Catherine, 1940-
     Happy as the grass was green / Catherine McColl.
ISBN 1-4120-1120-5
     1. McColl, Catherine, 1940- —Childhood and youth.  2.
Brussels
(Ont.)—Biography.  I. Title.
FC3099.B795Z49 2004           971.3'22         C2003-904487-4
```

TRAFFORD

This book was published *on-demand* in cooperation with Trafford Publishing. On-demand publishing is a unique process and service of making a book available for retail sale to the public taking advantage of on-demand manufacturing and Internet marketing. **On-demand publishing** includes promotions, retail sales, manufacturing, order fulfilment, accounting and collecting royalties on behalf of the author.

Suite 6E, 2333 Government St., Victoria, B.C. V8T 4P4, CANADA
Phone   250-383-6864   Toll-free   1-888-232-4444 (Canada & US)
Fax   250-383-6804   E-mail   sales@trafford.com
Web site   www.trafford.com   TRAFFORD PUBLISHING IS A DIVISION OF TRAFFORD HOLDINGS LTD.
Trafford Catalogue #03-1499   www.trafford.com/robots/03-1499.html

10   9   8   7   6   5   4   3

Happy as the Grass was Green

- *a memoir* -

Catherine McColl

with illustrations by author

TRAFFORD PUBLISHERS • VICTORIA

For Doug and Elayne, who walked that way with me.

For Andrea and Pamela, who made the journey worthwhile

For my mother and father, who are remembered with love.

Contents

All This and Fresh Air Too 7
Cheap at Twice the Price 26
Googy-Buzzy 41
Brother Can You Spare Some Time 54
And Then There Were Two 62
No Place Like Home 68
Once More With Feeling 92
The Good, The Bad, and the Bugly 102
Run Fast, Run Far 116
Good Old Golden Rule Days 124
The Ugly Duckling of the Diamond 144
Free to be Kids 149
Cowboys, Culprits and Cheap Candy 158
Aunts in the Cottage 165
Season of Plenty 188
A Pinch to Grow an Inch 199
Another Pretty Pickle 206
Scary Kids 213
I Just Go Nuts at Christmas 221
Hogmanay 239
Getting Plastered 248
Poultry in Motion 254

...CONTENTS

The Killer Tent of Doom   264
Blessed Diversions   270
Scaredy-Cat   279
The Little Dog Laughed   287
Fun and Games   296
It's Simply Not Cricket   306
God's in His Heaven   313
Dangerous Attractions   331
Skating On Thin Ice   341
On With the Show   350
Changes In Attitude   360
TV or Not TV   374

Preface

There is no real excuse for my writing this memoir. I have not achieved celebrity status in sport, politics, entertainment or, as it may soon become apparent, literature. I suppose I just wanted to go home again despite Thomas Wolfe's warning, and I didn't want to go alone.

My story begins sixty years ago in the spring of 1942, when everything was bigger and life was less complicated, at least for me. It is meant to be a celebration of the childhood I remember, with the family I loved, in a Western Ontario village for which I have a particular fondness. There could have been no better time and no better place in which to grow up. Of that I am certain.

Wide green lawns and overarching trees gave a sense of cosy togetherness to a village that provided far more freedom than privacy. The sweet, fresh air that brought our little family to the village in the first place, was thick with the scent of grass and flowers and spicy with the honest, earthy smells of the farm.

I begin my tale at the age of two, when I was on intimate terms with table legs and adult knees, the younger of two children, raised through the uncertainties of a far away war by two homesick British immigrants. The village I knew in the 1940's has changed since that time, but I can still trace its broken sidewalks in my memory and move through every room of our old house as if I'd never left. A fence, when I encountered one, was for climbing over. Property lines blurred by time were rarely taken seriously, creating a village-wide playground to explore with impunity.

Growing up is a time of firsts. First pet, first responsibilities, first trip to the dentist, first day of school, first fire drill, first home-run, first Christmas shopping spree, first feelings of love, loss, guilt and fear and first encounters with vice as well as virtue—none of it life threatening, all of it life affirming.

Acknowledgments

My deepest and most sincere thanks to my husband Steve for his patience and perseverance through the lengthy and gruesome job of editing. I could not have completed—or come to think of it, started—this book without your love and encouragement.

The title 'Happy as the Grass Was Green' was borrowed from the poem *Fern Hill* by Dylan Thomas (1946).

An Introduction

A strange mingling of fact and emotion, my memories of childhood return in waves, sometimes distant and elusive, sometimes close enough to touch, magnified by the passage of time.

I remember endless sunny days without a thought to yesterday or a worry about tomorrow. I lived every happy moment in the present tense, taking for granted my safe, cherished place in the universe. But idylls don't last forever, and little girls grow up.

During the turbulence of my teenage years, the restlessness began and the end was inevitable—boredom, apathy, followed quickly by a bad case of wanderlust. I could not wait to leave it all behind. Like a young bird breaking free from its shell, the getting out seemed more important than the reasons why.

* * * * *

The Toronto bound train was twenty minutes late. The first train of the day was often late in January, when the snow drifted across the tracks farther west toward the lake. Mother had come to the station with me, still hoping I'd change my mind. I did not. As if this one train were the last one out of my childhood, I had to be on it or die. I wasn't running from my parents, or even from my home town. I was running *to* something, something out there. A job was waiting. The world was waiting. How long could I expect them to wait?

"But growing up is your real job, don't you see?" My father's insistent voice still filled my head from one of the previous week's *discussions*. One of the many.

"Doing that well will take all your time and patience, and most of mine too," he added, in case I couldn't see what he was about to lose. My father had an enormous amount of patience. Patience is the virtue I have struggled with all my life.

The novelty of working in our store after school for little more than the experience had long since lost its appeal. My older brother, enrolled in college in Toronto, would be close by if I needed him. At least that was one of my best arguments and one I slipped in whenever my parents lost sight of my brand of logic. It had already been decided. I would not be going to college. Why then was I waiting? At a time before educational loans or drug plans and with my father's health in decline, my parents' finances were already stretched to their limit.

"If I had a real job with a real pay cheque, I might be able to help you a little," I reasoned, only half believing it myself. But there it was. I'd played my trump card and didn't even know it. It was also my last card, so if they launched a new offensive I would be in real trouble.

They did not. It's all in the timing. I had won. Or lost. It depends on your point of view.

In time they consented, though still somewhat reservedly. Now with no time for second thought and armed with little more than my high school typing skills, I left behind the safety and familiarity of home for the thrill of the unknown. While it was true my parents could have used a little financial help, my reasons for leaving were entirely selfish. If I had been a boy in the nineteenth century, I would have been running away to sea with my belongings tied to the end of a stick.

We stood sheltered from the wind against one wall of the CNR train station, just as we had done a hundred times before. Ours looked similar to most other small western Ontario train stations, single storied, with a bay window facing the tracks and the maroon paint faded to the colour of dried blood.

Mother fumbled for something to say, but it had all been said. She gave me last minute instructions regarding deportment and finances, and with all relevant topics exhausted, asked if I had a clean handkerchief—anything to fill the silence. I smiled at her honest concern but I didn't look. Snuggling deeper into the collar of my good winter coat, I thought about the choice I had made. If I stay, I'll be buried alive like Mother and never get out. That was easy, I thought. Leaving is the answer. At eighteen I thought I had all the answers. Unfortunately, I hadn't heard all the questions.

It had been a struggle to make them see my side of things, though there were moments on that cold, dark platform when I wished I hadn't tried so hard. I checked my watch two or three times, willing the train to come, to make it final. Despite my best efforts, a twinge of doubt crept in to send my confidence into a tail spin and give the cold a chance to seep into my bones. Suddenly I wanted to go home, to forget the whole thing. It had all been a horrible mistake. What could I have been thinking?

But it was too late. We could see the train through the bare branches of the trees along the tracks, rushing to make up for lost time, its lonely wail plunging me deeper into despair. Mother was already saying good-bye as it screeched to a stop in front of us. I felt her comforting warmth through my coat and a large part of me didn't want to let go.

The conductor swung down to the station platform but kept a firm hold on the hand rail. He was in a hurry too.

"Board!" he shouted, rather too loudly, and presumably at me, seeing as how I was the only one there with a suitcase. It was time to go.

I chose a seat on the station side of the single passenger car, close to Mother, but already miles away.

"I'll call tonight," I mouthed through the grime on the window as the train shuddered into motion. There wasn't enough room on the short platform for the usual cinematic cliché. As dramatic as Mother liked to be, this time she had to be content with disappearing in a cloud of steam, still waving, after only four strides. The effect was the same. Reaching into my pocket for the handkerchief I hoped would be there, I found it rolled into a tight little wad around a ten dollar bill. Mother had given me the return train fare in case I changed my mind along the way. I forced a smile for the benefit of the other passengers who were probably enjoying this gut-wrenching scene so early in the morning, and busied myself stamping the caked snow from my boots.

Slowly we creaked past the livestock pens, picking up speed as we passed the place on the tracks where I had played with my friends only yesterday—or was that ten years ago? Faster and faster, deeper and deeper into the countryside we sped, past miles of snowy farm fields asleep now until spring, through hamlets of scattered houses and stations even smaller than ours.

Can't go back. Can't go back, teased the speeding train, breaking into an excitable clatter as it roared over a culvert. *Rickety-plan. Rickety-plan, Rickety-plan,* it taunted. I stopped listening.

For the right or the wrong reasons, this was how I chose to end my childhood. Soon my head would swim with language unfamiliar to a village so far from the city—subway tokens, rush hour, egg rolls with plum sauce, HONEST ED'S Annual Going Out of Business Sale, and SAM THE RECORD MAN. Life would never be the same again, and I was counting on that. The excitement of the moment crowded any anxiety I might have felt into a remote corner. From where I sat my future looked rosy. But that may only have been the sunrise.

The four hour train journey gave me plenty of time for reflection. I did not know then, nor did I worry unduly about what lay ahead. Everything I did know I had just left behind. I began to tell myself these stories to ward off the homesickness that threatened to overtake me at the two hour mark of my journey, and through the years I've been afraid to stop.

Because my vision is far-sighted, looking back sixty years to my childhood is the right distance for me. Dusty images struggle into focus, familiar voices, unheard for decades, fill my head as if heard moments ago.

All This And Fresh Air Too

In the beginning, Mother did not totally embrace the concept of healthy country living. The prospect of moving to a sleepy village, far from the bustle of the city promised her absolute, agonizing monotony.

"I've been buried alive!" she despaired to my father a month after our arrival.

"There is nothing to do here, nowhere to go—everyone is related to everyone else. Where have you taken me?" My father weathered this storm the way he weathered the real ones, by respecting its force, but showing little fear of a direct lightning strike. However, deep down he knew her words held some truth.

Most of the residents of the village had lived in the community for generations, and over the years many had melded into large extended families. The village offered few amenities, the low cost of living being a direct reflection of that fact, and one of the reasons we moved from the city in the first place. This, and of course the clean, fresh country air.

We arrived by train from Windsor in the warm sunshine of the summer of 1942, leaving behind the familiar trappings of the twentieth century, stepping back into some slightly tarnished golden age. But for all its drawbacks, this world was the first I would recognize and the one for which I would feel the greatest affinity.

The following stories are my recollections, though I will admit to remembering the earlier events only through recountings from the older members of my family.

* * * * *

Our train chuffed past a collection of huts and open pens nestled in the tall, dusty grass a short distance from the tracks. It came to a jolting stop in a great cloud of steam in front of a dull red building on which hung a large black and white sign.

"Brussels!" announced the conductor on his way through the passenger car. "Brussels! This way out."

I could not remember hearing that word before and I wasn't sure I liked the sound of it. Brussels.

"We're here!" exclaimed my father with unnatural enthusiasm. "We're home!" I don't remember anything about our former home. My life began on that train to Brussels, as surely as if I'd been born there.

Mother wore a dark blue dress and a strangely resigned expression. The five hour train ride in the choking heat had taken its toll on our appearances and our moods. She swept the dust from my clothes with her once white gloves, running her hand over my hair in an attempt to make me look presentable. I was almost two at the time, and not averse to crawling up and down the aisle of the passenger car on my hands and knees whenever my parents were looking the other way.

"My God! Where are we?" Mother groaned to no one in particular, as she struggled to lift me onto the rug covered orange crate that served as the back seat of the only taxi in town.

"Even the Devil won't follow me here," she mumbled, somewhat desperately, giving a fairly picturesque description of her first impression of the village. The vintage black automobile waiting by the station was there to take us to the vacant store my father had rented by telephone, and to the vacant apartment above it that was to be our first home in the village.

Over the years, we would get to know that taxi and its driver well. She was the one who drove us the five miles to the CPR train station in the tiny hamlet of Walton where we boarded the train for the day-long journey to visit Mother's sisters in Niagara Falls. Because this train passed through Walton so early in the morning, the taxi driver arrived at our door dressed in her best chenille bathrobe with curlers securely fastened in hair the colour of new snow.

What I remember most clearly about her—other than her high-pitched, penetrating voice—was her set of badly fitting false teeth, which seemed to be leading a life of their own, jumping up and down with little connection to the words coming from her mouth. Of course I didn't stare, and naturally I didn't let on I noticed anything peculiar, though I imagined those teeth to be kept in place with a rubber band that at any moment could snap, forcing us to dive for cover or risk being chopped to bits. Not that I paid much attention. Even now I hardly ever think about it.

For want of a better place, I will begin with my parents' story. My mother and father arrived separately from Britain in the mid-1920's, settling in Niagara Falls, Ontario. I suppose one could say they met on a blind date, but that wouldn't be strictly true. You see, my mother did not expect to be on a blind date that night. She had agreed to date someone else entirely. Because her date had a change of plans at the last minute, rather than cancel he sent his best friend, my father, in his place. A daring plan to be sure, and one that worked in my father's favour. The man with whom Mother had the original date had to settle for being best man at their wedding some years later.

Cautious to a fault, it took my father several years to propose marriage. And then, each time they saved enough money to start their life together, something unforeseen happened. On several occasions, a death in one of their families dictated a year's mourning and their savings found more urgent uses.

Just when their future began to look promising, along came the Great Depression, and their little nest egg, saved so carefully but unwisely invested, vanished forever. Hardly a unique situation for the times, but it did mean there could be no wedding for another six years.

Mother moved away to New York City where she found a position as a governess for a family in Scarsdale, while my father stayed in Niagara Falls to begin his apprenticeship as a watchmaker with a local jeweller. His apprenticeship project involved constructing a working clock, its many parts being made from a single sheet of brass. This had to be done in his spare time. Attending to the jeweller's customers came first. For his sixty-hour work weeks, my father was paid the staggering sum of ten dollars, laughable by today's standards but not entirely uncommon for an apprenticeship during the Depression years.

Through those uncertain times my parents continued to correspond, seeing each other when they could scrape together the bus fare. But money or no money, Depression or no Depression, Mother could not wait forever. She was already thirty-seven. If they hoped to have a family of their own, it would have to be soon. Eventually, even they ran out of disasters. In April of 1936, after an engagement of ten years—time enough to fill two hope chests—they were married in Niagara Falls. Their honeymoon to Toronto had to be cut short when the jeweller lost the keys to his store. Since my father had the only other set, he was recalled immediately. My parents were never able to resume their honeymoon.

Not long after this, the jeweller retired, making it necessary for my father to find someone else with whom to continue his apprenticeship. The search resulted in a move to Windsor, Ontario, where in time they began their family.

My fair-haired, blue-eyed brother Doug arrived first, bringing joy to the world around him. Two years and three months later I came along, as dark as Doug was fair, no doubt protesting loudly at being an afterthought.

The years of sacrifice and bitter disappointment prior to their marriage served to steel them for what lay ahead.

And what lay ahead was World War II. My parents were part of an unlucky generation who endured more adversity with less money than any generation before or since—and they did it all without benefit of cars, television, blue jeans, or birth control pills. Inconceivable.

Born in the closing year of the nineteenth century, my mother was a strong, capable woman—tall and broad shouldered, accustomed to swimming in the cold lochs of her native Scotland. She wanted more than anything else to become a geologist, but having lost her parents by the age of ten, the money needed for the years of study was not available. Instead she worked in the office of a Clydeside shipbuilding firm until she left Scotland for Canada in her early twenties. Three of her sisters were already living in Niagara Falls.

My earliest recollection of Mother is of her shiny black hair drawn into a lustrous coil at the nape of her neck, in the style of the 1940's. Her expressive dark eyes could warm a room with a twinkle or bring it crashing down around its foundation with one angry glance. Although her generosity was legendary, taking advantage of her was done at your peril. She made me a lover of music, flowers and stories, and a keen observer of nature, from the tiniest insect to a sky-ripping, rip-snorting thunder storm. The name Jean suited her.

My father, an infinitely gentle Englishman, laughed easily and enjoyed being around people. Dealing daily with the public came naturally to him, but his debilitating fear of failure and his horror of debt kept his business small and relatively safe from any threat of prosperity. Being the eldest of six children, he started his working life at the age of fourteen in order to help support his younger brothers and sisters. Working at first in a bakery, he later apprenticed as a last maker in the shoe industry of his native Northampton. Eager to find a more secure future, he left England for Canada at the age of twenty-one.

Even as a young man, my father had only a fringe of black hair, with a few lonely strands on top. These he covered carefully with a grey felt fedora whenever he ventured outdoors. Every man wore a hat of some kind, and because hats were only worn outside, there were hat racks inside every front door, shelves for them in church, and hatcheck girls in restaurants. My father's hats always had three tiny colourful feathers on the side, which I played with until they molted.

Firmly believing his station in the community demanded it, he dressed in a suit and tie before opening his store every morning at nine o'clock. With his limitless patience, he took pleasure in the hours of meticulous work involved in making a watch run on time. Under the little circle of light from his bench lamp, he worked late into the night repairing watches whose tiny pieces could barely be seen. His few leisure hours were filled reading Shakespeare, the classics, his many books of poetry and any newspaper within reach.

Asthma plagued my father for most of his life, but when my brother contracted the same ailment at the age of two, my parents made the decision to leave the polluted air of Windsor—air that drifted constantly from industrial Detroit across the river. This move meant starting a business of their own, with two small children and very little money. The uphill battles that were a part of their past now looked as if they would be part of their future.

A lengthy search for an affordable store to rent brought our little family to Brussels, a village of eight hundred in the clean, fresh air of the western Ontario countryside. Mother saw the move as merely a beginning, a springboard to a larger community when my father's health improved. But it did not improve. Not substantially. And so they stayed in Brussels—happy most of the time—for the next thirty-four years.

The adjustment to Brussels proved to be an arduous one. It was especially hard for my mother who had lived for years in the cities of Glasgow and New York. Several years into the War, with scarcities growing daily, my parents opened the doors of their new store, uninitiated to the complex politics of village life and known to no one but each other.

With his homemade workbench and watch repairing tools, a few items of stock and an unshakable faith in God, my father opened for business on Turnberry Street, next door to the bake shop. Starting a business such as ours, in a village well removed from the main highways and populated largely by retired farmers, was a financial risk my parents accepted in order to find a healthy place to live. It had not been intended as a 'get rich quick' venture, and just as well. Although Brussels with its lack of industry was naturally healthy, there was no question that we were in the wrong business in the wrong place at the wrong time to get rich quick.

* * * * *

Split down the middle between the townships of Morris and Grey in the county of Huron, Brussels sat quietly on the banks of the Maitland River, deep in rolling farm land—land that had been scraped clean by receding ice-caps sometime before we arrived. The village had once been a thriving centre with industry enough to support a larger population. But that was before a fire wiped out most of the business district at the turn of the century, seriously decreasing the size and significance of the town. By 1942, a fifteen minute walk in any direction took us well out of the village, and I did not walk quickly in those days. Still, remnants of its former glory gave Brussels something of an air of faded prosperity. Ragged cement walls, crumbling and long forgotten, spoke eloquently of industries that years ago had enlivened the community. Yellow brick buildings of three or more stories exist to this day on the main street, but in most cases only the first two floors have been occupied for seventy-five years. Two hotels, 'dry' since the era of Prohibition, catered to a few stranded commercial travellers who called on local businesses, while most of their once bustling rooms remained empty.

Turnberry Street ran through the business district and was wider than most, possibly designed to handle the crush of traffic that once had been. Without a traffic light or even a stop sign at the main intersection, nothing kept potential customers from whizzing through the village and out the other side without stopping to see what it had to offer. Sometimes they didn't even slow down.

Every store on Turnberry Street had at least one display window, even if chicken feed was the only product being artfully displayed. Although most windows hinted at the line of merchandise for sale within, the window of one vacant store featuring a display of stretched crepe paper faded to the colour of cement, apparently advertised a fresh shipment of sick flies, dizzily buzzing on their backs or peacefully decomposing among the rosettes.

For the most part, the businesses on the main street reflected the needs of the village. There were three family-owned grocery stores smelling deliciously of oranges and celery, the way grocery stores ought to smell, and an old fashioned general store displaying, under a glass dome, the largest wedge of cheddar I'd ever seen. Deeper into the gloom, to the rear of the store, I'm sure we could have found both soup and nuts.

Four garages kept busy at a time when few families owned cars, and managed to stay that way until the demand for them became real later in the decade. Filling our need for the four basic food groups—salt, sugar, chocolate and grease—several restaurants and two lunch counters stayed open far into the night.

One of the lunch counters sold the only hamburgers in town, the other the only milk shakes. Why the two lunch counters did not combine forces to serve both hamburgers and milk shakes seems an example of short-sighted business thinking. But then again, specializing allowed them to be independent while avoiding any personal animosity.

Wimpy's, the smaller of the two, sold the best hamburgers on the planet, while hiding a mysterious darkened poolroom behind two swinging doors. Children were not permitted behind those doors, but we could hear the balls clacking against one another and could pick up strange scraps of male conversation that made no sense to us at all, "Five in the corner pocket." Clink!—Clump! What could that mean? The waves of tobacco smoke wafting over the swinging doors threatened to overwhelm even the heady aroma of frying onions, though it was an empty threat.

Coleman's Restaurant, with its sticky, high-sided booths and the only juke-box for miles around, sold authentically English fish and chips, sprinkled with salt and malt vinegar and wrapped in newspaper. They were greasy, but we considered them delicious beyond belief.

In addition to the restaurants, the business district in the 1940's included two hotels, two attractive clothing stores, a butcher shop, and a bakery—a place permeated with the best smell in life—bread. The bread was sold unsliced and unwrapped, the way God intended, with tops dark and crisp. We liked it as warm from the oven as we could get it, and since we lived next door, this wasn't hard. We consumed tons of it, its spongy white monotony broken only by the occasional surprise we found in it—paper, string, a bottle cap, and once a cigarette butt. These were the days of happy-go-lucky baking, and those bakers were as happy-go-lucky as you would find anywhere.

Several barbers kept the male population looking neat while smelling sweet, and a pretty millinery shop thrived at a time when it was still necessary for women to wear a hat to church. A busy cobbler mended everything from saddles to dress shoes, his shop bearing an unequalled smell of shoe polish, sweaty feet and horses. There were two drug stores in the village, each smelling of wintergreen. One had a pot-bellied stove that attracted a steamy circle of men on snowy mornings. We had a well-stocked furniture store that doubled as one of our two recession-proof funeral businesses, two hardware stores, a busy branch of the CANADIAN BANK OF COMMERCE, and a blacksmith's shop for those who held onto the past more out of necessity than nostalgia.

Brussels could also claim a well-subscribed, family-run weekly newspaper, *The Brussels Post*, whose occasional typesetting error kept the village smiling for days, ensuring that every word was read with interest. One such item, made more provocative by a slight rearrangement of letters, announced: *The Garden Club of the Majestic Women's Institute met on Thursday afternoon to exchange pants and slips.* I could not possibly make that up. Nor could I do without this addictive six-page letter from home when I moved away from Canada for a few years. It was mailed to me in bundles of four every month.

Brussels had a relatively extensive public library for a small community, a mysterious Gentlemen's Club (which I hear had a working spittoon), a busy town hall with a lonely, unused jail cell, a sturdy red brick Post Office smelling of brass polish, a telephone switchboard in use since 1909, plus two or three long-suffering telephone operators, four busy churches, and after the War, two tireless and fast-driving family physicians. Ever mindful of our safety and welfare, the lone village constable in his navy blue uniform with the silver buttons proudly patrolled the streets of the village on Saturday nights. The rest of the week, out of uniform, he doubled as the village bell ringer and general custodian.

When one is seven, there are few things in life more amusing than the mention of a bodily function, however benign. Words printed on a tiny sign, *Irene Pease Upstairs*, spoke more eloquently than necessary of the only hairdresser in the village at the time. Even without taking the spelling of the name into account, we considered the sign to be lie-down-and-die-laughing hilarious. With only one style in her repertoire, Miss Pease, as she was universally known, worked diligently to make every woman in the village look exactly like every other. Waves, pin curls and no complaints freed her from the drudgery of learning any other.

On the wilder side—and what community didn't have one?—we had a flourishing boot-legger who kept a certain clientele happily weaving through life while covering his tracks with a legitimate, if disorderly, business. We were told a shady character lived in that junk yard, but before I knew what a boot-legger was, I thought him to be a sort of shifty cobbler, someone who had been hanging around the wrong feet.

The residential areas on either side of the river lay green with dappled shade in summer and deep in snow in winter. Of indeterminate age and style, the houses ranged from modest to ornate, from one-story frame cottages to gracious Victorian mansions with wide, sweeping verandas dripping with gingerbread and widow's walks, just for show. All properties, large or small, had gardens alive with colour. Small barns stood behind most of the larger homes, memories of the horse and buggy days.

Life in our village was intensely communal. Having no movie theatre and few other diversions, we enjoyed church concerts, baseball games, card parties, dances and each other. Like living life in a fish bowl, few details were hidden and not much came between us and the intimate details of our neighbours' lives. Whether comic or tragic or somewhere in between, we had only each other for entertainment.

* * * * *

We lived at first in a dismal apartment above our rented store, as much out of a lack of available housing as out of a lack of funds. I remember little about it other than its dingy yellow colour, a shade that seemed to be on every wall in town at the time. With no cupboards for storage or shelving of any kind in the apartment, my mother put her irreplaceable crystal stemware on a card table in one corner of the living room, a place she considered to be safe from harm. However, she had not bargained on my two-year old curiosity for things shiny. Before she could save us, we lay in a splintered heap beneath the upturned card table, some of us in more pieces than others. If I earned any scars from that incident—either mental or physical—they have long since blended with the rest, though the incident remained indelibly etched on my mother's mind for life.

My brother's playmates came from the families who lived in and around the business district. Together they spent the first long winter digging tunnels inside the snow banks that lined both sides of Turnberry Street. A long line of children entered the tunnel system, crawled for five minutes through a pale blue twilight and emerged at the other end a block away. It may have been a marvel of engineering or just good luck, but to my knowledge, everyone who crawled in crawled out at the other end.

Many mornings we awoke to the sound of bells. The bells were coming from the harnesses of the snowplough horses, a team of great furry animals with feathered hooves, stamping down the main street, snorting out clouds of steamy breath as they pulled a V-shaped wooden plow laden with field stones. Even with this extra weight, they could only shear off the top layer of snow, leaving behind them a shiny, snail-like silver trail for the farmers' sleighs to follow. There were still many horse-drawn sleighs in use, and early mornings were merry with bells as area farmers arrived with loads of wood for sale or grain for the chopping mill.

Still too little to play with my brother and his friends in the snow tunnels, I kept busy in my red woollen snowsuit, dunking little icebergs I found while sitting in the middle of the freezing puddles behind the store. I don't remember feeling the slightest hint of discomfort, though I must have been soaked to the skin with ice water most of the time.

Snow removal in Brussels in the 1940's was left to the whims of nature, April often arriving before the last of the snow banks disappeared completely. As the days lengthened into spring, the time seemed right for me to get to know my neighbours, beginning with those most approachable. Left alone for a moment, I found my way onto the knee of one or other of the older gentlemen who lazed about each day on the green wicker armchairs lining the verandah of the Queen's Hotel.

When they asked my age, I told them my father said I was half-past two. The name I provided them was the one I had chosen for myself. Long before I heard the story of Paul Bunyon and his blue ox, 'Babe' was the name I preferred. So Babe it was for as long as we lived on Turnberry Street.

My new old friends did nothing all day, getting warmed up for a time when they'd be doing less than that. They smelled strongly of liquor, pipe tobacco and old age, diametric opposites of my father, who smelled of shaving soap and silver polish. I listened to the stories they told each other, eagerly accepting all offers of linty gumdrops from each of their vest pockets. Most of their days were spent playing cards in one of the back rooms of the hotel, emerging late in the afternoon for a little fresh air and a bout of political fisticuffs with anyone who happened by. Having no grandfathers of my own, and with no limit to their time or attention, I found their attraction an irresistible one.

Sadly, these happy hours with my adopted grandfathers were drawing to a close. As spring turned to summer, my family prepared to move again, this time from the cramped apartment above the rented store to a roomy house on the edge of town, where we would be even closer to the clean, fresh country air.

Cheap at Twice The Price

HOUSE FOR SALE—$700 AS IS—INQUIRE WITHIN. The hand-painted sign, nailed to the maple tree in the overgrown front yard advertised a 'fixer-upper', but one with undeniable possibilities.

When my parents bought this house as is, the 'as is' part meant no central heating, electricity or inside plumbing. It appeared to be solid enough for my father, seeing as how the brick walls went all the way to the roof and none of them were missing. Mother recognized its well-hidden qualities right away and these seemed to ease the sting of having to buy the house 'as is'. Barely within their budget, they spent every cent they had to purchase their first—and as it turned out, last—house. With no one in whom to confide, they took a chance on it being a sound investment and worked tirelessly to make it appear that they knew what they were getting into—which of course is doubtful. And so we moved from the comparative bustle of the main street, to the quietest corner of the village.

Nestled in one corner of a double lot, this two-story yellow brick house became our family home for the next ten years. A neat row of white currant bushes separated our two lots, one considerably wilder than the other but both of them in desperate need of taming. Two old apple trees, several maples and a domineering spruce provided us with wormy fruit, ample shade, and a pleasant woodsy smell.

The house had two floors of rooms of assorted sizes, a musty little cellar with an earthen floor, an old fashioned hand pump over the kitchen sink, and a family of field mice in the pantry—all for seven hundred dollars. A steal at twice the price. Kerosene lamps were used at first to light the small dark rooms, while a square galvanized tub, used as a rinse tub on laundry days, doubled as our only bathing facility. Mother set it up in the warmth of the kitchen next to the wood stove, our only supply of heat and hot water. This was the extent of the plumbing, making it as difficult to achieve cleanliness as it was to achieve godliness.

Set off by itself in almost a half acre of neglected wilderness and bordered on two sides by open fields, our new home offered a peaceful existence, our fortress against the world. Happy to have their first real home at last, and with far more optimism than experience my parents set to work immediately to drag the house into the twentieth century. 'Immediately' had more to do with intent than reality. A home owner with the nerve to start a project of this type during the War was asking for delays of unknown duration. Nothing ever happened in a hurry in Brussels at the best of times, but in the early 1940's no major renovations were being done at all.

Finding an item to improve our living conditions was hard enough, but finding someone who knew how to install it turned out to be the real quest. Most of the tradesmen who had lived in Brussels were serving overseas in the armed forces, leaving us at the mercy of the few remaining pre-war supplies, often years out-of-date, and workmen who had forgotten most of the skills they claimed they once had. Dubious indeed were the credentials of the few local tradesmen, their installations more a matter of faith than of any guarantee.

After one or two disastrous starts, further frustrating situations were avoided by turning them into work-bees, cheerfully undertaken by my mother's three Scottish brothers-in-law, all with years of hard-earned experience in repairing their own homes. A carnival atmosphere spread through the house as we prepared for their arrival. Mother called for an organ tuner in anticipation of the musical evenings that would surely follow the busy days. Because tea made the world go round for my family, enough ration stamps were found for an emergency supply. Makeshift cots were set up in my parents' large bedroom for my brother and myself, leaving our bedrooms free for our relatives.

We adored them all. No amount of disruption in our daily lives diminished the pleasure of their visits. They brought with them laughter and music, and a bit of city sophistication lacking in our country-bound lives. Although I will admit the sophistication was lost on me, their laughter worked like a tonic on all of us.

Uncle Hughie, my eldest uncle and husband of Mother's sister Lizzie, was the undisputed comic of the family. At first, because I could not pronounce his name, I called him Uncle Shooie. My cousin Caroline, having a similar problem, called him Uncle Fewie. In retaliation for either our impertinence or our inconsistency, he called us Brat Number One and Brat Number Two. I was Brat Number Two. Ever the afterthought. It was easy to tell Doug was his favourite. Uncle Hughie called him Oor Doogie, when he wasn't calling him Son. In my heart of hearts, I would have preferred the name Hen, or at least Brat Number One, but he just didn't get it.

I remember Uncle Hughie as a small, round man with laughing brown eyes, a fringe of greying hair and a Scots brogue that edged dangerously toward complete indecipherability. Because his visits to our house were rare, it took my brother and myself several painstaking days to get used to his broad Scottish accent. On one of his visits he greeted us at the front door with an enormous bear hug each and a string of Glessca patter that didn't come anywhere near the English language.

"Och aye! Ma tae brrraw bairrrns. Ayrrr ye guid the dee or didya nae moo the coo?" (Or something just as impenetrable.) Then he peered at us through his bushy eyebrows expecting a response. We were struck dumb. He could have been speaking Norwegian for all we knew. Uncle Hughie tried again—this time louder.

"What's rang wi' you tae? Dee ye nae speak the tongue or ayrrr ye frae Ecclefechan?" Since only he got his little joke, he ended this harangue with a wheezy "Hee, hee, hee," that shook his whole round self. We were either being teased or lectured about something, but we weren't sure which or for what, so we stood there looking contrite, amused and dumbfounded all at the same time.

"Jeannie! Yer wanes willnae speak tae me? Arr these tae daft the dee? Och, naever mine. Awa' wi ya noo and play, you tae. Jeannie? I could murrdurr a scone! Whurr's ma tea?"

Now 'tea' we understood. Mercifully Mother appeared at his elbow to steer him toward the Brown Betty tea pot and the plate of scones awaiting his approval. We were momentarily saved from further embarrassment, but we knew it was only a matter of time before he'd feel the need to communicate with us again.

A definite man's man with years of service in the British Merchant Marine at the turn of the last century, Uncle Hughie had a real tattoo and very hairy ears.

During his off-duty hours at sea, he kept himself busy by knitting. This was not as strange as it sounds for seamen at the time. When I wasn't imagining him with a parrot on his shoulder, I was imagining him visiting every port around the world—not for the usual pier side entertainment you understand—but for more yarn. Aunt Lizzie and many of his seven sisters-in-law wore the creations he had made while sailing off to Singapore, Shanghai, Bombay, or Durban.

As loud and boisterous as any man we'd ever known, Uncle Hughie played with us by his rules and only his rules. He gave us whisker rubs that left us protesting and rosy cheeked. He tickled and flung us around like rag dolls. But if we suggested he play one of our games—where we might have the upper hand for a change—he always gave us the same excuse:

"Awa' wi ye noo! Cannae run aboot wi a bone in ma laig! Jeannie, I've nae tea!" So, with nothing better to do, I crawled up onto his knee to inspect his hairy ears at close range. Uncle Hughie's hearing deteriorated as he grew older, perhaps explaining why he conversed with everyone at the top of his lungs. I suspected he couldn't hear because his ear holes were too full of hair, and one day I told him so, justifying his pet name for me.

Occasionally he'd let us help with the renovations, running to bring him a hammer, a screwdriver or another cup of tea. Because he seemed to have a language all his own, we were forever complying to requests we didn't fully understand. Once he sent us to the hardware store for apunna hoofinales. We didn't know what he wanted, nor did Aunt Lizzie seem the least bit interested in interpreting.

"Apunna hoofinales! Hoofinales!!—Away wi' ye noo, I'm busy! Lizzie! It's hot up heerrrr. Whadja dae wi' ma bunnet?" And those seemed to be his final words on the subject.

We practised the mysterious request all the way to the hardware store.

Apunna hoofinales. Hoofinales. Apunna hoofinales.

"Uncle Hughie sent us for apunna hoofinales, Mr. Gillespie," Doug requested, hoping he would know exactly what we wanted.

"What was that again? Good grief! What did you say?"

"Apunna hoofinales, please," Doug repeated, somewhat louder, hoping that the same decibel level as the request was given would somehow make it clear. It didn't.

Mr. Gillespie stood behind his counter thoughtfully stroking his wiry grey mustache, every bit as mystified by our request as were we.

"Apunna hoofinales you say?"

"Yup! Apunna hoofinales."

"Who sent you for this?"

I tried this time, putting more emphasis on the apunna, in case that was the key word.

"Uncle Shooie sent us for APUNNA hoofinales."

"What exactly is your uncle doing at your house?"

"Drinking tea," I replied. "On the roof."

"Uncle Hughie is fixing the roof," Doug corrected, with an older brother's exasperated tone. He never had any trouble with our uncle's name either.

"Hoofinales apunna, hoo-finales, apunna hoof-inales. For the roof, you say?" he repeated our words over and over again as if determined to crack the code. Finally, after much deliberation with himself, a smile crept across his face.

"Hoof! Roof! I bet I know what he wants," he exclaimed with a note of victory in his voice, "roofing nails of course. A pound of roofing nails it must be."

"O.K." we agreed in unison, happy to be done with the whole thing, and not eager to explain our uncle's strange command of the English language.

The mystery had been solved. Mr. Gillespie's eyes crinkled with good humour under his shaggy eyebrows. We ran all the way home to present Uncle Hughie with his punna hoofinales. When we tried to explain the trouble we'd had with his request, we found little sympathy.

"Och, yer daft! Awa' an' bile yer heids! Hee, hee, hee!"

Doug and I hee, hee, heed at that one too. Boil our heads indeed! We were beginning to understand him. Scary.

When the renovations were complete, it was with a sigh of relief that Mother flipped a light switch to put behind her the daily chimney cleaning and wick trimming chores of the former century. Caring for the kerosene lamps had been explained to me in such detail that I lived in fear of the time I would assume the task on my own. With the installation of electrical wiring, the lamps were relegated to the top shelf of the pantry, and we peered into dark corners where no light ever shone before.

* * * * *

After several summers of these family work-bees, our house began to accumulate most of the modern conveniences available at the time. The sprawling gardens, where Mother had been busy working her special magic, began to take shape too, growing in size and number with her experience. As hard as she tried to keep up with garden, house, two small children, and her duties in the store, it became clear she could not be everywhere at once.

One particularly busy day when she had laundry to do and baking in the oven, I grew tired of my swing and my sand box and decided to visit my father, figuring he'd have more time to spend with me. After all, he did nothing all day but sit at his workbench looking through a funny black thing and fiddling with shiny little wheels.

As the summer temperatures soared, I began to develop an aversion to shoes and clothes of all kinds, scattering them in every direction. This being one of the hotter days, I had already shed my sweater and my shoes and socks, running through the damp grass in my bare feet. The hem of my dress, now wet with dew, stuck to my legs after crawling under the currant bushes to retrieve a neighbour's cat. It too had to go. That left me in underwear that hung a little too loosely even when dry, which wasn't a constant state. Off they came. The back lawn was beginning to resemble an exploded laundry. Without a word to Mother, I toddled off down the familiar streets toward our store dressed only in my hair ribbon. I don't recall meeting anyone, though startled glances would hardly have stopped me.

I'm not sure who was the more surprised, my father or I. He did not seem to be as thrilled to see me as I had hoped. Instead of his usual smile, he made the same face I saw only when he hit his finger with a hammer. He rescued me from my struggle with the front doorknob, wrapped me in his suit jacket, and whisked me to the 5¢ to $1.00 Store across the street to buy something for me to wear. Strange as it may seem, he could not find child-sized underwear. This being wartime, maybe somebody had sunk the underwear boat. As painful as it must have been for him to pick through the piles of ladies' panties, he finally found a pair small enough for me to wear if he pinned them over one of my shoulders. I was once again presentable, or as close to it as my father could manage.

Mother did not seem pleased either, being called away from her work to be summoned to the scene of the crime. They agreed that I had to be kept under closer supervision until the cooler weather removed any tendency I might have to disrobe at will. So I became Mother's shadow as she weeded, kneaded, vacuumed or shopped. And she didn't like it any better than I did.

* * * * *

Faced with the food rationing system during the War, Mother planned our family meals for the week around what ration stamps she had on hand. Meat and staples were suddenly at a premium, resulting in a meatless meal at least three times a week. Millions of pounds of food were being shipped to Britain to help feed the civilian and military populations, making it necessary to ration butter, sugar, tea, coffee, meat and gasoline here at home. Ration books, which included the stamps a family would need to buy these necessities, were issued monthly from the Wartime Prices & Trade Board. If someone had an extra tea coupon but needed an extra sugar coupon, the swapping began. Shopping had become a challenging, more time-consuming process.

By continually observing these shopping techniques, I learned the purpose and value of ration stamps, which seemed to me to be even more valuable than money.

Being able to shop without the bother of rationing stamps became a dream of women faced with more and more shortages as the War years dragged on. From my standpoint, the system worked well. I had all I needed. In fact, I had too much of certain things. Getting me to eat what Mother had provided took some ingenuity along with a good dose of Christian guilt.

"Get those carrots into you," Mother ordered at one mealtime. "Don't you know children are starving in Poland."

Actually, no. I'd never heard of Poland. But whoever they were, they could have had my carrots and my dessert too, for that matter. That day we were having JUNKET, a horrible watery clot of a thing, halfway between milk pudding and JELLO, but not far enough either way. That sacrifice I'd have made without a whimper. Wasting food, according to Mother, was a mortal sin, and not tolerated within her range of sight, or voice. Often I had to sit for an hour after the rest of the family had finished, trying to choke down a serving of root vegetables. If they did not disappear at that meal, I saw them again at the next. Mother was becoming the cooking-pot dictator of the dinner table.

In Brussels at the time, the birth of a baby was big news. Babies were noticeably less common during the War years with the absence of the younger male population, so the birth of twins in the village was reason for celebration. Unfamiliar with the term 'twins', Mother explained to me that instead of having one baby to take home, the young mother would have two. I thought about this phenomenon for a minute, remembering all those frustrating shopping trips with Mother, and how seldom we could bring home two of anything. Then it dawned on me. Two babies at once could mean only one thing. The rationing was off.

This revelation gave my parents a chuckle for a day or two. Certainly the news broadcasts provided little levity. Many families, touched cruelly by the War, lived under a pall of sadness for the duration and forever after.

* * * * *

One evening shortly after VE-Day, a lively crowd gathered in Victoria Park to burn Adolf Hitler in effigy. As a child, ignorant to the atrocities of war and still uncertain about who was on what side, the importance of the occasion was not obvious to me. Well-primed with bottled enthusiasm, the crowd danced wildly around an enormous bonfire in the centre of the park, holding high a limp but vaguely human figure. From my vantage point, I could not tell it was just a straw-stuffed dummy, so this whole scene terrified me. The noisy crowd sounded menacing and I feared for the safety of the strange little man.

Whenever I found a situation threatening to myself or to anyone around me, I screamed until the threat went away. Doing so at the top of my lungs made little impression on anyone but my parents, who attempted to console me with the explanation that the dummy was just a pretend Adolf Hitler. At not quite five, my knowledge of the War that had just ended was somewhat deficient. I had never heard of Adolf Hitler, never seen a bonfire that large, or for that matter, a crowd of any size. Unable to stem the flow of tears, my parents took me home before the fist fights started, and I'm ashamed to say I forced them to miss the rest of the VE-Day celebrations they had been looking forward to for so long.

Up until this time, there had been few men in the village. Those who were left behind were old and quietly sad, like the village itself. Suddenly it filled with young servicemen in strange coloured uniforms, who stood around on the street corners, laughing and scratching and gazing wistfully at the children around them. If I felt uneasy with this noisy invasion, I was in the minority. Everyone else revelled in it. People kissed and hugged in broad daylight, thrilled to finally have this thing called peace. Rowdy dances were held right on the main street, and 'Welcome Home' parties filled the town hall, with the inevitable bloody brawls before, during, and after.

So this was peace? All this shouting and burning, all this dancing and fighting? Wartime seemed quieter somehow. Life varied little for me during those first days of peace—the sun rose over our maple tree and splattered its light onto my bed, just the way it had done on every other morning. And when I'd had enough of daylight, darkness came and sometimes rain fell. Still I could tell something was different. I could feel it. For one thing, the ration coupon book which had never been out of Mother's purse for as long as I could remember was relegated to the top drawer of my father's desk, where it stayed for ten years, just in case.

By Christmas the uniforms had disappeared, but the dancing and the fighting, like that thing called peace, were here to stay. In time I learned to recognize the subtle changes in the village and to accept the fact that some things would never change.

Googy-Buzzy

Dogs think they are people.
Cats know they are gods.

I can't remember where I read that, but whoever wrote those words had a keen knowledge of cats. If you're living with one, you are living on its terms, and the best you can hope for is that it will give you the same respect it would give an equal. Independent by nature and inclination, cats tolerate us only if and for as long as they choose. My larger than necessary tomcat chose to tolerate me, most of the time.

One morning quite unexpectedly, a local farmer presented him to me as a tiny, squirming lump in the bottom of a burlap bag. The smell of the burlap caught in my throat, but the pitiable cries from the lump could not be denied. Taking the bag from the farmer, I set it down on the grass and stood back to see what would happen.

"On you go then," he urged. "Open it."

Carefully, I drew back the burlap to reveal a most pathetic little creature no more than a few days old. Its eyes were not yet open and what fur it had lay flat and matted against its tiny body. With little thought to the kitten's dignity, the farmer picked it up, turned it upside down and proclaimed it to be male.

"It's a he. A tomcat," he said, returning him to the relative comfort of the burlap bag.

"D'ya want him or not?" he asked impatiently. I nodded my head, meaning that I most definitely did want him more than anything in the world, and I dove back into the burlap bag to haul him out.

The rest of his litter mates had been drowned, a common practice on farms when the cat population threatened to outnumber that of the mice. Some miraculous will to live had saved him from the fate of his siblings. The farmer told Mother he didn't have the heart to try it a second time. For years I wondered how he had survived. Why had he been chosen to live when the others had drowned? Could he swim? Could he hold his breath? Or was he simply born under a lucky star? In light of future experiments, the latter is probably true.

I could hardly be expected to assume the sole responsibility for this new life at the age of four, so Mother came reluctantly to my rescue. She had never been fond of cats, making no exception in his case, but neither could she resist the babies of any species. Wrapping the little tomcat in a towel, she fed him hourly from an eye dropper, a mixture of milk and corn syrup. At night he slept snuggled against a hot water bottle in a cardboard box under the kitchen stove. Soon his coat grew soft and shiny, and began to take on the brown and black stripes he wore so proudly as an adult.

Because he had been given to me, Mother suggested I think of a name for him.

"Tom!" I answered, having heard the farmer use that name for him.

"Well yes, that's what he is. He's a tomcat. But you can choose another name for him if you like." I thought about it for a while, wondering why he needed a name. I never found it necessary to call him. He was always right there getting mixed up with my feet. But this would at least be different than naming my army of dolls, who for some inexplicable reason were all female.

I picked him up, buried my face in his fur and held him closer than was comfortable for him probably. The sensation of touching his fur always made me grind my teeth, so while grinding away at my enamel I rubbed him back and forth across my face and thought and thought and thought some more. Suddenly a name popped into my head. Well, it was more a feeling than a name really, but I liked the sound of it.

"Googy-Buzzy! Googy-Buzzy!" I announced triumphantly from behind clenched teeth. My family stood in stunned silence, while I, still wearing the cat as a mustache, kept mumbling this strange incantation. Maybe they expected me to levitate too and zoom around the room, but I didn't.

Because Googy-Buzzy grew to be a cat of such large character and proportions, Goliath might have been a more appropriate name for him, but he was, even as a kitten, one of a kind, and Googy-Buzzy said it all. Much of his tail had been cut off in an incident with a screen door early in his life, serving to enhance his overall wild appearance in adulthood. He had the black and brown markings of the ordinary tabby cat, but these were clearly the only things ordinary about him. Announcing the approach of all visitors with loud yowls of protest, he evolved into a sort of family watch-cat, bearing the largest head on the thickest neck of any cat in the neighbourhood.

Googy-Buzzy became an exceptional mouser, an important skill to have, living as we did at the edge of town across the lane from open farm fields. In autumn, the field mouse population, in an attempt to keep warm, moved in with us. I didn't really mind sharing the house with the field mice. They were shy little creatures, which when discovered, hid their faces in a corner hoping not to be noticed. But Mother's disapproval was audible. Googy-Buzzy was now worth his considerable weight in gold.

Springing into action like a prize fighter, he dispatched every mouse he could find, dropping each limp victim at Mother's feet for approval.

"Oh, my goad! Here he comes again with another poor wee thing," she'd grimace. Then as if remembering something important, she'd add, "Yes, all right, good cat."

To say she viewed these presentations with mixed emotions was an understatement, but she praised him half-heartedly anyway, in case he lost interest in his one and only job. At the sound of her voice, Googy-Buzzy went into raptures, tying himself in knots of pride in his achievement and in her grandiloquent praise thereof.

He was demonstratively affectionate with the whole family. Purring like a tractor he lurched against our legs, arching his back and rubbing his hard head against our shins with such force we nearly toppled over.

Mother rarely called him by name, but when she did it was a special name she kept just for him.

"You filthy brute!" echoed through the house as Googy-Buzzy bolted out the back door to the safety of the wide open spaces. He'd been caught spraying the furniture again.

It must have been a relief for him to be scooped up just in time by me, even if I did it just so I could dress him in doll clothes—frilly little dresses, bonnets and booties. He went limp waiting for his chance to escape, and when that chance came, there we were, one cat in full regalia up a tree trying to shed his layette, with me in hot pursuit. When I caught him again he seemed more resigned to his fate, so I covered him with a woolly blanket and took him for a long ride in my doll buggy. Inquisitive passers-by viewed us with the usual adult interest shown to little girls with doll buggies. They stopped to discuss the weather and always asked to see my baby. Googy-Buzzy was used to this procedure.

One day I met the elderly Downing sisters walking home with their shopping bags full of groceries. They were retired school teachers, who wore lovely clothes in all the pastel shades of the rainbow with their hair tinted to match—one week a hint of frosty blue, the next a touch of lavender or pearly grey.

"Hello there, how are you today?" Elizabeth, the taller of the sisters asked most politely, flashing a knowing smile at her older sister.

"And how is your baby this fine day?"

Bending low enough to pull back the covers, the sisters' first glimpse of Googy-Buzzy gave them a start.

"Land sakes!" came the flustered response in stereo.

"What is it?" they inquired of each other. But when Googy-Buzzy made no attempt at retaliation, they quickly regained their composure, though they backed away to a respectful distance just in case. I assured them we were both fine and pulled up his blanket to cover him again so he wouldn't catch a chill, the way I'd seen other mothers doing it.

"And what is your—I mean—its name?" urged Elizabeth, now almost recovered and willing to play my little game.

"His name is Googy-Buzzy. He's a boy," I replied, gazing down lovingly at him sucking thoughtfully on his blanket and vibrating with purrs.

"Goo-Goo what?" Elizabeth mumbled in consultation with her sister. "Did you catch that, Hattie?" Hattie shrugged and shook her head.

"Buzzzz-y!" I answered, careful to enunciate all the zeds and probably more loudly than was necessary.

I repeated his name again, this time much more slowly, "Goo-gy-Buzz-y."

"Buzzzz-y, Goo-goo-Buzz-y?"

"Is that English, Elizabeth?"

Hattie had regained her power of speech by this time and together the sisters turned to me for an answer.

"Noooo—it's not English." I said in disbelief. "People are English. My daddy is English. Googy-Buzzy is Cat!" And with that explanation to ponder, off they went with their overflowing grocery bags, muttering something about what had happened to the English language since they quit teaching.

.

As long as Googy-Buzzy had his blanket to suck on, he stayed in the doll buggy, his enormous head snug in its dainty pink bonnet, dozing away the afternoon. I ignored most of his strange practices, but it was hard to ignore this dependency on his blanket. Any blanket would do, even Mother's best one, the white woollen one she kept folded in the linen closet, taking it out only for company. He liked nothing better than to crawl up onto the shelf, knead a part of it into a little nipple, then curl up and suck himself to sleep. When Mother discovered his forbidden pleasure, she had another occasion to use his special name.

Mother explained to me that Googy-Buzzy was the way he was because he had been taken away from his mother too soon, and had been searching for a substitute ever since. But when that substitute turned out to be her best company blanket, his excuse was not good enough. Down the stairs they roared, around the corner and out the screen door once again. I loved Googy-Buzzy in spite of this idiosyncrasy, and all the others that cropped up regularly.

Rarely did anyone pay a veterinarian to have a cat spayed or neutered in the 1940's. As a result they happily went about the business of doing what cats do naturally, resulting in a constant stream of people at the door trying to give away kittens. That is, after all, how Googy-Buzzy came to live with us. Cats were a real bargain in those days. They were free for the asking and ate table scraps, though not many of those if you wanted a good mouser. With the possible exception of a rabies vaccination, a cat cost nothing at all.

When Mother and I took Googy-Buzzy to the veterinarian for his vaccination, we put him in my doll buggy with his favourite blanket. Mother carried a sizeable piece of rope in case he tried to escape, but it was not necessary to leash him. The visit ended before he knew what had happened to him. Back in the doll buggy, once he had time to think about it the experience left him somewhat resentful, and it took many great slurping sucks on his blanket to calm him down.

Unaltered by human hands, Googy-Buzzy had all the usual bad habits of any male cat of his generation. Every few months he disappeared for a few days. When he managed to drag himself home again, his velvety ears were in shreds and his fur was dirty and stuck into matted clumps. Not worrying too much about his appearance for the moment, Googy-Buzzy ate until his belly touched the floor, then curled up and went to sleep for twenty-four hours. Emerging from his drowsy stupor, he spent many hours grooming himself and making sure every piece of fur faced in the right direction. This done, he struggled to his feet, stretched out all his body parts and settled down again for a nap, smugly confident that his sordid night life remained a secret.

Googy-Buzzy was without peer in the marking of his territory. Whenever he could manage it, he crept into forbidden territory—usually the living room—backing up to the furniture with an air of nonchalance. Then when he was sure no one was looking, he arched his back and anointed with glee.

I could hear the ruckus long before I saw it, because it often took some time for Mother to round him up. Despite his size, he could scoot under the sofa when he considered it to be the shrewdest move. But before long both of them came bursting through the screen door, back out onto the lawn, Googy-Buzzy with his stub of a tail stuck high in the air like a flag, Mother with the kitchen broom over her head, slamming it down on the grass in the place he had vacated just moments before. Around and around the lawn they stormed, both wearing the same wild expression. How Mother delighted in using his special name! Once again he was exiled to the woodshed for the rest of his life, or until the next day—whichever came first.

Like most cats, Googy-Buzzy had an acute sense of who was and who was not a cat fancier. With the exception of my mother, whom he loved inordinately, he could spot anyone less than enthusiastic at fifty paces. At the first opportunity he hopped up onto their lap, kneading with all his might until their thighs were soft enough for napping, then he curled up into a ball, yawned and closed his eyes. Because claws extended seemed to be his constant state, coming to the rescue too soon could be dangerous. We learned to watch and wait until after he yawned before lifting him from a poor ravaged visitor.

One summer morning, I filled the laundry tub to the brim with water and set it in the sun to warm. All afternoon I splashed and waded in the sun-warmed water with anything I could find that would float. Googy-Buzzy wouldn't float. If he had ever known how, he had long since lost the knack. I tried to teach him, but he was not a willing pupil. As soon as his paws hit the water he went berserk, writhing and snarling, spitting and kicking in every direction, with total disregard for life and limb. Especially mine.

For over three years, he tolerated my dressing him in doll clothes. He had been chastised for seeking the comfort of his beloved blankets, and been driven from the house for no other reason than for keeping the living room free from invaders, but this, this ultimate violation of his dignity crossed the line. One trial by water was enough. He refused to test his luck again. I never saw him more indignant, and his mood discouraged any further attempts to broaden his horizons. I probably still have a scar or two from that episode.

Keeping his claws in fighting form took up most of Googy-Buzzy's time. He sharpened them on anything that stood at right angles to the floor, whether it was a piece of the living room furniture or one of my legs. He was a happy, totally undisciplined cat, who refused to have it any other way.

One of his more curious habits was to spring at me as if I were his prey, with teeth bared and claws unsheathed. He sprang at no one else but me. First, he had to stalk me, slithering across the lawn on his belly, tensing for the leap and winding his mainspring. Then at just the right moment this inner spring uncoiled and he shot through the air at me as if propelled from a gun. And there he hung, until I disentangled his claws from whatever part of me he happened to be clutching. This behaviour, bad enough when he was a kitten, became intolerable once he grew older. No amount of scolding would change what for him was a natural behaviour and one he had for the rest of his life.

When I arrived home from my vacation one summer, it happened again, but this time in front of several adult witnesses. What had been normal play for him suddenly became a more serious and painful matter for both of us.

This time he drew blood, quite a lot of it, having tapped into a vein or artery or some such vital pipeline. Now I have never been good around free flowing blood at the best of times, but when that blood happened to be my own personal supply, I thought fainting entirely justified. This I did, right there on the lawn, leaving the adults to clean up the mess.

I awoke as our family doctor prepared to give me a tetanus shot—not the greatest timing in the world you have to admit. I called for Googy-Buzzy to come to comfort me, but he didn't come. Not then and not ever. I never saw him again.

Past the crisis, Mother told me he had gone on an unscheduled vacation and would not be returning in the foreseeable future. A vacation from what I wondered? He did nothing all day but sleep. No one seemed to want to explain further, and I couldn't be sure I wanted to know the truth anyway, so I stopped asking.

I've thought about him many times over the years, wondering if this violent streak toward me could have been the direct result of my sticking him with a name like Googy-Buzzy. Not many juries would have convicted him.

Brother, Can You Spare Some Time

Our house was my castle, and the gardens around it the realm I shared with squirrels, birds, butterflies and every other creature that hopped, scurried, buzzed or flew. Beyond the gravelled laneway bordering two sides of our house lay a world that was still a mystery to me. A warning from Mother at any one of our twenty windows kept me well within bounds.

Little traffic used this laneway, with the exception of the milkman's wagon on his daily rounds, or a wooden snowplough in winter, both pulled at a snail's pace by huge, hairy workhorses. Horses meant one thing to Mother. Beautiful roses. Occasionally the horses dropped their bounty in front of our house and Mother lost no time in spading it in around her roses. But traffic or no traffic, the laneway remained off limits to me for the first year we lived in the house. The field beyond it, glorious in a mantle of goldenrod, remained the forbidden kingdom I longed to explore.

Most of the time Doug ignored me. I had nothing much to offer him in the way of rough and tumble boy's play.

I played alone much of the time, exploring the mysteries of the outdoors and the in. There were wild corners of the garden that Mother had not yet had time to clear. One grew a marvelous assortment of weeds and long grasses, and sometimes vegetables that no one had planted at all and that I claimed as my own. I shooed away the butterflies and the grasshoppers and bent the long grass down so the sun could shine in. One year it rewarded me with a long vine of cucumbers, another year some yellow beans. Gardening was easy. I didn't even have to plant anything. I would learn.

Inside the house I discovered darkened closets for hiding in and bright sunbeams with dust motes dancing. There seemed to be an infinite number of objects that creaked or folded, opened or shut, and ornaments that when touched, mysteriously fell to pieces. I found a low cupboard in the dining room sideboard that always smelled of HP Sauce. This I could open by myself, and smell it any time I wanted to, which was often and for prolonged periods of time. In the end, this new-found attraction was designated off-limits to me after I crawled inside one day and shut the door. No one could find me, and that was so much fun I didn't tell anyone where I was for the longest time.

Getting Doug to play with me was harder, though I wasn't above begging. Whenever he relented it took no time at all before I ran crying to Mother with a bruise or scrape or some other kind of grievance. More often than not Doug received the blame, and occasionally—all right, rarely—I accepted some myself. It is little wonder I felt lonely. He knew I'd never be proficient at making kites from newspaper, string and two pieces of wood. I knew nothing about constructing model airplanes and ships, setting up train tracks or making a soap box car using the scrap found in the wood shed. He knew a great deal about all these things. In fact, Doug excelled at everything, it seemed to me. There could be little doubt that a younger sister had been a serious disappointment. But like most sisters, I'd rather be bruised than ignored, so I continued to pester him until he gave in and played with me, if only for a few minutes.

One morning he allowed me to tag along with him on a tour of the promised land across the lane, where thistles grew as tall as trees and the milkweed blazed with butterflies. The long grass towered over me, knife-edged and alive with grasshoppers that leapt about like tiddly-winks. We stumbled upon a mound of earth at the entrance to a large hole in the ground, a hole that looked big enough for me to tumble down inside like Alice in Wonderland.

"Groundhogs!" Doug exclaimed. "Stay back. Maybe I can get one to come out."

He knelt down poking a stick as far into the hole as he could reach, shouting threats that I imagined were intended to frighten the animal into submission. I peered over his shoulder into the darkness, not sure if I'd recognize a groundhog even if one came running out with its paws in the air. No groundhog appeared of course, though even the birds fell silent in anticipation. We moved on.

Several smaller holes looked less threatening, so I jammed my stick into one of these the way Doug had done, hoping against hope that it wouldn't touch something soft at the bottom.

"Those are SNAKE holes!" he teased, jumping back to a safe distance. I jumped back too, and threw my stick into the long grass, thinking better of my foolhardy probing. I had no reason to fear snakes. I'd never even seen one. But there was something in the way he said it that made me shiver.

Nearby, four tawny cows had been chomping happily on thistles, but now they shuffled off to the far corner of the field, leaving behind them a collection of flat, brown pancakes I'd never seen before.

"Cow patties," Doug warned. "Don't step on them or Mom'll kill ya'."

"What are they?"

"It doesn't matter. Just don't go near them." They were already covered with flies and stinking to high heaven, so the warning was hardly necessary. Only having seen the cows from our distant upstairs window, I could hardly believe how big they were at ground level and was relieved they wanted no more to do with me than I with them. Instead, we examined the milkweed pods, pulling one apart to see what could be inside that interested all those butterflies. Thousands of tiny seeds on silky parachutes blew away with the first breeze. The head from one of the teasel plants stuck in my hand when I tried to pull it from its stem. Several drops of blood taught me that plants can fight back.

"It bit me," I whined, in a bid for sympathy.

"It did not. It's a weed."

"Did too."

"It didn't."

"Did, did, did and did too," I insisted. It felt so good to have the last word, it was almost worth having a sore hand. But if I expected to get much sympathy from him, I was barking up the wrong brother. I licked off the blood and spit it into the long grass. It tasted like nickels.

Despite this little drama, Doug bored easily with me in tow.

"There's nothing to do here. I'm going home." he announced, far too soon for me but with a definite finality in his tone.

My first intriguing journey into the wilder side of the laneway had come to an end, but it would not be without memories. My hand hurt, my socks were covered with prickly burrs and my shoes were caked with mud.

At least I think it was mud. Struggling through waist-high tangled grass, we headed for home, pausing along the way to lop the heads off a few thistles, sending clouds of thistledown billowing away on the wind.

At home in the back yard, when I managed to keep his attention for a few minutes, we played in the sandbox with an army of tanks, trucks and soldiers and some cups and spoons I confiscated from the kitchen. I built my sand castles on his road system and Doug drove his convoy of tanks through the middle of them. Then if that were not bad enough, he bombed them with pebbles, making those rude explosion noises that boys do best. I rebuilt my castles, and he repeated the offensive. This seemed to be a big waste of time, but Doug wouldn't play house with me so I had to go to war with him. The only thing this exercise taught me is that war is never neat, seldom fair, and always noisy.

On rainy days, we played what must have been the most dangerous game ever created for children, certainly one that went out of its way to glorify war. It was called BOMBS AWAY, a totally unapologetic propaganda tool.

But when Canada was at war with Germany, attitudes were different and regular toys were few.

The game consisted of a square board made of a soft, wooden composition know as beaver board, gayly painted with a map of Germany showing the main industrial cities, each with a picture of something, that if bombed, would impact the War—munitions factories, buildings for aircraft manufacturing, and railroad bridges. The other game pieces consisted of a binoculars device with a mirror inset to reflect the map when it was held over the board. Most alarming were the two wooden bombs with sharp, metal pins on their weighted ends. They were inserted in the front end of the binoculars. The object of the game was to stand over the map, look through the binoculars, find a probable target, press the button and, well you get the idea—Bombs Away! We bombed Germany until we couldn't identify the country, much less the munitions factories. Each time a bomb dropped, Doug made that explosion noise and another piece of the map hit the living room rug.

Now I make no excuses for such a bizarre game, but I am fairly certain that neither of us identified our bombing raids with any real harm to anyone. There were few if any children's games for sale at the time because most factories were refitted and retooled to manufacture items more in keeping with the war effort. Obviously, the few who did make toys had a clear message to deliver. BOMBS AWAY was simply another in a series of noisy war games designed primarily for boys, who without exception, loved them to bits.

Every time I pressed the button, I bombed my feet— and because I was barefoot most of the time, I was the only one being hurt. Whether or not I ever finished a game before running to Mother for a band-aid, I'm fairly certain I never won any. Losing at BOMBS AWAY was something at which I excelled. Everybody's good at something.

And Then There Were Two

My wooden swing hung from a branch of the apple tree in the back yard above a sea of forget-me-nots. In spring, a chorus of bees accompanied the creaking of the ropes as they wore deep notches on the branch above. Many an idle afternoon was spent twisting the ropes around and around, until only the tips of my toes touched the ground. When I lifted my feet, I spun out of control for a moment or two, eyes shut, hair flying, before coming to a shaky stop. At the spinning stage, more times than I care to remember, my hair became entangled in the ropes, stranding me on tiptoes until my frantic cries brought scissors to the rescue. Ragged strands of my hair decorated these ropes for most of my childhood—every year my hair got a little shorter.

Up until the time I met Elayne, all this swinging had to be done on my own. In fact, all the things little girls do, I did alone, or with Doug if I could catch him in the right mood—clearly a situation that needed improvement. I was spinning on my swing one evening when I caught my first glimpse of Elayne. Actually I saw two of her and thought she was twins until my vision cleared. But there was just one of her, and she was so special one was enough. Her parents were talking to mine at the time, and knowing how badly I needed a playmate, Mother called me over to meet her. We discovered our birthdays were only two days apart—a good reason for an overindulgence of cake and ice cream at least once a year. Elayne was almost four years old. I was almost five.

I showed her all my favourite things in the back yard, but she showed no enthusiasm for my sandbox, having seen enough sand at her family cottage by the lake. My swing raised more interest. It took all my strength to haul her up onto the wooden seat, where she sat feet dangling, waiting for something to happen. Nothing happened until I gave her a push. Suddenly I felt older than someone else for the first time in my life.

"Moo-cows!" she said, pointing to the cows in the pasture across the lane. I could see I had my work cut out for me. Baby talk had always been discouraged in our family. Without a moment to lose I set about the task of teaching her my version of the English language.

"There is no such things as moo-cows," I explained. "There is just plain cows. Moo is what they say and cows is what they are. Now, say cows." She did and I praised her the way Mother praised me when I surprised her by doing something right.

"Rum-brello!" she said, pointing to an open umbrella drying by the back door.

"It's not a rum-brell-o. It's a rum-brell-a." And so the lessons continued, not always to her betterment. Before long she could speak in whole sentences that contained actual verbs.

Having Elayne for a friend was even better than having a cat. At first I thought she was a gift, like Googy-Buzzy had been, and was disappointed to discover we would not be living together in the same house. Instead, she had to live with her parents and older brother in an apartment above their clothing store. Sleep-overs at Elayne's apartment overlooking the main street were as exciting for me as they were for her at our house, overlooking the cow pasture.

It never occurred to me that I might have two friends. I thought everyone had just one, like a nose, and Elayne was mine. When another little girl asked if she could be my friend, I said, "But I already have one." And that was that, until I discovered that having two friends is like having friend insurance. Even best friends have an argument once in a while.

Not satisfied with being best friends, Elayne and I wanted to be twins, and our matching wardrobes reinforced the fantasy. Every morning we synchronized our outfits for the day by telephone—most of our dresses differing only in their colours. When our moods changed, so too did our dresses—sometimes three or four times a day—causing a sudden increase in washing and ironing, and driving our mothers to a matching distraction.

A large maple tree with inviting branches spread its cool, deep shade over one corner of our lawn. Mother taught me to climb it when she trusted me not to fall out of it and break something. As soon as Elayne's legs were long enough to reach the first foothold, I taught her how to climb it too. Our favourite branch extended parallel to the ground at a dizzying height of five feet. Sitting together on this branch we thought we could see forever. Sometimes we hung upside down from the backs of our knees side by side like two bats.

"If you two fall out of that tree and break all your legs, don't come running to me," Mother warned from an upstairs window. And with that bit of wisdom imparted and her conscience clear, she closed the window and never bothered us again. We called it our 'thinking tree', and we never did fall out of it. We jumped out of it *many* times, but we did that on purpose.

Generally ignored by everybody else, the spruce tree by the wood shed maintained its solitary existence by oozing great clumps of sticky resin from its trunk, making the climbing impossible and the chewing an acquired taste. I broke off a hunk and offered it to Elayne.

What good is a younger best friend if she can't be your food taster? She had trusted me until then. Apparently WRIGLEY'S need not be concerned about this particular competition. She spit it out on the grass right away and kept on spitting for five minutes. From then on, adding a pleasant Christmasy smell to the yard all year seemed to be this tree's sole purpose in life.

In spring, from the cedar chest under my bedroom window, we watched adult robins swooping in and out of the spruce boughs trying to keep up with their nestlings' demand for food. After several weeks of frantic activity, the little ones fluttered down to the lawn where they continued their incessant chirping. Still on call, the distraught parents attempted to keep their growing brood fed and out of harm's way until they could fly to the safety of a tree.

Googy-Buzzy, by now up to his fighting weight, could shatter this domestic scene with one well-timed pounce. When we were too late to stop him, the outcome seldom varied. A lifeless bundle of speckled feathers, who moments before had gobbled down a worm, now hung limp from the cruel jaws of death. This senseless bit of violence offered Elayne and me the perfect excuse for a somber funeral later in the day.

In autumn, the maple trees in our part of the country transformed themselves into extravagant blazes of colour. We raked every one in our yard and imported armloads from beneath the neighbours' trees to pile into a mountain under our favourite branch. One at a time, or sometimes together, we launched ourselves into space like the baby robins had done, landing in the middle of the leaf pile with a teeth-jarring thud. No matter how high we piled the leaves, the landing never got any softer. Many of the leaves found their way down our necks, causing us to do the leaf-dislodging-shimmy, which never really caught on as a dance.

By the first snowfall of winter, the untidy mountain of maple leaves had been swallowed up by Mother's compost pile, to be transformed into rich soil for the next year's gardens. Again we clambered onto our branch, this time in snow pants and black, buckled galoshes. Here we told each other our secrets, even though neither of us had one worth telling. Still, they seemed important to us, and more fun now we could share them.

Elayne was in my life to stay. She is mentioned many times in this book because I cannot think of my childhood without thinking of her. From that first meeting, we were best friends and inseparable for many years.

No Place Like Home

The cement walkway at the front door wandered ten or twelve feet into the lawn looking for a sidewalk, but never found one. As it was the only cement surface of any length near our house, this is where I learned to roller skate. The leather ankle straps of my skates, when tightened to my satisfaction, cut off all circulation to my feet. The skate clamps which held the skates to my leather shoes had to be screwed so tightly they buckled the soles, while the metal skate key for tightening those clamps banged freely from a length of butcher string around my neck, leaving mysterious bruises I could never explain. No safety precautions were taken, no helmet or knee pads ever worn—there was simply an abundant supply of band-aids in the medicine cabinet to stem the flow of blood.

Skating on our front walk allowed for only three glides before I ran out of cement and catapulted headlong into the grass. There my shoes slipped out of the metal clamps, and the skates, still attached to my ankles, whacked great gouges in the lawn and one or two in my shins. Before long I felt bold enough to try longer sidewalks farther from home, and thanks to a good rain and the band-aids, the gouges healed over time.

* * * * *

Whoever built our house in the early 1900's had not foreseen the popularity of the electric light, compensating with a disproportionate number of windows. By no means a grand house, ours had twenty of them in assorted sizes and styles.

The living room had two large bay windows, one facing an expanse of lawn and flower garden, the other facing the lane and open fields beyond. We heated this room with a tall round coal stove, its stateliness enhanced by bright accents of chrome. The slender stovepipe meandered a few feet across the ceiling before disappearing to warm my parents' second floor bedroom on its way to the chimney. Warm is a relative term.

In winter, even with storm windows in place, ice formed inside most of those twenty windows, though frostbite was rare.

Hanging on the only wall in the living room that did not have a window, a picture of Highland cattle wandered the bonnie hills of Scotland, the entire scene rendered in various shades of green. Not only had I never seen cattle with hair covering their eyes, I had never seen cattle in this or any other shade of green. They seemed too exotic even for Scotland. Mother gazed lovingly at this picture, saying it reminded her of home. For too long I figured Scotland was completely green. Grass, hills, sky, cattle, bagpipes, haggis, people, every bit of it green. And then I thought about children playing in the grass and getting lost and not being able to find their way home because everything around them was green. I loved that picture more than any other in the house.

Every Christmas, we replaced the large Boston fern from one of the bay windows with the Christmas tree. All of our trees were bought on faith, paid for weeks in advance and left at the back door a few days before Christmas, sight unseen. Almost without exception, these trees were so crooked they had to be tied to a window sill to prevent their careening unexpectedly into the middle of the room. On more than one occasion our tree looked like one from a painting by the Group of Seven, with all of its branches on the same side, as if it had lived its life in a hurricane. But no matter whether they were spruce or pine, straight or crooked, sparse or full, if they were at least green and had that familiar aroma that is so much a part of Christmas, they were perfect in my eyes.

A heavy coal pail held the tree upright, filled to the brim with shiny black nuggets and gallons of water. Mother strung the multi-coloured lights evenly through the branches, carefully placing each familiar bauble in just the right spot, then wired the star to the uppermost branch, which wasn't always in the middle. An old white sheet draped around the pail represented a snowdrift.

Leftover evergreen boughs, cut from the tree in an attempt to make it look more symmetrical, were tied together with red and green ribbons to festoon our front door, the mirror over the sideboard and the picture of the green cattle. The scene was set for Christmas. When the tree lights were turned on for the first time at dusk, emeralds, rubies, sapphires and topaz sparkled on the snow outside the window like the overflowing contents of a treasure chest.

A lone street lamp stood at the front of our house, its pale light swarming with snowflakes. I watched as my father emerged from the shadows into this pool of light on his way home after work. His delighted reaction to the decorated tree was all-important. He never disappointed me.

* * * *

An old pump organ sat askew near an unused door, doubling as a draft catcher in winter. Mother had the ability to coax a tune from any instrument, so she could play the organ well enough to be called upon to accompany the inevitable sing-alongs when our Scottish relatives came to visit. Struggling to find the correct keys through her tears, she stumbled through *Annie Laurie*, accompanying her older sister Lizzy as she sang. This ballad sent the younger generation fleeing to the far corners of the house, its sentiment totally unappreciated.

"Let's get out of here, they're gonna lay me doon and dee."

> *Maxwellton Braes are bonnie,*
> *Where early fa's the dew,*
> *And 'twas there that Annie Laurie,*
> *Gied me her promise true,*
> *Gied me her promise true,*
> *Which ne'er forgot shall be,*
> *And for bonnie Annie Laurie,*
> *I wad lay me doon and dee.*

Whenever we could talk Uncle Hughie into singing 'The Vulgar Boatman' in his basso profondo, the tears dried up in a hurry. Years later I learned *The Volga Boatman* told of a peasant fisherman toiling at his nets on the Volga River, and that it had nothing to do with an offensive fisherman as first imagined. I listened closely when Uncle Hughie sang the song, but with his accent, the only words I could understand were Yo Heave Ho, which did little to enlighten me.

In the era before television, we gathered as a family around the large wooden console radio in the living room listening to Jack Benny, Phil Harris, and Fibber McGee and Molly. The radio stood in the corner next to my father's armchair, the honoured position in the room. I can still see him perched on the edge of his chair, staring into the radio and slapping his knee with merriment at everything Phil Harris had to say.

Even more than the comedy programs, Dad enjoyed the *Gillette Friday Night Fights* from Madison Square Garden, sometimes featuring his all-time boxing hero, Joe Louis. On these occasions he had the living room to himself, teetering again on the edge of his chair, inches from the speaker, punching and jabbing the air in response to the commentator's blow-by-blow description of the fight. I found it incongruous that someone as gentle as my father would enjoy a sport as violent as boxing, but he did, and with no apologies. He called it the 'sweet science', the 'manly art of self-defence'. Mother claimed he liked boxing because he was English. Anything he enjoyed that Mother found repugnant she blamed on his being English. I stayed in the kitchen with her, watching through the crack in the door while Mother paced, wringing her hands in sympathy for the losing fighter. Eventually the fight ended and Mother proclaimed the living room safe once more for polite society.

Printed in bold letters on the radio dial were all the famous cities of Europe—Berlin, London, Paris and Rome. Of course we could never hope to bring in radio signals from any of these places, but just knowing they were there on the lighted dial encouraged us to try again and again. With the needle pointing to a city far away and our ears pressed close to the speaker fabric, we strained to hear a foreign accent. What we heard was a faint crackling and whistling as if the signal were being beamed at us from some distant galaxy. That was good enough for us. Even the static sounded foreign.

On Sunday mornings, from my place on the living room rug in front of the radio, I followed along while an announcer read the comics with all the proper voices and sound effects. Blondie and Dagwood argued constantly with their neighbours the Woodleys, L'il Abner and Daisy Mae continued their hill-billy courtship in Dogpatch, and later in the program, that lantern-jawed detective, Dick Tracy, rounded up the usual suspects. On weekday afternoons while my brother and I were at school, Mother caught up on her ironing listening to the latest crises in the lives of *Big Sister* and *Pepper Young's Family.* We were hooked on radio. So it is little wonder that when the announcer cautioned—"Uh, uh, uh! Don't touch that dial!"—we didn't.

* * * * *

Four folding French doors once separated the living room from the dining room, but they disappeared soon after my fingers were folded between them during a game of tag with Doug. The dining area stretched the width of the house. On one side of the room the massive oak table held a tall silver basket filled with seasonal flowers from Mother's garden. This table is invariably connected to the memories of my childhood. I can trace in my mind every inch of its immense surface and can run my fingers around each heavily carved leg. On rainy days Elayne and I sat underneath on the crossbar that braced the legs, the lace tablecloth providing the privacy we needed for our games of make believe. Some days we played house, choosing opposite ends of the cross bar, keeping our dolls and tea sets well within the proper boundaries. On other days we simply sat there secreted away for a while, until the sun shone through the window at just the right angle to form grotesque patterns on our faces through the lace in the tablecloth.

Mother cut out my summer dresses on the dining room table, finishing them on her portable sewing machine set up at one end. And it was here she sewed our costumes for the Variety Revue. But more about that later. Every Sunday we ate dinner at the dining room table, where Doug and I polished our table manners for company. But best of all were the times when both leaves were pulled out from either end, almost doubling its length. A special tablecloth appeared on those occasions. It meant our Scottish relatives were coming to town, an annual celebration. There would be music and laughter, extra nickels for ice cream, words I couldn't understand and dessert with every meal. Over time this dining room table became a large, comfortable member of the family, and no special event was complete without it serving as the centrepiece.

My father's glass-fronted bookcase stood against another wall, displaying two rows of Harvard Classics with gold lettering embossed on green bindings. Squeezed together on a bottom shelf were works by Hugo and Poe, Shakespeare, Dickens and Lawrence. The two books he read most often were his morocco-bound volume of *The Complete Works of Shakespeare*, printed on paper so thin I could almost see through it, and a battered, well-loved copy of *Seven Pillars of Wisdom* by

T.E. Lawrence. He bought most of the books in his collection during the Depression, at a time when he and everyone else had little money to spare for such luxuries. They were probably not new when he bought them, but still he felt he must justify this extravagance by claiming they were his escape from the mundane, his sole entertainment and his higher education.

He read them over and over again while sitting in his big green chair under the tall pink floor lamp—the one that came-a-cropper one day as I was practising my sliding technique on the recently polished floor. On this occasion retribution was swift. My father gave me one hard slap on the bottom before herding me away from the shards of broken glass littering the living room floor. Mother, the official disciplinarian in the family, did not appreciate being displaced from office, and did not speak to my father until his hand print faded from my bottom. She simply wouldn't have a perfectly good bottom marked by anyone, even him. I had never before heard my parents disagreeing about ways to discipline me, and I found the prospect of adult fallibility fascinating. This was the first and last time my father attempted corporal punishment.

On the far side of the room, a wooden telephone typical of a pre-electronic age hung on the wall by a window. It had a long black horn to speak into and a black bell-shaped receiver sitting on a cradle at one side.

Because of its location, anyone who used the telephone was forced to stand, ensuring all conversations were kept short. Our telephone number at the time was 2X, probably one of the shortest telephone numbers in existence, even then. Adults with more important things on their minds didn't always take the time to look up a number in the telephone book. They had confidence in the telephone operator, who knew the numbers of everyone in the village and most of everything else worth knowing. Whenever they cared to inquire, the operator kept them up-to-the-minute on local fires, floods, births and deaths, and she always had the correct time and temperature. This level of personal service was soon to go the way of the Tin Lizzie.

* * * * *

Through a windowless and often hazardous swinging door, the kitchen occupied the far end of the house. A tall window above the kitchen sink kept the room bright and airy, and in spring a lilac tree bathed the room in its special fragrance.

Dominated by a wood burning range, the kitchen was easily the busiest room in the house. Waging war against the ever-present cold in winter, the kitchen stove became the biggest gun in the battle. Mother fed it constantly from the wood box by the pantry door, and in turn it fed us. On winter mornings a great black bottomed pot of porridge occupied the largest hole in the stove top, giving way to soup at other times of the day. Pails of ashes were scooped from below the grate and stored in a bin to be added to the garden soil in spring.

On one occasion, and I must stress, only one, these ashes were used to make soap. They were mixed with lye and some other noxious substance, though what I remember most about it is the citronella Mother used as a fragrance. Because none of us could bear the smell, the soap seemed to last forever. Finally, in a desperate attempt to get rid of it, Mother shaved the last bits into the washing machine on laundry day. One thing for sure, we were unpopular with mosquitoes until the last sliver had disappeared. By a vote of three to one, soapmaking was outlawed. Mother refused to relinquish one moment of her pioneering experience, as if she were following a hundred year old rule book.

True to her Scottish heritage, Mother kept a large pot of mystery soup simmering at the back of the stove in a soot-blackened pot, responding to all requests for snacks with a nourishing bowl at any time of the day or night. What began as vegetable soup, may have been, by the third day, chicken noodle or vegetable beef or some combination of the two. I only know I disliked whatever it was, and begged her to buy the soup I heard was M'M! M'M! GOOD!

Our kitchen stove must have been designed by a genius. In addition to the regular baking oven and enormous cooking surface, it offered numerous practical features by way of towel racks, plate warmers, a water heating reservoir, and an oven door that could be folded down for drying mitts or thawing frozen feet. It was decorated with shiny nickel curlicues and ceramic tiles for no practical purpose other than to make it more attractive. None of us could remember when the temperature gauge on the oven door had last worked. Its red needle had melted at the 450 degree mark, but Mother knew when it was hot enough simply by putting her hand in the oven. Sometimes she added a little more wood to the fire-box when a higher oven temperature was required, or simply rearranged the wood inside the stove to allow the fire to die down a bit before baking.

From November until April we were drawn to the comforting warmth of the kitchen like no other room in the house. Here, over tea and raisin toast, Mother told me stories about the Scotland she had left behind and about the grandparents I would never know. Looking back past too many wars and too much death, she remembered her father, Peter Edmond, simply as two kindly dark eyes over a handlebar mustache—a quiet man who played the organ in the Kirk on Sundays. Her mother, Elizabeth, she remembered as a little round figure in a navy blue dress sprinkled with tiny flowers. But as often as she tried, she could not remember the face above it. She had a picture of her father to show me, but I never saw a picture of my grandmother. In my imagination I thought of the navy blue dress as being short like Mother's, but it would have been long enough to brush the floor at the turn of the last century.

Both of Mother's parents were dead by the time she was ten years old, leaving twelve surviving children, eight still at home. Her father died of pneumonia. Her mother died some months later from what was described as a broken heart. One brother drowned when he was still small, and the First World War a few years later claimed her three remaining brothers. Sitting beside a warm wood fire, listening to its comforting crackle, seemed to be the right place for remembering even the sad times.

* * * * *

Next to the back wall of the kitchen, a doorway opened into a small shelved pantry. This is where Mother kept her jars of dill and mustard pickles, pickled beets, and colourful jams, all the results of her labour in the garden. Heavy pickle crocks, canning implements and roasting pans, too large for storage in the kitchen, hung here on hooks or were stacked neatly on shelves. Away at the back on a top shelf, safely out of reach of anyone with a sweet tooth, a gallon jug of the darkest maple syrup sat awaiting the occasional Sunday morning breakfast, or our annual pancake supper on Shrove Tuesday to usher in the Lenten season.

As an Anglican, my friend Elayne understood that relinquishing something for Lent was intended to represent a personal sacrifice in her daily life. One year I decided to join her in this sacrifice. Not wishing to be left out of anything, even a self-imposed hardship, I thought and I thought about what I could possibly do without. Considering the forty days and nights I would be depriving myself, I decided to give up carrots. It was the least I could do, and I mean that literally.

Large enough for storage of all kinds, the pantry also housed 'the body'. Exactly Mother's size, the body was used on the rare occasions when Mother had time for dressmaking. A dressmaker's form is the correct term, but calling it 'the body' conjured up unspeakable crimes, and was the term I much preferred. After all, the body was headless, armless and legless. Most of the time it stood in a darkened corner of the pantry out of the way, naked and too embarrassed to show itself.

One afternoon while I was home alone, rummaging through the storage tins in the dark for something vaguely resembling chocolate, the body slithered down the wall, landing with a clatter at my feet. All thoughts of chocolate vanished as I raced from the pantry and out of the house in a state of near hysteria. The storage tins were safe from the cupboard bandit for a very long time.

*****

Through a narrow door in the pantry and down a set of wooden stairs lay a tiny, damp cellar with a ceiling so low my parents were forced to walk bent over like a question mark. Although the walls were whitewashed in an attempt to brighten the gloom, one tiny window forever curtained with cobwebs could only let in an anemic light even on the sunniest days. Not always in working order, a dusty light bulb was used more for its company than for its illumination. This cold, dank room felt like a tomb even in midsummer. Boards were strewn haphazardly around the mud floor to accommodate the faint of heart, though the cold rising in waves bathed small feet in fear and dread.

Here Mother kept her carrots from the garden, buried all winter in a covered tub of sand. After one encounter on the stairs with something she claimed was the size of a rhinoceros, Mother would not approach the cellar without a baseball bat at the ready and Googy-Buzzy at her side. He was, by this time, the recognized champion in the rodent extermination field.

I rarely ventured down to the cellar, and then only under protest. Forever on the lookout for something with more legs than me, I scurried back upstairs at the slightest unrecognized noise, slipping off a step in my panic and banging my shin on the bare wood. In this part of the house, every day of the year was Hallowe'en.

* * * * *

The shed leaned against the house at the kitchen door, a lazy construction of silvery barn boards with a swayback roofline and an interior on three rickety levels. The wood for the kitchen stove was split here and neatly stacked against an outside wall.

In an era of cooking from scratch and washing dishes by hand, I soon learned that household chores were an important part of growing up. The work of running a home required a great commitment of time. An extra pair of hands—even small ones—were welcome. Before the advent of automatic washers and dryers, Mother relied on a copper wringer washing machine and a tub of warm rinse water, both of which were set up in the shed. The duty of guiding the flattened clothes into the rinse water with a paint stick fell to me. It was always splashy work and I loved it.

"Look what you're doing or I'll need to wring us both out when we're done. That's right! Och, you're worth a dozen of them," Mother crooned. Who the 'dozen' of them were was never revealed, but of this I am certain, with encouragement like that I would happily have stirred those clothes until I dropped over dead. We were a team, Mom and I.

In winter, the clothesline strung across the back lawn sagged under the weight of everything from flannelette sheets to long fleecy underwear that flapped in the breeze until it froze solid into strange, flat caricatures of each of us. After a few hours the stiffened laundry had to be wrestled through the kitchen door and stood against the wall to thaw. Then the wooden clotheshorse, wrapped around three sides of the kitchen stove and draped with limp laundry, finished the daylong chore. The ironing would begin the next day. Everything was ironed, even the bed linen. But that wasn't as arduous as it sounds. We had a mangle. My job was to sit in front of it and guide my father's handkerchiefs over the roller. When they appeared again they were flat and shiny and ready for folding. Soon I graduated to pillow cases and tea towels, but Mother took care of the tablecloths, the sheets, and even my father's white shirts—all perfectly ironed on the mangle.

Outside the shed, a slight incline stretched from the door onto the lawn near the spruce tree. On Easter mornings, Doug and I rolled our Easter eggs all the way to the bottom. Our eggs were the real things, boiled and dyed as many colours as Mother could find in the kitchen cupboard. Sometimes we dyed them in a blend of several colours, creating hues that could not be found in any crayon box. Khaki for instance. At least during the War, combat eggs were appropriate. No matter whether they were khaki, orange or sky blue pink, all of them were eaten for Easter morning breakfast with lots of salt and the traditional hot cross buns.

* * * * *

I remember the linen closet in the bathroom as the best place in the house for leisurely browsing on a rainy day. Only the top two shelves held anything vaguely resembling linens. The other three held an assortment of gadgets, bottles, vials and boxes, tubes and rolls and brushes galore. There were brown bottles of cough medicine in varying degrees of fullness, a clear bottle of liniment Mother used to ease the aches and pains after spring planting, and several blue bottles of MILK OF MAGNESIA, each with white crusted drips running down their sides. I found bottles of aspirin, antacid crystals, a dark sticky bottle of FLETCHER'S CASTORIA, a jar of VASELINE and a little wooden box of CARTER'S LITTLE LIVER PILLS. They were pink, as I remember, with a touch of floral on the nose, chalky and sweet on the palate, with a mild medicinal finish. I thought only adults had livers, so my reason for trying them was simply that they were tiny and pink and there. Who knows? Maybe they worked. As far as I know, my liver is fine to this day.

.

Behind these I found a fever thermometer in a silver case with tooth marks on it, a bag of chalk powder used when Mother hemmed skirts, and a large tin of dry mustard for the dreaded mustard plasters I knew so well. A large bar of red carbolic soap sat on one shelf, casting off even more noxious vapours than Mother's homemade lye soap with citronella. If the smell did not discourage cleanliness, the colour surely would have. I do not remember it ever being used, nor do I know why we would need it—but if we ever did, we were ready.

There were atomizers, nose plugs, ear syringes, an enema bag, several rubbery hot-water bottles, and a white crockery steamer we used with a towel draped over our heads during winter colds. Battered toothbrushes still good enough for cleaning jewellery stood in a cup next to a pumice stone for wearing down calluses. Toward the back there was a jar of Mother's homemade burn ointment which the neighbours borrowed when they needed it, a small box of boric acid, a tin of tooth powder I considered ancient even then, two eye cups, rolls of gauze bandages and wads of cotton batting. A tiny, dangerous looking bottle of iodine with a skull and crossbones on it sat next to old prescriptions by the dozen. The linen closet smelled like an old fashioned drug store, the carbolic soap winning the battle for supremacy hands down. The collection grew over the years because no bottle or box was ever thrown out before its contents were used up, and that happened rarely.

* * * * *

My tiny bedroom on the second floor, overlooking the back lawn, served several purposes over the years. With so few rooms in the house, no one could afford to be territorial. One winter I was moved to the guest room down the hall, and the ping-pong table was set up in my bedroom with only inches to spare on all sides. Not intended for ping-pong, my room became the semi-permanent home of Doug's electric train set. He had been collecting bits and pieces of the set for years without having a place to set it up for any longer than a day at a time.

On cold winter nights, we stood watching the little train puffing real smoke as it chugged around the track, stopping to fill up at the water tower or racketing past papier-mâché mountains and through tiny towns. Doug had assembled many of the buildings for his towns from the forms printed on the back of the shredded wheat box, fastening them together with two tabs marked A and B and painting them appropriate colours. We ate a lot of shredded wheat that winter as I remember.

I moved back to my own bedroom in the spring, with the train packed away for the summer. Mother made a gathered skirt of blue-dotted-Swiss to cover my new vanity—two orange crates with a board the same width across the top. I was instructed to sit here and brush my hair a hundred strokes every night to make it shine. I did it once, with debatable results, deciding instead to take my chances with dull hair. I had higher priorities.

Most evenings my father read poems to me from my favourite book, instilling in me a genuine appreciation for poetry, preferably read with an English accent. My request seldom varied. I always wanted to hear Polly Boyden's *Mud:*

> *Mud is very nice to feel*
> *All squishy-squash between the toes!*
> *I'd rather wade in wiggly mud*
> *Than smell a yellow rose.*
> *Nobody else but the rosebush knows*
> *How nice mud feels*
> *Between the toes.*

Mud was not only my favourite poem, but also the subject matter closest to my heart. I made dozens of pancakes with it and three-layer muddy wedding cakes which I decorated with daisies I found growing on the lawn. I fed it to my dolls on little tin plates, and once I painted the neighbour's white house with it, as high up as my arms could reach, before being ordered to hose it off again. But when the opportunity arose I waded in it too, just like the yellow rose.

In winter I slept under no fewer than five quilts of assorted thicknesses, often feeling tired in the morning from holding them up. Because of the low overnight temperatures in our house, Mother insisted on my wearing a long flannelette nightgown, which next to a set of flannelette sheets made the simple act of turning over almost impossible.

The quilts we had on our beds were homemade. Mother covered a flannel sheet with squares of material from clothes we had outgrown or simply grown tired of, securing each piece with snippets of yarn drawn through the two thicknesses and tied in a knot. These all-weather quilts were easy to make, inexpensive, and warm enough if piled on the bed five deep. Mother called them 'memory quilts' because we could look at them and remember when we wore the clothes that now appeared in quilt form. Some of the scraps were heavier than others, resulting in a feeling of warmth in a curious checkerboard pattern.

Sometime during the War my parents scraped together enough extra money to buy two warm, woollen Hudson's Bay blankets. They were soft and thick and best of all, new, and I couldn't wait to snuggle under one. We spent days admiring them, sticking our arms between the folds to feel the instant warmth. But before I had a chance to sneak one up to my bedroom, they were packed in a box held together with that lick-it-and-die brown paper tape and shipped to our relatives in England. I knew better than to argue. Imagining our English relatives snug in their beds under those glorious Hudson's Bay blankets gave me a warm feeling, even without them.

As it turned out, the blankets never arrived to warm our relatives. They may still be lying somewhere at the bottom of the Atlantic, or perhaps they were sold on the black market, as so often happened during the War. From all accounts our English relatives did not freeze to death despite their loss, and survived unscathed to face a meagre peacetime.

Once More With Feeling

The massive turn-of-the-century organ holding court in our living room was at the very least an impressive-looking instrument. With ornately carved pillars at each side and two shapely legs in front, it made a definite statement. The most probable statement being: "I bet you can't move me." A matching stool on wheels, with a seat that could be swivelled higher or lower, sat neatly under the keyboard when not in use as my personal merry-go-round. A row of white knobs called stops could be pulled out or pushed in to alter the tone of the music that found its way mysteriously into the room. Acting as a bellows, two carpeted foot pumps produced the sounds that were made by the keys. The whole instrument was fascinating, but totally bewildering to someone not quite five.

I knew that pumping with both feet made the instrument work, but because I could not yet sit on the stool while pumping with both feet, I stood on the floor and pumped furiously with one foot, pulling out and pushing in the stops for hours on end. This did not produce a note of music, but that didn't matter. It was enough just to hear the wheezing sighs I could coax from the foot pumps and to be in control of an instrument of this size.

While we owned the organ, Mother enrolled Doug in piano lessons. The two keyboards were similar, though playing the proper keys while keeping up the necessary rhythmic motion with the foot pumps was a trick not unlike rubbing your tummy and patting your head simultaneously. Because I had by this time developed some skill at manipulating the foot pumps, Doug suggested I take over that part of the process, freeing him to concentrate on his keyboard skills. Happy to be included in any of his activities, I knelt obediently under the stool and pumped with all my might to keep the bellows full and the volume up.

This system, for the first few minutes at least, seemed workable. I performed my duties well, if all my huffing and puffing were any indication. Sometimes I pumped with one hand on one side only. At other times I pumped with one hand and one foot, just to be fancy. And sometimes I pumped the way I'd been shown, rhythmically with both hands. But I was easily distracted from my duties by a passing cat, and once in a while Doug's urgent key strokes brought nothing but muffled thudding from inside the organ. A brotherly nudge on the forehead with the heel of a running shoe brought me back to reality and pumping again with something resembling enthusiasm.

In the long run this proved to be a less than perfect solution, because the punching and kicking that resulted from one too many brotherly nudges set the development of music back five hundred years. I was relieved of my duties and ordered out of the living room during succeeding practice sessions. As soon as an affordable piano could be found, it took the place of honour in the living room. I missed the organ at first, but what the piano lacked in asthmatic wheezing and foot pumping athleticism it more than made up for in pretty, tinkling tones. It wasn't new of course. Nothing was ever new.

Suddenly music was accessible even to me. I didn't need a stool to play this instrument. Nor did I have to pump with one foot while teetering on the other in order to hear the music. I could simply stand at the keyboard and play. And play I did, from morning to night. I played all the popular songs I heard on the radio, by ear, with one finger. My sudden interest in music thrilled my parents, but for some reason playing it without sheet music caused Mother increasing distress.

"She's picking up bad habits, Bill. We'll have to do something soon." she complained, whenever my father praised me for mastering a new pop tune, if only a single digit mastering.

I stood watching while Mother played, glancing at the notes on the sheet music, then back to her fingers. Once in a while she crossed her hands and played a few notes that way, just to be fancy. Then she'd look down at me and smile, as if to say, "Try that little trick sometime." I did, the next time I had the piano to myself, but it didn't sound pretty when I did it. It didn't sound like music at all. Soon I was back playing by ear with one finger, happy that at least this way the tunes were recognizable.

When I was five and a half, Mother enrolled me in classical piano lessons, to become it was hoped, a multi-fingered, note-reading, rule-adhering pianist. Before my first lesson she presented me with a music case, just like my brother's but in a different colour. At first I had nothing to put in it but my two quarters for the lesson, and it dragged on the sidewalk unless I kept my elbow bent. But I felt like a pianist, albeit a short one.

Our piano teacher lived in a large, red brick house on Tory Hill, the upper section of Turnberry Street, probably named for the predominant politics of the area. The rooms were filled to capacity with pianos, ornate furniture, paintings and fireplaces. It didn't look a bit like our house. I waited in the darkly panelled waiting room with Doug, keeping busy sliding on the polished hardwood floor in my socks.

Through the French doors I could see a little girl with a cloud of coppery hair and a very intense expression, sitting at a funny shaped piano, playing real music with both hands and at least ten of her fingers. Suddenly I got the piano bug bad. I had to learn to play like that, even if it took a whole year. I returned to my chair, folded my hands and waited for the magic to happen.

When her lesson ended, the little pianist appeared at the waiting room door. Behind her stood a stern looking man with a drift of unruly white hair. Taller than anyone I had ever seen before and bent as if he were still sitting at the piano, he reminded me of the heron I'd seen wading in the Maitland River. Doug stood up and followed him into the music room. To my relief he didn't acknowledge me. The door closed behind them. I tried to sneak a peek at the little girl's hands to see how many fingers she actually had, but she put on her mittens and left before I had the chance.

Younger pupils with doubtful or as yet undiscovered talent were instructed by a tiny woman with curly white hair and dresses in all the prettiest colours in Mother's garden. Sometimes she wore a dress with all the colours mixed up together in stripes. She introduced herself to me as Mrs. Thompson, and led me into a sunny room full of plants, pictures, two upright pianos like the one we had at home, and several white kittens romping among the pillows of an armchair.

For the most part, she was kind and patient, but she kept a ruler close by for tapping erring fingers. Soon I had a beginners' book with funny squiggles and light and dark circles, which had as much trouble staying on the lines as the letters I tried to print at home.

In the weeks to follow, she taught me practice scales and a simple piece to play with the fingers of my right hand, all the while instilling in me what she considered to be good piano-playing habits.

"Lift those wrists—arch those fingers—try not to fidget, Catherine—keep your back straight, please!" I could hear her voice long after the lesson ended. First with one hand and then with the other, I practised the scales she gave me, trying hard to remember which fingers struck which keys. I wasn't always successful.

During an early lesson, my teacher placed a mysterious triangular box on top of the piano, wound it up and started it wagging. A whole new world opened to me. The fragile wand with the sliding weight wagged its tail right into my heart. Back and forth, back and forth, back and forth. The piano paled by comparison. My instrument of choice was now the metronome. Setting the weight high on the wand made the rhythm slow. One-and-two-and-one-and-two. Setting the weight low on the wand speeded things up to a ridiculous one-two-one-two-one-two. I was mesmerized! Trying to keep my head wagging at the same rate as the wand gave me a delightfully dizzy feeling, the best part of the lesson that day. This sudden interest in the metronome did not go unnoticed by Mrs. Thompson, who stopped it immediately and put it away out of my sight. I preferred playing the metronome to the piano, but I soon learned I had to master one of my lessons before I would see it again. With incentive like that, I was willing to play a whole set of scales without too many mistakes in order to have it brought out and started.

The children's classical pieces and the discipline of practicing my scales a whole five minutes a day were beginning to stifle my creative instincts. And I was most unhappy to learn that all the pieces in my practice book were written by composers who had been peacefully decomposing for centuries. More than anything else I wanted to play the kind of music I heard on the radio, with both hands and all my fingers at once.

For my generation, the introduction to classical music came in the form of cartoons shown before the main feature of most movies. At the time I did not realize this was classical music. It fit so nicely with characters like *Bugs Bunny* and *Mighty Mouse* that I considered it to be simply cartoon music. Because Brussels had no movie theatre, even this form of music was not available to me on a regular basis. Classical music concerts never came within fifty miles of Brussels, nor did I know anyone who had classical records to play at home. With the absence of any outside stimulation, my enthusiasm for this type of music failed dismally.

There were times when my teacher found it necessary to leave me on my own to practise my scales while she attended to another student. Alone and unsupervised, my discipline broke down altogether. Taking advantage of this new-found freedom, I abandoned the piano and my practice scales to romp with the kittens on the floor. After one of these unsuccessful lessons, where my mind along with the rest of me wandered right into another room, I was sent home in some disgrace. My disappointed parents were advised to wait a few years until I developed some self-discipline. Then perhaps, just perhaps, my latent, if any, musical talents would be assessed once again.

I returned happily to my former bad habit of playing what I wanted to play, when I wanted to play it, with as many fingers as I deemed appropriate. Keeping time on top of the piano, wagging its little wand at me, sat our nearly new metronome. Life was good!

During recess at school, I played the "Heart and Soul" duet on the school piano with any one of fifty girls who were all born able to play this song, whether or not they had ever had a piano lesson, or for that matter, a piano. As the years passed, I added a few legitimate pieces of music to my repertoire, painstakingly taught to me by Elayne from one of her music books. They had to be memorized because I no longer had music books at home, but at least no disapproving teacher stood over me with a ruler. And for that I was grateful.

A few years later Mrs. Thompson agreed to try again, giving me a second opportunity to learn to play the piano properly. This occasion proved only slightly more successful than the last, because now I could lie with the best of them. At every lesson I claimed to have practised a full hour each day, fooling no one, especially Mrs. Thompson. I guess now I had become an underhanded, multi-fingered pianist. Off I went to my weekly lesson prepared with nothing more than a rosy outlook, hoping my teacher wouldn't notice how many mistakes I was making. She did of course. She always did. Cock-eyed optimism is no substitute for hard work. I felt guilty about lying, and left my lessons full of resolve—a whole hour's practice every day without fail I told myself, closing the music room door behind me. But by the time I walked the three blocks to our house, I didn't give diddly-squat about my resolution, and the next lesson was as disastrous as the last.

Parental coaxing and cajoling, and on many occasions threats and bribery made little difference to the final outcome. Even my parents finally lost interest, and my piano lessons were discontinued, this time for good.

Without missing a beat, Margaret, the little girl with the copper-coloured hair—and only ten fingers as it turned out—became not only a pianist but a professional singer in her teens. As she was now a close friend, I spent many Saturday afternoons sitting with her while she prepared for an important recital or upcoming television appearance.

I could wait until the cows came home—nothing magical was going to happen to me until I became as dedicated as Margaret, and that wasn't likely to happen, suffering as I did from a particular lack of perseverance. It would have taken more than magic for me to attain Margaret's level of excellence. My love for the piano was just not as deeply ingrained as it needed to be.

If nothing else, my friendship with Margaret and my on-again-off-again love affair with the piano left me with a deep respect for the instrument and a love for all music that has grown throughout my life. Maybe that's enough.

The Good, the Bad, and the Bugly

O the green things growing,
the green things growing,
The faint sweet smell of the green things growing!

Dinah Marie Mulock Graik (1826-1887)

The winters of my childhood were long and cold, and the onset of spring eagerly awaited by anyone with a lick of sense. Early in a still wintry February, colourful seed catalogues arrived by mail to be pored over for possible additions to the gardens in spring. This became a winter tradition, and in many households gave promise of warmer days to come.

Serious decisions had to be made. Pages of order forms begged to be filled. Mother's list, always totalling to some astronomical amount, had to be slashed over and over again to a more affordable sum. Still, this procedure took weeks of exquisite planning, making spring seem closer and our winters not quite so interminable.

One day in April a soft wind began to dry the ground, and within a few weeks the soil could be worked in anticipation of planting time. The grueling chores of spading and cultivating, fertilizing and raking was undertaken by Mother, though toward the end of the job not always with the greatest enthusiasm. These soil preparations continued well into May, when a vast assortment of seeds and bulbs arrived to be planted.

Not entrusted with the exacting work of setting out stakes and string to ensure eventual straight rows, my job was sprinkling tiny lettuce seeds along the string line or pressing onion sets into a little trench. Sometimes I placed pieces of potato, each with three eye sprouts intact, into holes in little hills of soil. Carrots had to be planted too, because everyone knew eating them allowed us to see in the dark. During the War, wasn't it carrots that helped the Spitfire pilots spot enemy planes at night? Of course it wasn't. The real magic was radar, but that was top secret for a long time, and the theory of improved night vision through the consumption of carrots died hard. Mother was still using that ploy on me years after the War ended.

Planting the garden lasted several back-breaking days, though the real work had just begun. As the daily weeding and watering began to produce results, little green shoots appeared in the dark soil. Mother thinned and weeded along the rows every day until tiny blossoms appeared amidst the bright green foliage. Soon the fight against the relentless garden pests would begin.

The assailants came in all sizes, colours and shapes, and few plants were completely safe from them for an entire season. Mother took the infestations personally. Whether they crawled, burrowed, flew or hopped, she always had a system of eradication.

Only too eager to share the mysteries of nature with my brother and myself, she carefully revealed the intimate details of each tiny creature, even if their futures were less than secure. The strategy worked for the most part, though I never cared to be on intimate terms with any of them. Once in a while a cry of anguish could be heard from the garden as another predator was spotted devouring its favourite vegetable. But when Mother discovered her first plump green tomato worm, her horror knew no bounds. You would have thought her garden had been invaded by Martians. Tommy, an elderly neighbour with sixty years of gardening experience behind him, gave her a quick lesson on the creature's habits and how best to control it. By the time she got around to sharing the knowledge with us, she appeared to be in complete and fearless control, holding the worm in the palm of her hand and gently rolling it over with her thumbnail to reveal its natural, if well-concealed, beauty.

All this thinning, weeding, dusting and squashing resulting in the most amazing array of vegetables, freshly crisp and tasting the way they should taste—three minutes from garden to kitchen.

* * * * *

"You are nearer God's heart in a garden, than anywhere else on Earth." Those words by someone I can't remember became a mantra for Mother, who had a special fondness for God and flowers. When she could afford the luxury, she worked from morning to night in her flower garden, stopping only long enough to make a cup of tea. She possessed a clear understanding of each plant's needs, and they rewarded her with an endless profusion of blooms from May till October. Delphiniums and lupines in a variety of pinks, blues and purples grew in charming chaos in the large central garden bed. Sun-drunk honeybees, dizzy with scent, sorted through the petals hunting for nectar, filling the air with a busy humming. Looking to me more like flying flowers than insects, the butterflies who visited the hollyhocks made no sound at all.

Watching this frantic activity from a child-sized clump of alyssum, I encountered my first bumblebee. He had been busy minding his own business gathering pollen, when a five year old bottom interrupted his work in an unexpected way. Using the only weapon he had at his disposal, he retaliated. I was no happier about the situation than he—though considerably more vocal about it—and a crumpled stinger was the least of his worries once I located my assailant. That first encounter with a bumblebee proved to be a bitter experience for both of us.

One spring, Mother discovered a fur-lined rabbit's burrow, well-hidden among the delphiniums in the central flower bed, with several tiny babies curled up inside. She delighted in relating how the mother had softened the burrow by plucking pieces of her own fur from her breast. Only too aware that later in the season the babies would invade her vegetable garden, Mother nonetheless had a tender spot for all of nature's younger generation. I promised to be watchful of the whereabouts of Googy-Buzzy, who was at the time the Ghenghis Khan of the animal kingdom. To my knowledge, the babies remained safe, busy as he was with the field mouse population in the wilder parts of the garden.

When my parents bought the house, Mother inherited an abundance of goutweed which had been planted as foundation cover. She was successful in exterminating this stubborn plant on two sides of the house, but the situation at the back remained hopeless despite her constant digging. When she eradicated the scourge in one place, it sprang up twice as strong in another, and for its trouble earned the nickname 'Dancing Betty'. I preferred this more picturesque name, and felt some sympathy for the plant that could thrive despite Mother's unrelenting efforts to destroy it. The tenacious Dancing Betty may have lost a battle here and there, but she definitely won the war. The plant continued to grow ten years later when we sold the house, and upon recent inspection I found it thriving still, after fifty years.

Mother began to construct a compost pile long before it was ecologically fashionable to do so, extolling its virtues on anyone within earshot. Our pile, a small pit six feet square bounded by low wooden walls, hungrily devoured grass clippings, garden refuse, fallen leaves and rotting apples all season. Despite its distance from the house, the compost pile could be a noisome thing in the heat of summer if the wind happened to be blowing from that direction. But the gardens, happy recipients of Mother's special mixture each spring, bloomed their thanks all season.

In the formal garden, pink climbing roses covered the white trellis in an impenetrable jumble of blossoms, while red floribundas bloomed in beds under the bay windows from June through September. About once a month, Mother spaded a mound of long-spent tea leaves in around their roots, claiming that like herself, the roses needed this boost once in a while. It was and still is a strange thing about our dependency on tea. Mother referred to it as a wonder drug, and perhaps she was right. It warmed her when she was cold, cooled her when she was hot, raised her spirits when they were low, and calmed her nerves when she was upset. At least one and maybe two wars were fought on the strength of it, and everyone knows another was fought because of it. Simple, glorious tea.

* * * * *

When my mother's Scottish blood was roused, she heard again the distant skirl of the pipes and became a mighty foe indeed. The wanton destruction of one of her gardens caused one such Celtic outburst.

It took several years and an enormous amount of work for Mother to complete her rock garden, but by far the hardest part was hauling home each rock once she found it and hoisting it into place. Using Doug's wagon she carted home some of the smaller rocks from a pile at the edge of a farmer's field. But her favourite, a large granite specimen in a startling shade of pink, she found while on vacation at Lake Huron. I have no idea how she got that one home, but I imagined there was a taxi somewhere in desperate need of new springs. Mother placed it in one end of the rock garden where it sat like a sparkling exclamation point after a colourful statement.

This was no ordinary rock garden to Mother. She was interested not only in the flowers that grew around them, but in the rocks themselves, aware of their ages and the forces involved in shaping each one in her collection. Her obsession with rocks lasted for as long as she was able to bend over and pick up another one.

Like a floral brook, the rock garden ran along the road at the western boundary of our property, its tiny spreading plants tumbling up and over the rocks, or settled in orderly clumps between them. With the windows open on a summer's evening, the moist air carried in the spicy fragrance of night-scented stock, a sweet reminiscence of those hard, red Christmas candies we found in our stockings.

Two years after the completion of the garden, the village decided to pave the laneway that ran past our house. An improvement to be sure, since previously it had been given only a dusting of gravel and a glaze of oil when it had been remembered at all. The surveyors came one day, determined the right-of-way for the road, put down their stakes and went off to another job. No one said a word to Mother, who did not view the stakes as any kind of threat. A few weeks later, she came home to find that someone, in a master stroke of urban planning, had bulldozed a path down the middle of the rock garden. The fact that the area had been landscaped did not sway the bulldozer driver one bit. He saw his duty and he did it.

I found Mother heart-broken, sitting with her face in her hands on her large pink rock, now completely unearthed and lying on its side. Her lovely rock garden lay about her in ruins. Given time to consider the destruction, her despair changed to a jaw-tightening anger, and whenever that happened you had a potential for drama. A battle-scarred combatant in the war of life, Mother flung herself into the search for the culprits and the reason for the outrage.

It didn't take long to discover the reason. Too eager to see the results of her grand plan, in a moment of carelessness, Mother had not made certain the entire garden lay within our property line. Most properties in town were large. Where one started and another ended had rarely mattered before. Neighbours did not insist on protecting every square inch of a property that might in some cases encompass an acre. Rarely questioned, the memories of property lines faded over time.

As it turned out, a strip of the rock garden lay on property owned by the village, and apparently the village protected its property with a vengeance. Although their methods were heartless, they were simply taking back what was rightfully theirs. Right or wrong, Mother wasted no time in wringing an apology from everyone involved, right down to the bulldozer operator, whose eyesight—and at one point, lineage—

came into question. Under a relentless barrage, each workman in turn reeled back as if he'd stepped on the business end of a rake.

After that incident Mother had neither the heart nor the strength to restore her rock garden to its original beauty. So for the remaining years we were in the house, a pile of rocks in the far corner of the yard bore silent tribute to what once had been. I am thankful that time erases most distressing scenes, leaving memories once again bright with sunshine and gardens radiant with colour.

* * * * *

Beyond the vegetable garden and behind a row of spruce trees, stood the home of a much larger family. As children, we played together, fought together, and grew wild together all year. Rarely fewer than seven and often as many as twelve people lived in this square, white brick house, well within yelling distance.

At mealtime, the matriarch of the family, a woman of generous voice and proportions, approached the back step as if to centre stage. From here she summoned each of her children, whose names were shouted distinctly and with a fancy upward twist at the end. Most of the time she began with the name of the youngest child, working her way to the eldest. Sometimes she worked in reverse order. And occasionally she started in the middle and lost her way altogether. One thing for sure, with volume like that, her kids could have been playing in the next county and still made it home in time for dinner. Each day I listened carefully to the order of the names, hoping she might forget and mistakenly call mine. It would only be polite to show up.

To my father, cleanliness was not as close to godliness as good table manners. Accordingly our meals were sedate affairs, downright dull by comparison to those enjoyed by this larger family. For instance, no part of us other than our wrists was allowed on the table at any time. This rule would not have gone down well in our neighbour's house, where I've seen everything from the waist up on the table. But I think only one person at a time was allowed to do that. They did have their standards.

Because I have been a guest in their home, I can speak from personal experience that mealtime there was a three-ring circus. From seven to twelve places were set for every meal around an enormous wooden pedestal table in the kitchen, over which a colourful oilcloth was tacked securely in case it slipped out from under a dozen plates and a multitude of heavy serving bowls.

On one occasion which included me, lunch for the younger children consisted of warm bread fresh from the oven, edges blackened and crisp, slathered with butter and liberally sprinkled with brown sugar. This was a rare treat indeed, for as often as I begged, it never appeared on any menu in our house. My father had definite ideas about food. We were to eat bread with everything, except sugar. If we had to have brown sugar at all, it belonging on our porridge and not as part of a main course at any other time of the day. His eccentric food preferences covered every meal. If he had had his way all of our food would have been boiled, especially the vegetables, to a nice mushy consistency. Salads and all fresh vegetables were suspect to him, not being familiar foods from his childhood in England. Mother saved me from scurvy.

During meals in our neighbour's home, amid orders to pass plates for second helpings and directions to sit up and eat, came wails of frustration from aggrieved sources as arguments and the occasional fist fight erupted. These altercations were commonplace, generally passing unnoticed by parents too busy making sure they were getting their fair share of bounty.

Elayne and I, and sometimes my brother and his friends, played but more often fought with these children all summer, spending long hours hurling insults at each other from the relative safety of our respective back yards.

"You're not our friends anymore, you bunch of snot rags, and you can't come over here ever again. So there!" came the colourful threat from their side, accompanied by the traditional impish facial expressions—heads tilted, eyes closed, noses wrinkled and tongues stuck out.

"Ooooh!—I'm broken hearted—I almost farted!" floated vulgarly across the garden from the good guys on our side, backed up by outrageous body language of our own, and just to be sure we had the last word, a good old fashioned raspberry or two.

"Pbsspbt!!" "Pbsssppbbt!!"

"We're telling! You swore!" raised the confrontation to new heights—especially if it were followed by a thundering retreat through their back porch and into the house.

"Hey, Mom! They swore!" could be heard shrieked in unison at the volume of a band saw. This never failed to cause a stampede to the safety of our shed, where we peeked through a variety of knot holes in the boards, giggling at the cranky, if massive, reinforcements now gathered on the front lines. Verbal abuse launched in our direction kept us under cover until the General had her say and withdrew with her little platoon of tattle-tales.

Almost immediately the kids who hated us now more than anything returned unaccompanied to the property line, each with a delicious slab of homemade bread and jam to be eaten in full taunting view of the enemy. Us. It was time to forgive and forget.

So okay, maybe it was for the wrong reason, but there was a limit to how long we could hold a grudge where homemade bread was concerned. A clearing of the air such as this—along with a general sharing of the snack—ensured that peace would be restored, for the next couple of hours at least.

Run Fast, Run Far

A first trip to the dentist is just another in a series of unavoidable childhood learning experiences, though the lesson I learned that day had little to do with the dentist.

Despite claims by Doug and me that we had perfect teeth, Mother went ahead and made an appointment for three dental checkups the following Saturday, one for each of us. Without a car, this meant a thirty minute train ride to Wingham where the dentist had his office. The train schedule dictated the length of our stay at two hours, lots of time for three appointments. In Mother's absence, my father agreed to stay alone in the store, balancing his time between his customers and his watch repairs, all for the sake of our good dental health. Owning a car would have simplified matters, but my father remained adamant about avoiding debt at all cost.

"We'll buy a car," he promised, "the minute our ship comes in." And because he'd never lied to me before, I took him literally, watching for that ship whenever we were near any sizable body of water.

Having seen the dentist the year before, Doug was clearly not thrilled about the prospect of seeing him twice in one lifetime. And because nothing I can think of is as contagious as an older brother's fear, it was my fondest wish that Saturday would never come. Just to spite me, it dawned especially bright and sunny right on schedule, the day after Friday.

Trains, in my experience, had always been associated with good times—pleasant family visits to Niagara Falls and shopping trips to Toronto. I had never thought of trains before with any sense of menace. But this time I watched the station disappear with a niggling fear in the pit of my stomach. If my brother's premonitions were correct, this trip would not be one I'd look back on with pleasure.

Mother would condone no more whining about our sad plight, and instead busied herself rearranging the two bench seats in the passenger compartment into a little room for the three of us with a window of our own. The seats, I remember, were dark red and prickly, with heavy white antimacassars draped over the back of each one. In winter these seats felt warm and comfortable, but in summer they were torture on small bare legs. I sat on my hands trying to avoid the prickles, but they went to sleep in two minutes and I had to shake them to get the circulation going again.

Wobbling down the aisle like a large blue wind-up toy, the conductor took our tickets, tore them in half, and slipped the stubs into the bottom edge of the green window shade. I told him we were going to the dentist.

"Better you than me," he said, smiling at Mother. I didn't get the joke. Maybe it's just as well.

Doug and I spent most of our travelling time drinking copious amounts of foul tasting water from flimsy conical paper cups, and the rest of the time flushing the toilet to watch the railroad ties whizzing by beneath the train. Eventually even those good times had to come to an end.

"Wingham!" shouted the conductor, struggling to keep his balance as he weaved his way through the coach, "This way out!"

We climbed the creaking stairs to the dentist's waiting room on the main street with less than our usual speed. Blinds lowered against the strong morning sun intensified the stuffiness of the room, giving everything a sickly yellow colour, including us.

Mother was at her reassuring best, smiling too much and patting me on the knee, something she did only when she knew I was in for something painful.

"It won't hurt a bit, you'll see," she promised. I'd heard that before. She'd used it for everything from removing a sliver to getting a needle from the doctor. It hadn't worked then and it wouldn't work now. Although, just to prove her point about having nothing to fear, she offered to see the dentist first—probably not the wisest thing she'd ever done.

With no receptionist to calm our jitters, Doug and I were left on our own to dredge up the required amount of courage, the ultimate test of our mettle. Unfamiliar smells of antiseptic and the closeness of the little room did not help. I tried to concentrate on the children's book I'd been given, but it wasn't easy with the high pitched whine of a demented wasp in the next room.

"It's not a wasp," Doug corrected, "It's a drill."

"A drill? What drill? Why? Tell me!" I insisted, beginning a rapid descent into hysteria.

The only drills I had ever seen were jack-hammers drilling holes in the road outside our store. They made a terrible mess. Poor Mother. What would she look like the next time we saw her? Even with my ear pressed hard against the door to the examining room, I could hear only a muted voice that didn't sound like Mother's. There were no bloodcurdling screams like the ones he'd hear if he tried using that drill on me. She had been gone a long time.

Doug put down the book he'd been trying to read and began pacing the floor. He wore the same look I'd seen on a deer caught in the headlights of my uncle's car. Suddenly he stopped pacing, froze momentarily, then bolted toward the door.

"Where are you going?" I insisted, getting up to follow him.

"Come on. Let's go! Run!"

Doug had a pretty good idea I'd do anything he told me to do, and I saw no reason to disappoint him now. He ran out of the dentist's office, down the narrow stairway, up the street and into the park. I tried to keep up, but my legs were shorter and I kept falling behind.

"Where are we going?" I panted.

"I don't know. Hurry up, will ya?"

"Mommy will be mad," was my final plea for reason, but by this time he was a dot in the distance. I had never seen him so scared and I found it unsettling. Doug had always been the level-headed one and had never made a serious error in judgement, at least not with me along. Could the dentist be that frightening, I wondered? Why take a chance? Suddenly I was in complete agreement with his decision to leave.

We ran down one street and then another and another until we were completely lost on one of the residential streets, far from the dentist's office and the whining drill. Too tired to go any farther, we collapsed onto a shady lawn to consider our next move. We knew Mother would come looking for us as soon as she realized we were missing. And the longer it took her to find us, the more annoyed she'd be.

I couldn't bear to think of our father hearing about this. He was not the regular disciplinarian in our family, but then we'd never run away before. Maybe in this case, he'd make an exception. The best thing to do, we decided, would be to find Mother before she found us. Maybe even find the dentist, and throw ourselves on his mercy. But where was his office? We didn't remember how many turns we'd made or in what direction we were facing. We knew we couldn't just sit there, so we walked and we walked some more, hoping something would begin to look familiar. Nothing did. We walked for a long time.

But just when things were looking bleakest, the distant sound of a train whistle—ours as luck would have it—plunged bleak to a new low. This was followed shortly by the voice we'd been dreading. I knew it would be hard to talk my way out of this one, but I had to try.

"You two get back here right now!"

"Keep walking and don't look back." Doug whispered.

"We aren't supposed to talk to strangers."

"But that sounds like Mom. We have to talk to her."

"Do as I say. I'm older."

Well, he had me there. I walked faster, trying to keep up with him, but it was almost impossible not to turn around, lost, scared, and nosy as I was.

"I'm warning you. Stop right where you are!"

Doug glanced at me with that same trapped look he'd worn in the dentist's office. Then ever so slowly we turned around. It wasn't all bad. At least we weren't lost anymore. I decided to tell her it was so hot in the waiting room we went for a walk to cool off and couldn't find our way back. Yeah. That would work. There was a slim chance she'd even feel sorry for us.

Who was I kidding? She wouldn't fall for that. Mothers have built-in lie-detectors. It's a known fact. I blurted it out anyway, hoping to plant a seed of uncertainty, but clearly she was in no mood for excuses, lame or otherwise. Her eyes were two shades darker than I remembered them and that was scary. How could facing the dentist be worse than this? Holding us together in a grip like a vice, she reminded us in a strangely controlled fashion that we had not only missed our dental appointments but also the only train back to Brussels.

"Now get going, the pair of you, we have to find someone to take us home!"

We were herded into the back seat of a taxi, while Mother and the driver discussed the price of the seventeen mile trip home and something about motherhood that I couldn't hear. Whatever it was it made the driver laugh out loud, but he didn't look around at us. They were definitely in cahoots. For a moment I thought his laughter might change Mother's mood— laughter sometimes did—but this time it didn't seem to be working. She didn't look around either and didn't speak to us all the way home.

When the front door closed behind us, the silence was finally broken—and Mother could break a silence better than anybody I've ever known. You could say our dental appointments were even more painful without the dentist.

And the moral of the story? Often what you learn from a learning experience is something else entirely.

Good Old Golden Rule Days

Tis education forms the common mind:
Just as the twig is bent the tree's inclined.

. Alexander Pope

On a wide expanse of lawn on Alexander Street stood the Brussels Public School, an imposing two story, yellow brick building of Victorian vintage. From 1895 until 1950, every student in the village from grade one to grade thirteen studied here under a system known as the 'continuation school'. To the rear and to one side of the building lay our only sports facilities, two softball diamonds. Around them lay a playground of erupting tree roots, marble pots, exhausted clumps of grass, spindly weeds, and mud.

Over the span of fifty winters, the school took on its mottled grey appearance due to the continuous belching of coal smoke from a monstrous furnace in the basement. Bold and brooding, this building represented real structure in our lives, never-changing, rule-enforcing structure, and through the years it became as familiar to us as any of our homes.

Our school custodian, an English veteran of the Boer War named Jimmy, had a face deeply ingrained with the dust we created, and honest blue eyes that twinkled with good humour above a pipe-yellowed handlebar mustache. Late in the afternoons he swept the classrooms and halls until the creaking wooden floors were stained black from their daily dose of dustbane. Despite Jimmy's efforts, the school bore the unmistakable odour that can only be accumulated over decades of exposure to coal dust, pencil shavings, glue, overheated kids and the occasional puddle of vomit. Every spring the teachers brought in large bouquets of lilacs and peonies in a valiant attempt to mask the smell, but with limited success.

Grade one to grade eight occupied the upper floor of the school, several grades to a room. The high school students on the first floor, their classes small by comparison, came and left mysteriously, often by an open window. Rarely speaking to any of us from the upper floor, they went about the business of being ordinary teenagers far removed from our orbit. We did not see them at recess, and most were gone before we were dismissed for the day. We may have occupied the same building, but we were living in two separate worlds.

* * * * *

The lesson I had learned from my first trip to the dentist the year before was just the beginning. There were many still to come, some more educational than others. I began school at the age of five. And as if doing it once were not traumatic enough, I did it all over again the following year.

On the morning of my first attempt, at exactly eight forty-five, Mother deposited me at the door of the primary room in my new navy jumper with pleats fore and aft. There I stayed, glued to the spot, until I heard the school bell ring and was nearly trampled by a crowd of exuberant classmates. My teacher, ever vigilant for first morning nerves, pried my fingers from the doorknob and escorted me to a little desk halfway down the first row. I stood, hardly breathing, by my assigned desk, while a tone-deaf chorus of voices asked God to save the King. With the others I bowed my head for the morning prayer, but in my nervousness I couldn't remember the words. When the teacher read my name out loud during roll call, I remained silent, unsure what the word 'present' meant. I had never felt so foreign.

The whole concept of school was lost on me. I had been plucked from a world of play and plunged into one of constant supervision and discipline, with none of the gentle pursuasion that kindergarten might have provided. This, for me, only hastened the inevitable.

At first, I was under the impression I had a choice in the matter. If school did not meet with my approval, I could simply go home and forget the whole thing. But when that door slammed shut on my first escape attempt, I discovered the terrible truth. I would be trapped in a room full of strangers for the rest of my life, where it would be impossible to reach my mother no matter how great my need. Never again would I feel the soft grass beneath my bare feet, or breathe the fresh air of the open field. How could they expect me to put up with this outrage?

A desperate panic mounted inside me. I tried to blink back the tears that burned behind my eyes, but one squeezed through despite my efforts. I dabbed at it with the handkerchief I found in my pocket. Mother had thought of everything. How I missed her. Other tears formed behind that one and soon I could hold them back no longer. Tears flooded my eyes, spilled over, cascaded off my chin and splashed onto my desk top. This attracted a certain amount of unwanted attention from those classmates sitting nearby, who were regarding me with amused scorn. I closed my eyes tightly, as much to get away from their stares as to stem the flow of tears. Not knowing what else to do, to keep from sobbing out loud I held my breath for as long as I could. And I could hold it a long time. It worked. But it also caused my face to turn a bright red, and somehow that caused me to topple into the aisle in a dead faint. My alarmed young teacher telephoned my mother, who came to take me home, quite exhausted from my morning's ordeal.

With a strange feeling of satisfaction I imagined how pitiful I must have looked lying there in the aisle, a tear-stained champion for freedom. The rest of my day was spent at home, barefoot in the back yard without a care in the world, hanging upside down from my swing seat letting my hair sweep the dust into little piles. This was more like it.

The next morning, determined to try again, I waited to be returned to my classroom. I would wait a long time. Someone else had decided my future. School was to remain a mystery to me until the next September. Nothing could be done about it. I had to wait. So wait I did, for one long, interminable year. To make matters worse, by the end of that year, Doug so impressed his grade two teacher with his sporadic flashes of brilliance that he was allowed to skip grade three entirely and move on to grade four. Now he was three grades ahead of me and growing smarter by the minute, a fact he was prepared to demonstrate at every opportunity.

* * * * *

The butter-coloured sunlight of September, one year later, found me in the same navy blue jumper—somewhat shorter now—ready and willing to give school another chance. My second attempt at an education proved to be more successful. One extra year at home made me lonely for friends and hungry for learning.

The walls of our primary room were painted the same dirty yellow as the walls in every public building in town—as if somewhere there was a rule about it. Facing the front of the room and bolted to the floor, the small wooden desks with iron scrollwork on their sides were arranged in rows of six.

Our classroom included grades one, two and three, sitting side-by-side, eavesdropping on each other's lessons. The grade one desks were free of carved initials due in no small part to our deficient printing skills, though mainly to our lack of pocket knives. Generations of grade one students, maybe even the grandparents of my present classmates, had contributed to the wads of petrified chewing gum peppering the bottom of each book compartment. There were long grooves on the desk tops to hold our fat, black pencils and vacant holes where inkwells would have been, had we been allowed to get anywhere near ink.

Into these yawning inkwell holes we tossed apple cores, candy wrappers and orange peels, whenever they had to be disposed of in a hurry, creating an overwhelming dump-like aroma in the room. Adding to this ambiance, a thin film of smelly white paste coated every surface and permeated all of us to the marrow.

Mel, the little boy assigned to the desk in front of me, had a particular passion for the stuff. Needing little encouragement from the boys in grades two and three, he devoured a colourful assortment of crayons, washing them down with a generous slurp of white paste. Whenever he managed to pry his lips apart, he grinned a toothy rainbow to the delight of the older boys on the far side of the room. Mel's unique appearance was enhanced most days by his insistence on wearing a pair of his older brother's rubber boots, whose tops reached a spot well above his knees. With his unbendable legs stretched to mid-aisle on either side of his desk and his mouth a kaleidoscope of colour, he was not only a comical sight but also a serious hazard to navigation.

In two rows of little desks, the grade one students included Frances, Bill, David, Mary Beth, Carol, Harold, Mel, Murray and Arnold. Not to mention Sneezy and

Wheezy—two of the evil dwarfs if I remember correctly—though I sometimes don't.

Anything but a melting pot of ethnicity, my class was a simple mixture of second- and third-generation English, Scottish and Irish. I fell madly in love that first morning with the front half of a set of twin boys who occupied two desks across from mine. The next day the teacher changed the seating plan, and being unable to tell one twin from the other I simply had to forget about it and get on with life.

Even more unique than twins, a six year old aunt sat across the aisle from her six year old niece. How could this be possible, I wondered? I thought you had to be old to be an aunt. At any rate, these two little girls and the set of twin boys represented the exotic for us. We were simply ordinary 1940's vintage kids—clean when we had to be, well-behaved when threatened, occasionally scabby, sometimes warty, and too often boisterous, pigheaded and cruel.

For the most part, I enjoyed school that first year. I revelled in the pink plasticine the teacher gave me, rolling it into a long snake on the top of my desk until it reached the edge and fell to the floor where it broke into other snakes. I liked the smell of the white paste and the feel of the blunt scissors in my hands. But most especially I liked to clap the blackboard erasers. Only the best-behaved students were given this most enviable task, somehow excluding most of the boys in the room. Standing outside the back door in a huge cloud of chalk dust, I clapped the erasers until I looked like a ghost.

Our school primer contained the immortal saga of another set of twins, Dick and Jane, along with Sally their little sister, their dog Spot, and their orange cat Puff. From what I can remember of the dialogue, Dick and Jane were nasty little siblings who spent most of their time teasing their pets.

"See Spot chase Puff," said Jane.

"Run Spot Run!" urged Dick.

"See Puff climb the drapes," said Jane.

"Better luck next time, Spot," laughed Dick. Or something to that effect. We loved those stories so much that one or two of the boys stayed in grade one for another year just so they could read them again.

My first fire drill at school proved to be as unpredictable as all the other firsts in my life. While our young, inexperienced teacher explained the horrible fate that awaited us if we did not follow her instructions to the letter, she failed to clarify the meaning of the word 'drill'. So later in the day when I heard the jangling of the school bell, which was the signal for FIRE, I assumed it to be the genuine article and reason to panic in the extreme. The teacher formed us into single file at the classroom door as the excitement mounted.

"It is important to obey me class. Keep in line," our teacher instructed in her usual calm voice.

"Walk quickly and quietly down the back stairway and out the girl's door. Remember now. Do not run!"

This simple instruction would have worked well enough if only I had known that the drill was not associated with any immediate peril to me or my personal belongings. Remembering my new red coat hanging alone and vulnerable in the cloakroom—imaginary flames singeing its pretty silk lining—I forgot our recent instructions, and instead of turning left, I turned right and ran as fast as I could in the direction of my endangered garment. The remainder of the class, obeying orders to keep in line—fools that they were—followed me at breakneck speed into the cloakroom. At the end of this procession followed our teacher, her face flushed with confusion and embarrassment, yelling at each of us in turn as we yanked frantically for all manner of precious belongings hanging there.

When my little rogue band eventually assembled on the lawn outside, it was with our coats, umbrellas, marble bags and skipping ropes securely tucked under our arms. I expected to see flames jumping and playing on the roof, but the school looked the same as it had always done, and this was how I learned the meaning of the word 'drill'. I had still to master the word 'obey'.

* * * * *

Grade one students were not escorted to school after their first day, their safety taken more or less for granted. We did not yet view strangers with suspicion, but were offered friendship from everyone, irrespective of age or gender. It says something for quiet village life in the 1940's that stern parental warnings began and ended with this English children's song:

> *When you cross the road by day or night,*
> *Beware of the dangers that loom in sight,*
> *Look to the left and look to the right,*
> *And you'll never, never get runned over.*

While in grade one, I discovered our comings and goings had some mysterious connection to the large wooden clock that hung by the door. I gazed hopelessly at those stick-like figures all standing at attention. Unlike the fat, round numbers we were learning to print, these I's and V's and X's left me bewildered. In the end it really didn't matter. Our teacher told us when to go home for lunch or out for recess, and the school bell took care of the rest. The clock remained inscrutable to me for years.

In the spring of my first year at school, a public health nurse came to check our vital signs. Occupying the teachers' office at the end of the hall, she made arrangements to see each of us privately. We looked forward to this break in our daily routine once we discovered no pain was involved. The older boys in grade three tried to scare us by saying the nurse had come to give us a needle, but when the first victim returned unpunctured the rest of us followed willingly.

Some of my classmates must have been more vital than others because they stayed away a long time. My eye examination was not entirely successful. Although I could see the letters well enough, I could not exactly remember which letter was which. The nurse looked in my ears, in my mouth, in my eyes, and down my neck. Whatever she was looking for, I knew I didn't have it. This ordeal over, it seems I looked a fright, since she tried to make me more presentable by combing my hair with two popsicle sticks. This proved to be a more time-consuming business than necessary, though I suppose she had no option as she didn't seem to have a comb in her possession. She must have combed everyone's hair the same way, because it took her three full days to work her way through the school.

Some years later I discovered what the nurse had been looking for with the popsicle sticks. I expect one or two of us rewarded her in this search, but I never found out who. The girls tried the popsicle stick routine at noon hour, but the lime ones kept getting stuck in our hair, so the practice was abandoned. With the public health nurse no longer uppermost in our minds, we returned to our old bad habits within days.

About this time, I discovered I could cross my eyes at will. This talent was not revealed at the eye examination as I didn't want the nurse to think I was showing off. Besides, Mother forbade me to perform this fabulous trick, claiming that one day my eyes would stick that way and then I'd be sorry. But I didn't know any tricks that other kids couldn't do as well or better—only this one. It made me feel dizzy to see two of everything in the room, and even better, it made my classmates giggle out loud.

Although we didn't have group pictures taken until grade three, a photographer came one day to take individual pictures while we sat at our desks. When he asked me to smile for the birdie, something in me snapped. I couldn't help it. I crossed my eyes. "Click!" went the camera. "Thank you," went the photographer. "Next!"

I suppose he thought I looked that way all the time. The result is that the only picture I have of my first few years of school is that one with the goofy grin and the crossed eyes. Mother was right. I am sorry.

Grade three brought the mystery of the times tables. I can remember feeling disillusioned on learning that the product of one times one is still one. All that finger counting, all that mental gymnastics, and I was no further ahead. Having mastered the one times table, I applied what I had learned to the two times table and found someone had changed all the rules. It didn't seem fair. The other numbers held their own special terrors that had to be sorted out as the years went along.

* * * * *

In grade four, we encountered a teacher with an exaggerated sense of his musical ability. Along with this trait, he had an unhealthy mean streak that saw knuckles wrapped with wooden rulers and heads battered with hard-cover books. In his class talking was a crime, and any deviation from the norm inconceivable. He still appears in my memory as a hostile figure, spitting anger at every turn. In an attempt to avoid his wrath, we ducked and weaved, dodged and parried, all the way through grades four and five. While we couldn't appreciate it at the time, I imagine we have him to thank for our superior reflexes.

One late spring afternoon, when the call of the wild made it all but impossible to sit quietly in our stuffy classroom, the teacher promised us something special if we completed our assignments by recess. Could he be taking us for a nature walk in the woods behind the school? Probably not. The last time he did this, the boys ate every wild leek they could find, resulting in our near asphyxiation when we returned to the classroom.

Our teacher vowed he'd never take us anywhere again, and he was as good as his word. No, the something special was to be even better than that. As we were leaving the room at recess, he told us we would be treated to the *Moonlight Sonata*.

Defective listening skills aside—and with sincere apologies to Beethoven—we heard what we wanted to hear, and what we wanted to hear was the 'Moonlight Sinatra', starring the one and only Frank Sinatra. We had recently been shown a short film about the importance of keeping our nails clean—so the same projector and screen could be used for something important like a movie, couldn't it? With our assignments finished on time, we returned after recess with a greater than usual enthusiasm.

No movie screen had been set up in readiness. No projector stood in evidence. Instead, the school's upright piano stood at the front of the room with our teacher sitting at it smiling his smuggest smile. We were baffled by these developments. What happened to the movie?

A long-term veteran of the class, impervious to either learning or authority, Tom made no apology for his scepticism. He had seen it all. By the time I reached grade four he was a school legend, having been there for as long as any of us could remember. No one knew for sure how old he was. Even he couldn't say with any certainty. Rumour had it he was fourteen, but it was hard to tell.

His overall dusty appearance, the result of a two mile walk to school over gravel roads every morning, concealed any hint of a definite age. He had the class routine, if not the lessons, down pat by the time I joined him in the row next to the window. Recess was his favourite subject. The others he simply tolerated. He did not grasp the intricacies of mathematics—he lived beyond mathematics anyway. He knew precisely the number of steps it took to reach the edge of the mill roof, as well as the exact angle required to catapult out into space to land in the only spot in the flume that would not kill him outright. In fact, he seemed to know anything worth knowing outside the classroom. He could catch a difficult fly ball while running in a pair of L'il Abner-sized work boots, or snare a wary sunfish when no one else had seen one for days. Tom was just structurally challenged. We his classmates sat firmly in two camps. There were those of us who befriended him because our respect for him bordered on fear, and those who avoided him for the same reason. Nobody took him for granted. He was big.

Tom had won every schoolyard scrap he ever entered, though he did not start any of them. He had been given the strap by most of the teachers in the school at one time or another, for the horrendous crimes of talking out of turn, or not talking when it was his turn, or for—and this is my all-time favourite—being late for school with no excuse, fifteen days in a row. Tom put in almost the required amount of time, grade after weary grade, never really passing any of the lessons he sat in on. The grade four teacher took personally the fact that Tom did not understand the basics of grade four subjects, and tried every mean trick in the book to force him to learn. Adding insult to injury, Tom did not seem unduly disturbed by this or much of anything else.

As that painful afternoon wore on, we continued to sit up straight in the position of respect with our hands clasped together on top of our desks, listening while our teacher enthralled himself at the piano, eyes closed, swaying gently to the rhythms of his music. Tom sat idly flipping the pages of his reader, occasionally yawning a lion-sized yawn and staring longingly out the window at a world where he felt more in tune.

At the end of his recital, our teacher interpreted the exaggerated applause as a sign of sincere appreciation, if not a genuine display of good taste. So he favoured us with a medley of Cole Porter selections, *a cappella*. I can still see him standing there beside the piano, his delicate hands clasped to his chest, moved almost to tears by a captivating rendition of *In the Still of the Night*. Normally shy, if not always quiet, Tom took matters into his own hands in the middle of the second song, suddenly demanding to know when the show was going to start.

This abrupt departure from classroom conformity was exhilarating, and I had to think of something really sad to keep from laughing out loud. Both a strict disciplinarian and a proponent of corporal punishment, this teacher was not one with whom we cared to take liberties. But it did not bother Tom. He had transgressed before and lived to tell the tale.

With the rubber strap from his centre drawer grasped firmly in his left hand and Tom's shirt collar held tightly in his right, the teacher pushed Tom out the door and over to the principal's office across the hall. We had been shown the strap at the beginning of the year, presumably to make its use unnecessary, but nonetheless it had been used many times, even on the youngest students.

Several sharp whacks could be heard through two closed doors, but nothing else. Nothing like the ruckus I would have raised had I been on the receiving end of that strap. What came next was the sound of something heavy being thrown against a door—then silence. The whole class sat frozen in their seats.

The door burst open, clattering against the blackboard. Tom shuffled more noisily than usual to his desk by the window. We turned as one, to make sure he had all his moving parts in the right places. The teacher, somewhat unsteady, appeared in the doorway pressing a red-spotted handkerchief to his nose. He stayed only long enough to dismiss the class for the rest of the day.

'Hero' was added to Tom's legend that year, but it hardly mattered. He didn't return to school that September. Nor did the teacher.

* * * * *

Friday afternoons were even better than weekends. Saturdays and Sundays were reality, for better or worse, but Friday afternoons were full of promise and that was best of all. Through eight years of school, we had an art class every Friday afternoon right after recess, one of the few times in the week when I could relax, because it was my best subject.

Responding to a request to find a subject on which to try their skills, the girls arrived with a bouquet of pussy willow or daffodils. Too preoccupied with a baseball game or a schoolyard fight, most of the boys forgot. With the ringing of the last bell, six frantic boys dashed into a nearby garden, bringing screams of protest from the owner at their bald-faced assault on his tulips. By the time the neighbour could shuffle out to the scene of the crime, the culprits had disappeared through the boys' entrance and were back inside the classroom, mangled tulips in hand.

Feeling that distance might improve our completed masterpieces, the teacher tacked each one to the bulletin board at the back of the room. Here, flowers of vaguely familiar colours grew in snowy gardens, lashed flat by Arctic gales. What the original subject had been in most cases remained a mystery.

Without realizing it, the enjoyment of school began to overtake me, though I think the special days had a lot to do with it. No sooner had we tired of the novelty of our first month with brand new scribblers and pencils, than we were presented with Hallowe'en, and a variety of cats and bats and jack-o-lanterns to decorate the room. When all traces of black and orange disappeared, it seemed only a matter of days before red and green took their places and preparations for Christmas broke the monotony of the times tables. Once we returned from Christmas holidays it wasn't long before we were buying valentines and decorating the classroom once again, this time with lacy paper doilies and red hearts. In early spring when winter started to lose its grip, the girls brought in snowdrops to fill the vase that sat on the teacher's desk—then tulips—then lilacs—then we lost interest.

By the end of June the school year was over, and the moment we had either been waiting for or dreading had arrived. Report Card Day. Few of us ever failed, not because we were particularly bright, but because by this time the teachers were sick to death of us. That's simply an assumption on my part, of course.

The Ugly Duckling of the Diamond

We played softball before school and at recess every day, unless a sudden snowstorm covered the diamond to a depth of three feet. But try as I might, I could never play the game with anything resembling skill. Like opposing poles, the ball and bat repelled each other at every swing. And because my lack of skill was well known, the choosing of sides for team play tormented me all through public school. In fact, arguments used to break out over which captain had to have me on her team. At times like this I disliked everybody on the team—and I wasn't even crazy about the game.

Why play softball at all, you ask? Because softball was the only sport played at our school. You played the game or you watched others playing it, and that was just too pathetic, even for me. Being on the sidelines was not an option. Besides, I thought I might acquire some skill through osmosis if nothing else. When that didn't happen, I was assigned a bogus position somewhere behind right field, between the laneway and the neighbour's vegetable garden. Few balls ever came that far, though I suppose that was the whole idea.

As often as I wished for recess to be over, my turn at bat always came around with loads of time for me to humiliate myself. Had someone ripped up a tree and told me to swing that, I would have gripped it with as much confidence as I gripped the bat. In Brussels in the 1940's, baseball skills were picked up the same way we picked up a virus—out of the air somewhere. There were no real ball teams until we were in our teens, and by then it was assumed we had learned all the skills we'd need. I did not seem to have a natural ability for softball, so I avoided the game as much as I could, and as a result, the skills avoided me. No one showed me the correct way to swing a bat, or what to look for in a ball worth swinging at. So I swung at everything—at high balls, low balls, at balls miles outside the strike zone and balls so far inside they grazed my knees. Could anyone *be* more hopeless and still be breathing?

The opposing team took advantage of my turn at bat to tie their shoelaces, freshen their bubble gum and readjust their pony tails. They knew that for the next minute or two they would be free from having to dive for a ball.

Slap! Into the catcher's mitt sailed the ball.

"Strike three. You're—out!" How I hated those words. But how often I heard them.

In the middle of another day's game, I noticed the sky growing dark. A storm was approaching. Thunder exploded over us and fork lightning licked the open fields behind the school. It was only an electrical storm. Even if we *were* playing under two maple trees, they saw no reason to delay the game. These were hard-core softball enthusiasts.

"Who's up?" yelled my captain. "Oh...yeah..."

"A lightning bolt about here please, God." I prayed, pointing to my chest. But of course nothing happened because as we all know, God is a softball fan, and even He wanted to see how the inning would play itself out. It looked like I was on my own. And up.

The pitcher wound up and pitched the ball.

"Strike one!" yelled the catcher, who incidentally was also the umpire. Does that sound fair?

I tapped the plate with the tip of my bat, the way I'd seen the others do it, though I didn't know why, and steeled myself for another strike. At that precise moment, a clap of thunder burst above my head. I'm pretty sure it was thunder. What I'm not sure about is whether the noise startled me into swinging at precisely the right second, or whether the electrical energy surging through the atmosphere somehow galvanized my batting ions. But everything came together for the first time in my life. "Thunk!" went the bat as it hit the ball. The catcher, with unusual eloquence, murmured, "Ho-ly Shit!"

The right field position, attempting to pull up each of her knee socks to exactly the same height, was otherwise occupied. The ball sailed past her, unnoticed. I froze while it bounced wildly across the lane to hide in a neat row of cabbages. Someone yelled, "Run!"

Now there's something I didn't hear every day. Seeing as how I had only ever aspired to first base, I wasn't sure what constituted second. Searching my mind through past games, I remembered it lay somewhere near the maple tree, so I stepped on every root and slapped the trunk on my way past, just in case. Third base was easier—it was an actual base—a triangular piece of wood implanted in the ground by some softball enthusiast long forgotten.

The right fielder continued to search in vain through the cabbage plants for the ball, while my team jumped up and down like a row of pistons. Chugging faster than I thought possible, I crossed home plate just as fat raindrops began to splatter the infield dust, collapsing into the first pair of welcoming arms I came to.

A home run! Me! Imagine that! For one glorious moment I wasn't a charity case. I was one of the team. Doncha' just love softball! And what a kind, appreciative, truly wonderful bunch of girls I had on my team! The opposing team, now in a catatonic state, searched each other's faces for an explanation. Who would have thought they had to be paying attention while I was at bat?

I don't remember which team was ahead after my home run. It doesn't matter now. They chose me with new respect at the next recess. Not first mind you, they weren't exactly stupid, but not last either.

Alas, my popularity on the diamond was fleeting. The ball and bat resumed their contempt for each other and never again formed any kind of meaningful relationship. At subsequent recesses, the girls who exhibited some skill at the game were chosen first by the usual two captains. When it came down to their last grudging choice between me and a girl on crutches with a cast on her leg, my captain took her time. It was a hard choice.

I do not look back on grade school softball with any sense of nostalgia. In fact, one of my greatest pleasures in growing up is never having to play the game again.

Free to be Kids

In work of labour or of skill
I should be busy too
For Satan finds some mischief still
For idle hands to do.

Isaac Watts

Totally happy being victims of benign neglect, Elayne and I accepted our freedom to wander at will as nothing less than our due. Selective ignorance was the cornerstone of child rearing in the 1940's. Parents didn't keep their kids under constant supervision, because they didn't want to be scared out of their wits. Instead they remained aloof, watching from afar with a regal, benevolent—and lucky for us—nearsighted gaze. On Saturdays we took our chances with anything high, watery, abandoned or noisy. The old forgotten swinging bridge, fifteen feet above the shallow Maitland River miles from home, was a favourite spot until it lost too many foot boards for crossing to be anything but foolhardy. All long-abandoned farm houses within cycling distance were explored in the hope that in broad daylight at least one of these little shacks might be haunted. None were.

Weekends during the busy school year held the promise of new adventure. We were content most Saturday mornings to remain at home, since this was the best time of the week to explore the back alleys. Large, empty appliance boxes and orange crates bristling with slivers lay discarded behind many of the stores, waiting to be claimed by the first kids to come along. We must have been first a lot of the time, because we were rarely without a box of some kind. It took both of us to carry an appliance box to the patch of grass beside Elayne's parents' store, where we transformed it into a club house, with doors and windows that opened and closed, and signs printed in red crayon that read 'Keep Out' and 'Girls Only'. We sat inside our club house spying on Saturday afternoon shoppers, occasionally inviting a group of friends to squeeze inside with us until our club house burst at the seams, disgorging a knot of giggling girls onto the lawn.

When no windfall of boxes presented itself, we wandered up and down the alleys through a no-man's-land of broken bottles, rusty tin cans, and open bonfires that exploded regularly, scattering debris in all directions. Once we followed the lonesome strains of country music into Export Packers, where the sound of running water revealed an intriguing if gruesome sight.

A blizzard of feathers and a most disagreeable smell filled the air as three women in long, blood-spattered, rubber aprons stood plucking the feathers from hundreds of headless chickens hanging by their feet from a long assembly line. A dripping hose snaked across the floor, coiling itself around their rubber boots, waiting for the moment when it would be picked up and turned on, to send a torrent of water, blood and feathers whirling toward the central drain. Without much thought, we decided chicken plucking was not a skill to which we aspired, so off we went to find less grisly adventures.

If we looked hungry enough and asked politely enough, we were handed a handful of raw hamburger through the back door of the butcher shop. We ate as much as we were given, as often as we were given it, and never experienced more than a hiccup.

Unseen from the front street, the back alleys of Brussels fascinated generations of village kids. They were dirty, smelly, messy and dangerous. And the alleys weren't much better.

* * * * *

When I could find nothing more exciting to do, I ran errands for my father, collected the mail from the post office, rubbed out his pencil scrawl from dozens of watch repair tickets so they could be reused, and emptied the wastepaper baskets. Elayne had her assigned chores to attend to as well. But at precisely one o'clock every Saturday afternoon we collected our fifteen-cent weekly allowances from our fathers, promising half-heartedly to do more to earn them in the future. Whether or not we followed up on these promises, the offer to do so seemed to be enough to keep the nickels flowing. Meeting halfway between our fathers' stores, we sat on the curb to see how long we could keep from spending this not-so-hard-earned money. Five minutes is the record. After that, our eyes glazed over and we marched, arms outstretched like zombies, to the nearest candy store. What would it be today? Present joys or lasting pleasures? Ten cents would buy a conical holder of french fries smothered in salt and soaked in cider vinegar—a definite present joy. Coming under the heading of a lasting pleasure, a comic book also cost ten cents. Expenditures of this size left only five cents for enough candy to last the rest of the day.

With the largest selection of candies in town, Coleman's Restaurant usually won us over. Most of the candies in our price range were displayed loosely in trays inside the display case, or in large covered glass jars sitting at jaunty angles on the shelf behind the counter. At the front of the restaurant, a dish of tiny coloured mints sat centred under a fly-studded insect coil hanging limply from the ceiling. Helping ourselves to a few of these took the edge off while we made our selections, which always took a considerable amount of time.

Quantity seemed to be the most important consideration, though we tried to avoid candies that shared their jars with livestock of a crawly nature. The safer pre-wrapped candies did not hold the same appeal as did the gayly coloured gum balls or the hard, black jawbreakers. These, on account of their colour, were always suspect, but we were prepared to take the risk.

When the weather sweltered—as it so often does in the summers of my memory—we chose five-cent popsicles, usually lime, occasionally orange, but never banana. With the right snap of our wrists, we cracked each of them into two pieces on the edge of the restaurant counter and took them outside to eat in the stifling heat. Always a messy business. The coloured juice ran down our arms in long, sticky veins that had to be licked off so as not to waste any of the flavour. When the last piece of ice disappeared from the stick, the time had come to check our tongues for intensity of colour. Now you know why we did not choose the pale yellow banana variety.

Standing in front of our reflections in the nearest store window, we stuck out our tongues as far as they would go. Most of the time this exercise went unnoticed, but occasionally a short-tempered shopkeeper, intent on glaring at passing pedestrians who were obviously not shopping at his store, mistook our intentions for impertinence and stormed outside to vent on someone.

The expenditure of five cents for the popsicle left us with lots of money to squander on further indulgences requiring another decision. Would it be a toffee bar to last the whole afternoon? Or bubble gum wrapped in tattoo transfers? These when moistened and applied to our skin would last for days—as long as we were careful to wash around them. Both were lasting pleasures, though the possibilities were endless.

A towering four-scoop ice cream cone aptly named a 'from-here-to-there', the inspired creation of Papa Baker, the Old World proprietor of the New American Hotel, would be a present joy of the highest order. Even if it took our last cent, it was difficult to think of anything else once that idea took root.

Clambering up onto the red leatherette swivel stools of Papa Baker's coffee shop, we clinked our money on the grey arborite countertop to attract his attention.

"Vut'll it be, gentlemen?" he teased with his most formal Eastern European accent, the stub of a tired cigarette hanging limply from his lips.

"Two from-here-to-theres please Papa."

He struggled to his feet, set down his fly swatter on the counter with a flourish and shuffled over to the ice cream freezer in his bedroom slippers. From the hanging dispenser above the freezer he selected two cones which he held firmly in his left hand while he packed on scoop after scoop of ice cream with his right. Sometimes he chose one flavour, sometimes an unlikely combination of several, depending on his whim or his supply. This was entirely his own creation after all, and for ten cents we got what he gave us. If we quibbled about his choices, we got a smaller cone, simple as that, a rule every kid learned early.

Momentarily rejuvenated by this blast of sugar and inevitably out of funds by mid-afternoon, we searched for ways to supplement our incomes. Ahead of us lay a long Saturday evening of wandering the streets while our parents attended to their businesses. A stretch such as this could be fairly dismal without some incentive to stay awake past nine o'clock—the incentive of course being more sugar.

We knew who had lots of candy, and we also knew it was free. Everyone knew, though we tried not to take advantage of his generosity too often. The candies belonged to Jimmy, the school custodian. First we had to sit like ladies in his living room for a few minutes to exchange pleasantries and a bit of school gossip, before being led into an Aladdin's Cave of goodies. Every kind of candy imaginable filled each of the colourful antique dishes, placed at intervals around the edge of Jimmy's dining room table. One dish held chocolate buds, another jelly beans, while still more overflowed with sugary gum drops, licorice allsorts, peppermint patties, and those flat pastel candies with the intriguingly cryptic messages printed on them. Jimmy handed each of us a small paper bag at the dining room door before we entered, and instructed us to walk once around the table choosing one candy from each dish. There were so many dishes and so many kinds of candies that one trip around the table almost always filled the bag. Unfortunately, the small talk dried up once the bags were full.

Once in a while we brought flowers to Jimmy, flowers we picked ourselves from Mother's garden. And to prove we liked him just for himself, we declined the trip around the dining room table. Even if it nearly killed us. I'm ashamed to say we didn't do this often enough.

When Jimmy's candy was not available, we burst into the baby-walking business, offering a new mother a few minutes of blissful solitude for ten cents. Elayne and I took turns pushing the baby carriage up and down the sidewalk in tiresome circles until all three of us were dizzy as coots. That chore completed, we were ten cents closer to solvency for Saturday night.

Considered to be boys' work, mowing a lawn on a hot summer afternoon held little appeal for us. But a FRESHIE stand set up in the shade of a tree—now that was more to our liking. The back alley provided the orange crate that when stood on end became a counter, with a shelf underneath to store the wads of money we planned to haul in. The little matter of sugar, packages of FRESHIE, and glasses depended on whose property the stand would appear. Our mothers, both business women, were pleased to see us developing our enterprising sides and happily supplied the raw materials. A cardboard sign, scrawled in crayon and attached to the front of the orange crate by a thumb tack made it official. We were in the refreshment business.

Through the long, hot afternoon we drank most of the FRESHIE ourselves, shared some of it with a few thirsty friends—temporarily down on their luck—and sold the rest to our mothers who took pity on our slow business. Our earnings for two hours of sitting in the shade of a tree, doing not much of anything, was fifteen cents. Along with the ten cents we earned for disorienting the baby, the grand total for an afternoon of sloth amounted to twenty-five cents. It was a living.

Cowboys, Culprits and Cheap Candy

Built in 1872, the centre for culture as we knew it stood at the south end of the business district. Large by village standards, the town hall had an auditorium on the second floor with a proscenium stage at one end and four long windows on either side, each with a dark green window blind for blocking out daylight on occasions when movies were shown.

Before television became a fixture in every living room, periodic Saturday matinées drew noisy, rambunctious audiences of kids ready to be entertained. Eager to escape our familiar surroundings for a few hours, we were seated in the hall a half hour before the movie started. The boys who came considered it their sworn duty to make as much noise and create as much havoc as possible. Town boys fought with country boys out of habit, chasing each other on and off the stage, knocking over chairs, throwing hats around and generally making fools of themselves all for our benefit. Staying out of the line of fire by crouching down in the straight-backed wooden chairs seemed to be the wisest thing for the girls to do. In winter, the steam rising from a collection of wet mittens and galoshes piled on the central heating grate mingled with the aroma of cheap candy and overheated boys, creating a pong of epic proportions.

At last the green blinds were lowered and the production trademark appeared on the screen. This generated a louder roar than any heard from the MGM Lion. It took stern threats from the projectionist to quiet the crowd enough to hear the dialogue, as by this time the movie was five minutes into its plot.

Westerns of all kinds were popular and frequent. The suppliers knew their audiences well. The boys who loved these movies best were of two minds. Those who cheered for the ruggedly handsome sheriff in the white hat, and those who cheered for the not-so-handsome but still plenty rugged villain in the black. The girls cheered for the horses, regardless of colour.

Sword-and-sandals Biblical epics were much longer than necessary, but popular for several reasons. Most of my friends and I came to see the fabulous sets and the diaphanous costumes that floated about every female cast member from lowly slave to exalted princess. And of course for the love story. Not surprisingly, the boys came for the brutality of the arena, featuring wild beasts of every stripe and spot, and half-eaten slaves in varying degrees of expiration. I don't know of anyone who came for the message—Biblical or otherwise. At least once during the movie, a handsome slave—who almost without exception was slippery ol' Victor Mature, wearing little more than a pained expression and a gallon of olive oil—won the battle with the beast. As long as he lost the required amount of blood in the process, the boys roared their approval, stomping their feet and making those same retching noises they made during the love scenes.

My favourite was a swashbuckling pirate movie with a beautiful female star in whale-boned corset and low cut neckline, screaming none too convincingly and seeming to enjoy every minute of being kidnapped by the pirates. Naturally after several moonlit evenings aboard, she joined their merry throng, appearing at the helm this time with raven tresses loose enough to catch every breeze, short shorts held together by prayer, thigh-high leather boots, miraculously just her size, and a white satin blouse with a few strategic buttons missing. Articles of women's attire, you may assume, were easier to find on the average pirate galleon than buttons. That gives one pause. I noticed that many of the same actors appeared in all three types of movies, with only a change of costume and the gaining or losing of essential moving parts.

Almost no one but the major stars in these pirate movies had a full compliment of appendages. Ordinary pirates were severely disabled—eyes, arms, legs, tongues, you name it—gone. Not from the same pirate, you understand, but every one of them had something missing if you looked hard enough. Prowling the high seas must have been a hazardous occupation for the run-of-the-mill pirate. Those whose hands were still attached to the ends of their arms looked downright dashing, swinging through the rigging with their cutlasses in their teeth. If they still had teeth. We tried to duplicate these scenes in the maple tree at home, with homemade swords and mostly painful results. Any deficiencies the pirates may have had in the limb department they more than made up for in their use of smart accessories—brass hoop earrings, leather eye patches, tarry pigtails and colourful parrots worn, with a certain panache, on their shoulders. Aaahhrrr! Those sea dogs were a jaunty lot!

Occasionally an animal movie appeared, if one could be found that was sufficiently sappy. Life was no cinch for the animal stars either. Dogs and horses led horrendous lives, enduring hardships and biting the dust with great regularity. The directors must have known they could wring a lot more sympathy from a young audience with a doomed domesticated animal than, say, an alligator.

After watching 'Old Yeller', Elayne refused to leave the auditorium until her face recovered from two hours of crying over the poor unfortunate 'yeller' dog. I waited with her, feeling guilty for not crying as hard as she had, but knowing I had no choice, as my only handkerchief was soaked twenty minutes into the movie.

Elayne's compassion for animals appeared to be well developed from an early age. Perhaps having her obedient and faithful dog Blondie at home made her more sympathetic to the plight of animals. I had my tomcat Googy-Buzzy of course, but his sole heroic endeavour involved removing his claws from my leg.

Movies were not the only events held in the town hall. Every December, a member of one of the men's service clubs, wearing a moth-eaten red costume with a lumpy pillow and a good stiff drink under his belt, was talked into playing Santa in the yearly Santa Claus parade. His starring role was fleeting at best, our main street being just a little over two blocks long. In order to get the most out of all that dressing up, stuffing in and drinking down, he held court on the stage of the town hall, ho-ho-ho-ing on cue and distributing bags of Christmas candy to all outstretched hands. Because we celebrated every conceivable event with tons of the stuff, it is little wonder that after a few years our teeth began to rot merrily out of our heads.

On Variety Revue nights, courageous performances by the genuinely talented and the slightly less so were staged in the town hall auditorium. These were well attended by proud parents, long-suffering relatives, and the truly bored. More about those evenings later.

Dances were held in the town hall regularly, many ending in drunken brawls outside on the lawn. Because

Brussels at the time was 'dry', the only source of alcohol were bottles of bootleg liquor stashed under the front seat of most of the cars lining the main street. Often there were more people in the cars than on the dance floor, but the music played on and on regardless, and could be heard in every corner of the village on summer nights when all windows were open.

Two large front doors opening onto the main street revealed the volunteer fire station with its bright red engine, all but invisible under a collection of ladders and axes. On both sides of the station, rows of black rubber coats, helmets and boots stood ready to protect the volunteers as they fought local conflagrations with bravery and determination.

Brussels was no stranger to fire. Over the years fire had served to shape its boundaries, its economics and its history. Ragged skeletons of former industries gave clear evidence of blazes that raged through parts of the village in the mid 1800's, though none had the same impact as the devastation caused by the great fire at the turn of the last century. This one changed the face of the village forever.

Behind the town hall, hanging in an elongated tin pyramid, the village bell awaited its next performance. From a wooden cradle fifty feet above the ground, the heavy iron bell rang four times a day, except on New Year's Eve when it rang in the new year, or on Hallowe'en when it rang mysteriously at ten-minute intervals all night long.

Whenever we heard it at other than these times, a fire blazed somewhere in the area, the rapid pealing summoning the volunteer fire brigade to action. Arriving on the run from all corners of the village, they struggled into their waterproof gear while they clambered aboard the fire engine—its motor already warming up. Turning either left or right onto Turnberry Street, off they roared in the direction of the fire, every man hanging on for dear life, sirens wailing, bells ringing, people yelling—followed at great speed by cars, pick-up trucks, every boy who owned a bicycle, and dogs.

The bell, as a rule, told us nothing more exciting than the time of day. Because it tolled at seven in the morning, and at noon, again at one o'clock and six in the evening, the citizens of the village scheduled their activities around its ringing. If we timed it right, the Town Constable, whose job it was to ring the bell, allowed Elayne and me to hang onto the end of the rope while he pulled, and together we would summon the village to its various tasks of the day.

Aunts in the Cottage

During the spring run-off, the normally sluggish Maitland River transformed itself into a raging grey torrent, sweeping away everything in its path. By the middle of summer, the river having simmered under a hot sun for a few months, was reduced to liquid amber and in some places shrunk to a depth of a six inches. With the closest swimming pool fifteen miles away and our ship nowhere near coming in, the prospect of a two-week vacation at the lake came as a welcome relief from the heat. I packed my suitcase and was ready to go before the zinging of the cicadas could rise another octave.

Saturday morning found me stuffed into an overcrowded car with assorted relatives heading to Kintail, a modest collection of vacation cottages on the shores of Lake Huron. Eight of us rode in Uncle Bill's postwar sedan, loaded to the roof with enough provisions for a lengthy siege. Crowded as we were in the stifling heat, the car grew smaller with each passing mile, until by the end of the trip it felt about the size of a tuna tin.

Because the Scottish side of my family has always had an unusual attachment to water, it seemed only natural that these vacations should be spent at a cottage by a lake. Lake Huron seemed about the right size. At the end of the first week a few more pale faces arrived from the city, and the same number of pink ones packed to return home. The little cottage could hold just so many people, no matter how related we were.

My father remained in Brussels, peacefully oblivious to the fun we were about to have, doing what he wanted to do, when he wanted to do it. For some reason known only to him, he preferred to live a grim Dickensian existence on his own, dining each night on the oldest cheese and the stalest bread he could find, washing it all down with a glass or two of Canadian sherry. Maybe he read *Oliver Twist* too, while he ate this meagre fare, making even more realistic the harsh images Dickens portrayed. The food Mother prepared for his meals while we were away remained, for the most part, untouched.

On the morning of our departure, having packed my striped cardboard suitcase with anything remotely important to me at the time, plus the old patched inner tube I bought at Champion's Garage for ten cents, and my collection of SILVER SCREEN movie magazines, I was ready hours before my uncle's car arrived.

Quiet, dignified and ever the stoic Scot, Uncle Bill drove the four sisters and assorted cousins to their yearly retreat. The back seat of his sedan was spacious enough to accommodate folding jump seats that attached to each door. These were created by my uncle, who reengineered everything he touched, with inspired results. Still small enough, my cousin Caroline and I sat on these seats at a safe distance from one another for the duration of the trip. Mother and two of her Scottish sisters, Elizabeth and Isabella, or Aunt Lizzie and Aunt Bella as I knew them, sat in the back seat with us, oching and ayeing with enjoyment at being together again. The fourth sister, Aunt Cathie, sat between my brother Doug and Uncle Bill in the front seat.

Our three aunts, along with their three Scottish husbands had lived in Niagara Falls since coming to Canada in the early 1920's. Mother, ever the nonconformist, broke with tradition to marry an Englishman, then moved far enough away from the others to avoid most of the arguments. These happy, often noisy vacations, were a chance to get caught up.

While they were still young in Scotland, the daunting task of raising four younger sisters and a younger brother fell to Aunt Lizzie upon the deaths of their parents a few months apart. At fifteen she became the mother as well as the older sister to her five younger siblings, resulting in her appearing older and more serious than the rest, even though only a few years separated them.

A diminutive Scottish lady, Aunt Cathie was the youngest child in the family of thirteen, Caroline's mother and my namesake. She was also the aunt I knew best from frequent visits to her home in Niagara Falls.

"Och, ma' wane!" she murmured, greeting me at her front door and drawing me into a pleasant cloud of lavender. In the city, my three aunts wore dresses, stockings, often hats and gloves, and always smelled deliciously of white scotch mints and talcum powder. At the lake, their attire was slightly less formal, though I cannot remember any of them wading in the lake any deeper than their waists. Mother, the undisputed tomboy of the family, wore nothing more formal than shorts and bare feet when she wasn't neck deep in Lake Huron for her early morning swim.

With my brother sitting well out of trouble in the front seat, Caroline and I amused ourselves playing a favourite travelling game called 'Pretty White Horse'.

"Pretty white horse, pretty white horse, grant me a wish before the day's over," we chanted, scanning the passing fields for any animal vaguely resembling a white horse. Because each sighting could be claimed by only one of us, spotting the same white horse at the same time raised the hostility level to a point where any object placed between us would instantly self-destruct.

"The wanes are crabbit the dee," Aunt Bella teased in the quietly mocking tone that always made us giggle.

No one could change a mood faster than she, and soon we were smiling and happy again despite our competitive natures.

The incessant heat, which we endured with the windows tightly shut to protect Aunt Lizzie's new permanent, did little to help keep our tempers or anything else cool. It was a well known fact that the three sisters home-permed each other's hair to such an extent that it would have taken a force-ten gale to ruffle any of their curls, but for the first day at least, we deferred to Aunt Lizzie's wishes. She was the eldest though not necessarily the least combative of the four sisters, and we knew better than to challenge her.

Always a pleasant if somewhat prolonged journey, it took four hours to drive the fifty miles to the lake—with a short delay while the eight of us used the same garage washroom, with a stop farther along the highway for tea. Lots and lots of tea. The camp stove rarely cooled down during any of these family outings. Uncle Bill set it up on one end of a roadside picnic table, while the sisters busied themselves putting out enough food to attract every fly within a ten-mile radius. All the adults in my family loved picnics, exploiting any opportunity to have one. I have disliked them from the beginning. Who was it who said, "If God had intended us to eat with buzzing insects, he would never have invented screens."? It wasn't me, but it should have been.

Uncle Bill, in a moment of special inventiveness, built a stove into the back seat of his first car, a 1920's vintage limousine, so that hot tea was only moments, and in that case inches, away at all times. As risky as this sounds even at twenty-five miles an hour, the sisters considered the convenience to be the ultimate in luxurious living and were still raving about it twenty-five years after the fact.

Lake Huron appeared at first as a wavy blue line on the horizon above the wriggling heat of the road. With instructions from Mother and all permanents forgotten for the moment, we rolled down our windows to breath in the fresh lake air. Smelling vaguely of hay, damp earth and manure—much the way the world had always smelled to me—great gulps of it brought blissful expressions to all adult faces. Off to our left, gulls followed a tractor like feathers burst from a pillow, and still others dotted the earth in the wake of the plow.

Excitement rippled through the car as we made the last turn onto the narrow lane leading to the cottage. Young rabbits with white tails flashing led the way, darting ahead along the ruts and over the grassy centre strip. We considered this to be a fitting welcome and a good omen for the start of our holiday, rabbits feet still on the rabbit being especially lucky. Moments later we bumped to a stop on the soft grass of the cottage yard.

"Everybody oot! End of the line!" announced Uncle Bill, who made the same pronouncement at the end of every journey, whether it lasted four hours or four minutes. Spilling out of all four doors at once, we were greeted by the scent of juniper and hot sand and the gentle, familiar rustle of birch leaves. The white clapboard cottage that would be our home for the next two weeks bore the name 'Dew Drop Inn', probably one of a hundred cottages of the same name dotted along the eastern shore of Lake Huron.

At one time it had been painted dark brown, the remnants of its former colour showing through in more than a few places. With its squat profile and its speckled brown and white appearance, the cottage always reminded me of a broody hen nestled on a comfortable nest of junipers.

Three of the rooms in the cottage were bedrooms. The rest of the cottage included a kitchen and a combination living room and dining area. Kerosene lamps hung on sturdy hooks from open rafters, supplying enough light for reading or playing games around the large round table during the long evenings. A tidy whitewashed privy overgrown with honeysuckle and constantly buzzing with bees, sat in a glade of trees at the rear of the property. The 'wee hoose' as it came to be known was a two-holer and quite a novelty for the first few hours.

Clearly the mid-twentieth century had not caught up with the Dew Drop Inn.

Halfway down the hill a rusty pump provided water clean enough for washing dishes, if we primed it first then pumped with the necessary ferocity. At first it brayed like a donkey, but in the end rewarded us with a splashing torrent of cold water all over our warm feet. Filling the large pot we were given, we lugged the water back up the stairs to be heated on top of the wood stove in the kitchen. Not trusting this water with our lives, our drinking water came from a tap at the entrance to the property.

Eager to be free, everyone under the age of twelve raced down the fifty steps to the lake, scattering shoes and socks, never to be worn again until we returned to civilization. The warm sand felt comforting to feet confined to shoes for most of the year. Stretching before us as far as the eye could see lay moody Lake Huron, its beach a gentle curve of pale grey sand edged with coloured pebbles that rolled and rattled with each wave. Up and down the shoreline, little grey and white sandpipers scurried on toothpick legs, while high above them gulls wheeled and screeched over the water.

For a minute I stood drinking in that special air, spicy with the scent of juniper and cedar. A silver birch tree, its roots exposed by erosion, had lost its grip on the cliff and toppled down the hill during the heavy rains of spring. The beach looked slightly different each time we returned. Some years the fierce storms of autumn gnawed at the beach, leaving it narrow and strewn with pebbles. In other years, the waves washed it clean and left it wide and sandy. My family may have rented the same cottage every year, but we rarely saw the same beach.

Uncle Bill stood over the hood of his car studying his road map for the fastest route back to the city. This year some of his holiday would be spent tinkering uninterrupted in his workshop at home. He planned to leave right after supper.

The Dew Drop Inn came equipped with a wood-burning cookstove and unmatched dishes from at least a dozen different sets. The four sisters went about the business of setting up house, putting food away and assigning bedrooms. Familiar bedding gave each room the cozy feeling of home, with one important difference. Each leggy bed hid a covered china chamber pot, whose necessity would soon become apparent.

As the only sister accustomed to the task, Mother busied herself chopping kindling and starting a fire in the kitchen stove. Before long, the cottage filled with the comforting sound of the kettle spouting steam and rattling its lid with impatience. Vegetables harvested from our garden that morning were stored in the dumbwaiter, a tin-lined hole below the floor through which a box could be raised or lowered by pulley. In addition to serving as a cool storage area for vegetables, the dumbwaiter provided great material for two weeks of bad jokes.

The first meal at the cottage was more lavish than some we'd have later in the week, because we had not yet run out of anything. Despite the number of Scots already in residence, we did not once sit down to a plate of haggis or a bowl of cock-a-leekie soup. Thick slabs of cottage ham, potato salad, sliced tomatoes and warm apple pie were on the menu that first evening.

"Don't go near the water for an hour," was the first of many warnings we heard as we disappeared down the stairs to the beach after supper. That meant a full sixty minutes—not thirty-five or even fifty-five, but sixty interminable minutes. Otherwise, we were told we would drown immediately, even if we were in only up to our ankles.

Most of the time we were law abiding. But without a watch, waiting for the prescribed amount of time meant long climbs up fifty uneven steps to the cottage to check the clock. We held off for what we estimated to be forty-five minutes, then threw caution to the wind and sneaked into the lake a full fifteen minutes early, mad impetuous fools that we were. Sitting in a row up to our necks in the soothing water, we waited somewhat nervously for the cramps to begin. These would be followed, as we were told, by a slow descent beneath the waves to certain watery death. We waited and waited, and all that waiting around for the Grim Reaper took a lot longer than fifteen minutes.

We swam—or what passed for it—for an hour or until we turned blue, whichever came first. Without fail, one of our aunts was waiting for us on shore with dry towels and a 'shivery bit'. Cookies have never tasted better.

As a family we were inveterate beachcombers. An early morning search of the beach rewarded us with tiny shells that had been tossed up on shore by the waves during the night. Bits of broken glass, transformed into frosty gems of emerald and topaz, and silvery abstract sculptures of driftwood were gathered, to be stroked and admired when summer was just a memory.

I scanned the lake daily for a freighter that might be our ship coming in. And though I saw one or two every day, none of them came any closer than the horizon. Nor did I give up the search for a bottle with a scrawled note inside from a ship-wrecked sailor. That search continues.

Every evening when it didn't rain, anyone who felt they could stagger back up the fifty steps in the dark came down to the beach to admire the sunset on the water. Sometimes the sun appeared so fiery red I expected the water to hiss and bubble as it slipped below the horizon, but it always disappeared without a ripple or even a wisp of steam. Whenever we could talk Mother into lighting a bonfire, we gathered long twigs for the annual incineration of the marshmallows, an ancient family ritual. Toasting them to a golden brown was our intention, but they always turned out as black as cinders, and were eaten in spite of the sandy bits.

Bedtime at the cottage had a festive atmosphere. Caroline and I were allowed to sleep together, recent white horse hostilities long forgotten. Aunts unfamiliar with our regular nightly routines were easily persuaded to tell more than their normal share of bedtime stories. Because we loved Aunt Lizzie's Scottish accent so much, and were at the time attempting to perfect our own, Caroline and I concentrated all our efforts on her.

"Tell us a wee story, Aunt Lizzie. We'll be everr so quiet. We prromise."

"Och weil—Once upon a time there was a wee coo wi' a crookit horn..." she started, and just as we had promised we listened attentively until 'The End', enthralled as much by her accent as her story.

"Now say yeer prayers, and be quick aboot it. Ma tea's getting cold," she instructed, standing over us to make sure we did just that.

> "*Now I lay me doon tae sleep,*
> *I pray the Lord ma soul tae keep.*
> *If I should dee before I wake,*
> *I pray the Lord ma soul tae take...*"

This was too impertinent even for us, and we giggled under the covers at our barefaced attempts to fake a Scottish accent before the greatest of them all. Usually such cheek received an immediate reprimand, but we were counting on the fact that Aunt Lizzie did not hear well.

"Would the Lord really keep our souls, Aunt Lizzie?"

"Aye, nae doot, and soon," she replied, firmly tucking us in, "if you donnae stop pokin' fun at ma accent."

Then we got one prickly kiss each, and this started us giggling all over again. Surrounded by our mothers and three aunts apiece, we felt thoroughly loved and up to our knees in approval. The frequent threats to separate us dwindled to a trickle as we ran out of things to giggle at and drifted off to sleep.

Tea time for the sisters rolled around once again before they retired for the evening. The brew they preferred consisting of at least five tablespoons of loose tea tossed into a large Brown Betty teapot, one prewarmed with boiling water, the proper way. They could have danced on the resulting brew, but anything less was rejected as fortnight tea, or tea that was too weak. If one of the sisters awoke during the night, she had only to open her bedroom door, and the others still half asleep would stumble out of bed and into each other in the dark on their way to the kettle. Tea was served once again sometime around two o'clock in the morning.

After so much tea, it was inevitable that one if not all the sisters would need to visit the 'wee hoose' before morning. As unaccustomed to the darkness of the countryside at night as they were to chamber pots and wood stoves, the sisters elected Mother to lead the way with a flashlight. Since she was the tallest and most robust of the four, the others looked to her as their guide and protector on these nightly expeditions into the wilds of the cottage yard.

On their return from the 'wee hoose' one night, they encountered a nosy raccoon scouting the area for a loose garbage can lid, to be followed by a leisurely snack. Caught suddenly in the beam from Mother's flashlight, the raccoon pulled himself up to his full height and stared at them with the natural inquisitiveness of his kind. Approaching with a dignified lack of haste to investigate the strange noises coming from behind the flashlight, the raccoon took just one cautious step in their direction—a step that was later described as a fierce charge. The strange noises coming from behind the light were coming from Mother's sisters, who were nervously trying to climb up each other's backs. Within seconds, Aunt Lizzie, the most highly strung and vocal of the four, had managed to work her two city sisters into a frenzy.

"Ma Goad! I'm feart to death, Jeannie! Dae something!" she shrieked, attempting to hide her little round self behind Mother, not surprisingly at the head of the line. Mother searched for something to throw at the raccoon, but because she had on only her nightgown, she took off her slippers and threw them one at a time. The raccoon responded with a disdainful sniff and another step forward.

"AAAIIIEEE!" seemed to be the consensus of opinion.

"Jesus, Mary and Joseph, Lizzie! It's not a lion. Get off my back! Now see what you made me say!"

Mother allowed herself this reference to the Holy Family in events of dire emergency—like fires, floods and hysterical sisters—always followed by the same disclaimer, somehow absolving her of any blasphemy.

"Haud yer wheesht, Jeannie. He'll kill us all!" whimpered Aunt Lizzie, now on the verge of tears. Momentarily befuddled by the mounting hysteria behind her, Mother threw the only thing—other than her nightgown—that she had left. The flashlight. Unaware he was about to cause a stampede unlike any seen on the shores of Lake Huron, the raccoon disappeared into the underbrush. Everything else disappeared too, because their only source of light had just been tossed into the bushes, and it was three o'clock in the morning.

Now with only the sound of the lapping waves, the crackling of twigs as the raccoon made his getaway, and the knocking of eight Scottish knees, a wild fire of panic spread through the little group. Four squealing sisters, stuck together like some demented caterpillar, burst through the cottage door as if the devil himself were after them. Not even kids could sleep through that.

Freeing ourselves from a ton of blankets, we found them holding onto each other in the kitchen, arguing over who started the stampede and who should go back outside to bring in the only flashlight.

"You go, Jeannie. You flung it at the beast," Aunt Lizzie suggested, with a certain edge to her voice.

"Sure I flung it. But I flung it to save you. Remember? So you go. And see if you can't find my slippers while you're at it."

"I'm nae goin' oot there again tonight and naebody can make me. I may not go oot there tomorra either. I'm gonna hold it till I get hame to my ane bathroom, if it takes forever."

"Ah Lizzie, you're aye greetin'," complained Mother, reaching for the kettle.

All seven of us were awake by this point, and four of us were ready for more tea. With wild animals roaming the backyard no one left the cottage for the remainder of the night, and the three china chamber pots suddenly came into their own.

* * * * *

Without a car, and with the closest general store several miles from the cottage down a hot, dusty road, keeping food fresh became an obsession. Standing in one corner of the kitchen on four sturdy legs, the wooden icebox became an integral part of the operation.

Twice a week, long before breakfast, a rusty pick-up truck crunched its way down the gravel laneway behind the cottages. With the first toot of the horn, a cry rang out from one or other of the bedrooms.

"The iceman cometh!" Early or not, the day had begun. No cottager with an icebox as their only means of preserving food could afford to ignore the incessant honking. Screen doors were flung open and arms were waved in a frantic attempt to attract the iceman's attention.

With a pair of savage looking iron tongs, he grabbed a blue-white chunk of ice from deep inside the sawdust in the back of his truck, hoisted it onto a leather-padded shoulder and carried it into the cottage. Here it sat in the upper compartment of the wooden icebox, melting slowly over the next few days and keeping the perishables a few degrees cooler.

Following in the wake of the iceman, the milkman was the next salesman to call. The sign on his van read EARL E. RISER - DAIRY PRODUCTS and indeed he must have been. Kintail was only one of several beach communities he called on before breakfast, his metal carrier of glass bottles tinkling like chimes as he ran between the cottages bringing fresh milk for everyone's cereal. Sometimes he brought chocolate-covered ice cream bars we knew as Eskimo pies, which had to be eaten right away before they melted. That meant before breakfast. How perfect is that? As long as we ate the meals placed before us, no one worried much in which order we ate them.

* * * * *

One rainy night threatened to dampen more than our spirits. Since none of the others were as fond of thunderstorms as I, and as I was considered too young to stay up by myself to watch one, everyone went to bed at the same time—far too early. I lay awake listening in the darkness to the thunder, the drumming of the rain on the roof, the wind in the trees, and the crashing of the waves on the beach below. Watching all this from the comfort of the big wicker rocking chair on the veranda would have been more to my liking.

Not long after the last of the candles had been extinguished, a murmuring could be heard from the bedroom next to ours. None of the partitions came within six feet of the open beamed ceiling, so all conversations were more or less public announcements.

"I did nothing of the sort!" came the emphatic denial.

"Well, it certainly wasn't me!"

"Oh, for cryin' out loud! What next?"

Above the constant beating of the rain, we heard someone get out of bed, then soft padding steps, a rustle, a pop and within seconds, uncontrollable giggling from the other side of the wooden partition. Caroline and I, ever eager to be included in the fun, tiptoed to the bedroom next door to investigate. There lay our mothers, holding an umbrella over their heads, their bed covered with a plastic tablecloth. Sharp Ping! Ping! noises filled the room as drop after drop of water fell onto the umbrella, cascaded to the tablecloth and onto the floor. The roof had sprung a leak above their bed.

Unamused at being roused from a warm bed, Aunt Lizzie stood in the doorway glaring in at her two younger sisters.

"Look at the pair of ye. Yrrr fair drookit." And I suppose 'drookit' they would have been had someone not remembered to pack an umbrella.

Five pairs of hands helped shove the bed against the wall and someone ran for a cooking pot to catch the drops now falling with increasing frequency from a height of ten feet. The PLOCKETY-PLOCK! PLOCKs! changed to plinkety-plink! plinks! with the placement of a facecloth in the bottom of the pot. That seemed to signal the end of the excitement for the night.

By morning the rain had subsided, allowing the leak to be located and patched with the kind assistance of a neighbouring cottager. Mother and Aunt Cathie returned their bed to its original position in the room, and everyone looked forward to an uneventful night's sleep.

Sometime during the first hour, we were awakened by an unearthly crash and another reference to the Holy Family. Firmly convinced a truck had driven through the cottage wall, everyone bounded out of bed and into each other in the dark. Everyone that is except my mother and Aunt Cathie, who lay in bed laughing louder and harder than they had the night before. Aunt Lizzie reached for a candle, lit it, and opened their door. Five bewildered faces illuminated by candlelight peered into the darkened bedroom. One end of their mattress stuck high in the air above the end of the metal bedstead, sheets and blankets waving in the sudden breeze. Under a knot of arms, legs and pillows we saw the two sisters' heads pressed firmly against the partition at floor level, where they had slid down their mattress. Our family has always been vulnerable to the ridiculous and has a tendency toward uncontrolled laughter at times like these. It's a curse.

Given some time, we regained enough composure to help them out of their blankets and what was beginning to look like their nightly dilemma. As so often happens with flimsy bedsteads in rented cottages, when it was returned to its original spot after the leaky-roof incident of the night before, the frame had been knocked loose. Barely holding together, it collapsed when both sisters turned over at once. There's nothing like a good night's sleep. And this was nothing like a good night's sleep.

"Whadeeya have to dae aroon here to get some sleep?" grumbled Aunt Lizzie to anyone who would listen, as she climbed back into bed beside Aunt Bella. "I can't wait to get hame for a rest."

At the end of the two weeks, there were the inevitable lengthy good-byes in front of our house. No one was in a hurry when it came time to leave. It might be a year before we saw any of them again. Hugs were exchanged, hands were shaken, and promises to get together soon were extended. Ever so slowly, we began our journey to Uncle Bill's car, a distance of about fifty feet. Some progress was made until we neared the car, at which time the procession came to a halt when one of my aunts remembered something she'd forgotten, and off she went to retrieve it. Everyone dispersed, only to be rounded up a minute later to start the process all over again.

More hugs, more prickly kisses, more promises. Whatever wise Scot once said, "It's not the gangin' awa', it's the partin' at the pier", must have been referring to our family. Saying good-bye has always been a long drawn out process for us.

"Behave yoursels noo!" Aunt Lizzie warned one last time, before squeezing into the back seat next to Aunt Bella and releasing a mighty relieved sigh.

"Och! Ma Wane," crooned Aunt Cathie, pulling me one last time into her little cloud of lavender. A few complaints from the sisters about the stifling heat of the back seat got the engine started, and the car slowly drew away with everyone waving. I stood in the middle of the lane watching the car grow smaller until it turned onto Turnberry Street and disappeared. They were gone, and there seemed to be no reason to hang onto the Scottish accent I had worked so hard to acquire.

My father, left at home to fend for himself, had not died of malnutrition despite his Dickensian diet, and all other living things left in his care continued to thrive. Our sunburned shoulders, slathered with NOXEMA for days, had peeled off in sheets before finally developing into tans that would inevitably fade with the first thought of school. It took more than a week, but eventually we were able to rid our clothes, our shoes and our suitcases of the sand that had stowed away in every seam and crevice. But those treasured memories of our aunts in the cottage would last a lifetime.

Season of Plenty

We savoured the last days before Labour Day the way a condemned man must savour his last meal. As there seemed no way to slow the steady march of time, we had to face the fact that our summer holidays were almost over. And that could mean just one thing—school. When the muggy days of August gave way to crisp early September, we returned reluctantly to the structure of the classroom. The feeling of freedom that summer had given was quickly forgotten in the excitement surrounding old friends, blank scribblers, stiff new textbooks, and sometimes even a new teacher.

Within days our energies were focussed on the Fall Fair, a time set aside each September for a country-style exhibition of excellence. Wholehearted participation filled each hour with project preparations. On this special day, everyone from the community and surrounding district converged on the fairground at the edge of town to celebrate the bounties of the season. Many were there to display the skills they had acquired over the years, and still more were eager to judge those skills for themselves. The display tables groaned with everything from prize-winning apple pies all the way through the alphabet to giant-sized zucchinis. For inflating the population of Brussels, there is no question that Fall Fair Day surpassed the busiest pre-Christmas Saturday. A period of inclement weather had little effect on the day's activities. If it rained, we did in a sea of mud all the same things we would have done in the warm autumn sunshine.

At one o'clock on the appointed day, a visiting brass band or the local Canadian Legion Pipe Band led a long, impressive parade of floats and marching school children along the route from Victoria Park to the fairground a mile away. The rest of the community stood beside the road and watched.

As many as a dozen floats were entered in the competition, some manned by the entire student body of a nearby country school. Themes for these floats ranged from the patriotic to the playful, though a float bearing an outhouse with an EATON'S catalogue tied to the door was certain to please the crowd. Because we were barely a decade past their use in some of our day-to-day lives,

I imagine the appeal was more out of a sense of relief than of nostalgia.

Pulling the country school floats were enormous workhorses, still vital to many of the farms at the time. No small town parade would be complete without horses, and our farming community had no shortage in every breed, size, colour and temperament. They were brushed until they shone, their long, dark tails plaited with red satin ribbons for the occasion. Bicycles and tricycles, decorated with crêpe paper streamers in a combination of colours seen only in a bad dream, followed proudly at the end of the parade like the colourful tails of a kite.

Every school kid was told to assemble at Victoria Park the day of the fair, where we were given a simple uniform consisting of a red crêpe paper sash which crisscrossed in front and attached in back with a safety pin, and pillbox hats made from a strip of red bristol board stapled together and set at a jaunty angle. As long as we stayed out of a sudden downpour, our uniforms had a chance of holding together for the half-hour march.

By the time we were enroled in school, we had naturally developed a high degree of skill in movement of all kinds, but when asked to march we lost all sense of coordinated motion. The simple order to "Forward— March," threw us into a dancing frenzy as we tried to correct the unnatural wobbling motion that resulted from starting off with our right feet and right arms extended. In fact, whenever any request to move included the word 'march' we dissolved into a stumbling bunch of misfits.

After weeks of practice and much ranting from our frustrated teachers, we were as ready as we'd ever be. Turning corners had been mastered, but stopping as one still gave us trouble. With no more time for practice, the teachers must have hoped that once we were rolling there would be no reason to stop before we reached the fairground. Although the parade had to cross the railroad tracks to get there, I can't remember ever encountering a train. That was attributable either to good planning or good luck.

Concerned about how we would appear in public, the teachers marched beside each of their classes, counting out the required steps: left—right—left—right—with their heads held high—left—right—left—right—their arms swinging at the correct height—left—right—left—right—lifting their knees with every step—left—right—left—right—looking proud, terribly efficient and totally military to our parents—but altogether dorky to us.

We did try to march in a straight line, but we also had to follow a number of well-fed horses, so it was necessary to veer to the left or to the right every once in a while, taking the rest of the line with us. This little manoeuvre, widely known as the 'horse bun two-step', was practised by any kid paying attention. Some of us veered left and some of us veered right. But the keeners, obeying all orders to hold their heads high, marched straight through the still-steaming mounds, giving the rest of us a reason for living. As the parade pitched and rolled down the main street, our mothers stood at the curb waving encouragement and wiping away tears of pride and emotion.

Once at the fairground, we were judged on our smart appearance and our skill at marching by the school superintendent and a couple of village worthies. Some years we were more successful than others, but since our relatively large student body included a range of marching talents from expert to completely hopeless, I am certain we rarely, if ever, won first prize.

The area by the main fair building used for small animal judging teemed with entrants, spectators and owners, all of them vocal in their excitement, or in the case of the animals, in their outrage at being confined. Unhappy dogs and cats made known their feelings of betrayal by keeping up an incessant din of staccato barks and yowls. Secure in rows of straw-lined cages a short distance from the uproar, rabbits, guinea pigs and other small creatures cowered in their makeshift burrows gnawing nervously on carrots. There were tiny roosters with fancy feathers I had seen only on Sunday hats, snowy ducks and more types of geese than I thought existed. To one side of the building stood the better behaved calves and sheep, tethered to poles deeply set into the ground—each with a proud young owner attached, washing and brushing in anticipation of the honours to be awarded later that afternoon.

It was a scene of biblical proportions. Noah's Ark in this case was played by the fair's main building—the Crystal Palace—with its totally inappropriate name. Nothing in the building resembled crystal, and no one could say with any honesty that it reminded them of a palace, however run down. Whoever named the Crystal Palace must have had high hopes for this country cousin of the English original. High above the crowd, sheltered among the open beams and waging an ongoing guerilla war, the pigeon population—squatters in every sense of the word—led satisfying lives taking unerring potshots at anyone below.

The day before the exhibits arrived, a small army of women descended on the building with a truckload of cleaning paraphernalia, working miracles in a matter of hours. Normally draped in miles of cobwebs and months of accumulated dust and detritus, on Fall Fair Day the Crystal Palace shone with a magic it knew on no other.

To enter this building was to dive headfirst into a cornucopia. I remember the aroma best—the pleasing combination of fruit, flowers, home baking and the wholesome, honest smells of the farm. Fresh and perfect produce was displayed in eye-catching arrangements beside bouquets of asters, zinnias and chrysanthemums. There were pumpkins in all shapes and sizes sitting next to heads of cabbage, cauliflower and bunches of crisp carrots, all scrubbed and trimmed to look their best. Bushel baskets of jewel-bright apples and fragrant grapes lined the shelves along the walls waiting to be judged. Out of reach of greedy fingers sat fussy cakes with mounds of creamy icing, plates of homemade fudge and every cookie in a child's imagination. All of them were to be savoured by a judge and marked for their good taste and pleasing presentation. This was surely one of the more coveted positions on the judging panel.

The upper floor held hundreds of pages of carefully prepared school projects. Neat displays of printing and writing shared space with rows of brightly coloured artwork. Scrapbook collections on subjects as varied as warplanes and the recent royal wedding filled the tables lining the walls, alongside simple woodworking and craft items. Town and country schools entered the same categories for each class, though we townies were often soundly beaten by a smaller country school with a total enrollment of fifteen pupils. Elayne and I entered as many categories as we could to increase the odds of winning something. Separated by a school year, we never competed with one another directly, a twist of fate that surely protected our friendship through the winning and losing process.

Decades before we became aware of the Women's Movement and its long struggle, the girls in our grade seven class demanded the right to enter the woodworking competition that had been, up until then, restricted to male entrants. Woodworking was a required course in our school. We worked as hard as the boys, scrubbed off the same paint after class, removed the same number of slivers, and if I remember correctly, bled the same colour. Clearly the competition should have been open to all of us, though no one had questioned the rules before. Even the school principal did not want to upset the *status quo*. We arranged a meeting with the members of the Fair Board, who after hearing our argument agreed to change the rules.

Impressed with our initiative but still confident in their woodworking skills, the boys in our class thought it only fair that the girls be given an equal chance to lose to them. We entered our bird houses, our magazine racks, our candy dishes and our book ends, sweeping every category we entered. A little skirmish in the long battle for gender equality had been won. This just might have been a glimmer of the dawning of the modern Women's Movement, at least in Brussels.

Getting to the midway set up in the centre of the busy oval race-track proved to be even more exhilarating than the rides once we got there. Although the officials made a genuine effort to control the crowds of children driven on by a lust for cotton candy, we invariably found ourselves running for our lives as a snorting horse bore down on us at breakneck speed.

All the mechanical rides shook and rattled enough to scare to bits anyone over the age of twenty-five, but we didn't let a little thing like the threat of an early demise deter us. From the top of the Ferris wheel we could see all the way to the local dump. Even better than that incomparable view was the dependable thrill we got from riding the swinging chairs. With a growl from its engine and the acrid smells of diesel smoke, corn dogs and manure fighting for supremacy, the circle of box chairs swung into action. Around and around and higher and higher we soared until we were flying parallel to the ground and screaming for more. I *think* it was more we were screaming for. In any case, once the chairs had jiggled to a stop, we couldn't line up fast enough for another ticket to get back on.

As soon as we had devoured a cloud of cotton candy, a candy apple was a must. Out of guilt, we ate at least part of the apple after the red candy coating was gone. For a quarter, a boisterous man with a microphone offered to guess our ages within three years and our weights within ten pounds, and we actually fell for it. Rarely anyone other than teenage girls won the large stuffed animals, since the barker didn't dare try to feel how solid they were. Elayne and I were handed a cheap plaster ornament for the pleasure of being fleeced out of our quarters and were told to move along. We were happy enough with that. The ornament was what we wanted in the first place. At other booths we threw softballs at a line of wooden milk bottles, darts at a wall of balloons, and dimes onto a row of saucers, trying to win something. My deficient skills at hitting anything kept the prizes well out of reach.

Older farm boys showed off their strength by hammering the base of a thermometer-looking contraption, to see how high they could manage to send the metal weight. If they hit the base hard enough, the weight sailed all the way to the top and rang a bell. That sound won them another panda bear for their girlfriends who stood looking on adoringly from the sidelines, all but hidden under an armload of colourful plush. But mostly we rode the swinging chairs until neither of us could see straight. Hours later, with our funds and energies exhausted, we started the long walk home to reality.

In the evening when the school projects had been stripped from the walls and the farm produce and animals taken away, the Crystal Palace transformed itself once again, this time into a large hall for dancing. Shortly after eight o'clock, a small orchestra hired for the evening began tuning up their instruments, while a layer of powdered wax was applied to the wooden floor of the second story.

The gathering of another rowdy crowd so enraged the pigeon population—fresh from a generous gorging of popcorn and french fries—that they began hopping from one beam to another, cooing vindictively and adding their own slippery concoction to the floor. This then, is how the Crystal Palace earned its more colourful and clearly more suitable name—The Birdshit Ballroom.

For two short days out of every year, we orbited around this building like planets around the sun. The day after the fair, the Crystal Palace reverted to its lonely existence, staring out at us with dark vacant eyes, sadly resigned to a long wait until the next September.

A Pinch to Grow an Inch

The birthday parties held at the home of our family doctor and his five daughters were as eagerly awaited as any of our own. Their large Victorian house on Williams Street, built in 1887 as a replica of Scotland's Dunedin Castle, had a sweeping veranda and bay windows reaching all the way to a bell-shaped turret. We heard the house had so many rooms on its three floors that some were not used at all. Any home with space to spare had a magnetic attraction to those of us who lived in more modest houses. We couldn't wait to explore the darkened, vacant rooms in search of mysterious passageways we knew must be there. As hard and as often as we looked for them, we did not find a one.

Moving to Brussels shortly after the end of the War, Doctor Myers and his wife set up a family practice with a maternity ward in their home, subsequently bringing into the world most of the Baby Boomers in the district. Their daughters' birthday parties, always fun and occasionally thrilling, were social events we would not miss. Because space in their large house was not a consideration, the girls were encouraged to invite as many friends as they wanted—and I suppose they wanted a crowd, because they always had one.

Dividing the large front room were a pair of sliding pocket doors, which could be opened or closed to accommodate the number of people to be entertained. We treated these sliding doors as stage curtains for our impromptu plays, which we performed for the sole purpose of being able to use them. Three floors of rooms were available when we played hide and seek, some with bay windows, some with balconies. There were front stairways and back stairways and alcoves galore, even a stairway to the turret.

At one of their more noteworthy birthday parties, a baby girl was born between the sandwiches and the money cake. I am referring here to time—after the sandwiches were served and before the cake was served. She wasn't born right there on the table between the sandwiches and the money cake. That would have been enough to put us off birthday parties for life, or at the very least off sandwiches.

We were allowed to see the baby once she was presentable, one at a time and at the safe distance of the hallway. Now how can you top that for party entertainment? Several of my friends tried, but with the exception of the undertaker's daughter—who had a sleep-over birthday party at the same time as the deceased was laid out in the living room—no one even came close.

* * * * *

Most of us have at least one memorable birthday. My seventh birthday party, the first one I helped to plan, especially sticks in my mind.

"Because you will be seven years old in two weeks, you may invite seven of your best friends to your party," Mother instructed, somewhat naively.

I made a list. Then I made another list. And still another. It was impossible to narrow the number to seven. Who could be left off the list? Who could I afford to insult that year? I tried for a week to make Mother change her mind. Explaining my side of the situation didn't work. Pleading didn't work. Sulking didn't work. That never worked. It would be seven guests or no guests, and that, according to Mother, was that.

We planned my seventh birthday party for five o'clock in the afternoon of the 24th of September, a school day. I asked for different kinds of sandwiches so my guests would have a choice. Of course they would have to be crustless, using only white bread and cut on the diagonal. Never given a choice at other times of the year, I ate sandwiches on all types of bread, in any shape, crusts and all. Children were still hungry somewhere in the world, and Mother was prepared to provide a list of them if she saw the need.

After some negotiation—okay, pleading—my birthday cake was to be a money cake. The trend, after all, had been set. It also had to be chocolate. Mother agreed to slip coins wrapped in paper into the cake before serving it with Neapolitan ice cream. We selected the games I would play with my guests and how we would decorate the dining room with crêpe paper streamers and balloons. But most important of all, I promised to come straight home after school to help with the preparations.

I drew up a list of my seven best friends, trusting the others to either forgive or forget when it came time to invite me to their parties. My fondest wish was for my seventh birthday party to be the one everyone would talk about for the rest of the year.

The day for inviting my friends arrived. While I fully intended to invite only the seven girls on my list, when I saw all those expectant faces, I was overcome by a sudden *joie de vivre,* and invited all thirty-two of my classmates, and some in other classrooms too. No one had invited forty guests to their birthday party before, not even the doctor's daughters. Few children had other priorities where a party was concerned, and clearly no one wanted to miss this one.

I know I should have informed Mother of my sudden change of plans, but I couldn't begin to explain what had happened to me. I prayed for a really good excuse. What passed for temporary insanity had been used so many times before, I knew it would never work again. My mind went blank. But then that's what got me into the mess in the first place.

At school the day of my party, my popularity soared. My party guests gave me the royal bumps, my seven birthday spanks and so many pinches to grow so many inches, I began to wonder why these birthday rituals were considered an honour at all. They seemed more like assault and battery to me. So intrigued was I with my sudden popularity, I couldn't bear to let my new best friends out of my sight long enough to change into party clothes. Instead, we moved as one from house to house until everyone looked fresh and neat. Well, everyone but me.

Eventually we appeared at the top of the laneway with me in the lead like some disheveled Pied Piper. I could see my anxious mother standing in the bay window watching for me, as by this time I was an hour-and-a-half late. Long forgotten were my promises to come straight home to help with the party preparations.

Forty-one of us erupted through the front door like lava from a volcano, laughing and screeching and falling over one other in a race to begin the festivities. No matter how well Mother knew the parable of the loaves and fishes, when faced with the task of stretching food for eight into food for forty-one she knew she needed help, and fast. Assuming the role of Sergeant Major, Mother began shouting orders at my brother—who really must have been enjoying this spectacle.

"I'll call the hotel and ask them to make a couple of loaves of sandwiches. Get a cake too if they have one to spare. Oh yes, and two more bricks of ice cream—any kind—I don't care. Stop at the store and get some money from your father first—And come straight home, please, for goodness sake! What am I going to do with her? Oh, she'll rue this day!"

I didn't need to hear that prediction. I was already up to my eyes in rue. What exactly the punishment would be or when I could expect it was uncertain, but this I knew, some day, some way, I'd pay. For the moment I hoped none of my guests were noticing the drama going on about them, as the party had taken on a life of its own. The boys were riding the back of the sofa like a horse, three or four of the girls were plunking away on the piano at three different tunes, and all the rest were busy squeezing into corners at a safe distance from the opposite sex. Even over this kind of commotion, the news about my ruing the day sailed out of the kitchen and into the ears of my guests, who scattered like geese as Doug came bursting through the kitchen door on his mercy errand for more food.

"Why is your mom so mad at you?" Elayne asked, all too aware of a certain unexplained electricity in the air.

"Because I invited too many."

"How many were you supposed to invite?"

"Seven." I mumbled, avoiding her eyes. She looked around at my forty guests, and then at me. But she said nothing. This disaster was beyond words. All of my guests knew of my blunder, and some—all right, the boys—were revelling in it.

"You're gonna get it!" several of them mewed with that special sing-song mockery that boys of a certain age have. Mother and I made a point of avoiding eye contact during the party, though I could feel her displeasure, like an icy draft, from across the room.

It was almost dark when the last of my guests went home. The time had come to face Mother. For fifteen minutes she ranted at me about my thoughtlessness, then grounded me for the rest of my life, or until she was sick of looking at me. My father, attempting to read his newspaper over the ruckus going on about him, raised his head and stared at me over his glasses with that disappointed expression he saved for these situations. That look and his silence stung most of all.

Despite the embarassing outcome, my birthday wish came true. All my friends remembered my party for a whole year—not for its unique entertainment value, you understand, but because of their mothers' constant warnings never to pull a stunt like that.

Another Pretty Pickle

Smoke from roadside leaf fires spread a blue haze under the maples. It was early October, a time when pots bubbled and steamed on kitchen stoves all over town, filling the air with the heady aroma of pickling spices.

Thumbing through a dog-eared scribbler, Mother's friend pointed to favourite pickling recipes she had gathered through the years. Althea's skills at pickling were well-known. Mother had never pickled anything. But a bumper crop of cucumbers from the garden, overflowing an assortment of baskets in the kitchen, was about to launch her into unknown territory. Dill pickles, she decided, would be her first attempt.

She followed the recipe to the letter, with me in my usual spot, underfoot. Baskets of dark green cucumbers plunked into the kitchen sink, where I scrubbed at them furiously with a little brush to remove all the prickly whiskers. After each one had been towel-dried, Mother placed them into the large stone pickling crock she had bought at an auction sale the previous spring. She poured a brine solution, a mixture of coarse pickling salt and water over them, lay three or four cabbage leaves on top, and covered the entire concoction with a large dinner plate weighted down with a brick. According to the recipe it was necessary to keep every cucumber under the surface of the brine, and because they tended to float, this method worked best. A bouquet of fragrant dill hung upside down in the pantry beside the pickling spices, awaiting the final process in a few days.

Struggling under the weight of the stone crock full of cucumbers, the gallons of brine, and the brick, Mother found a cool, dark corner of the pantry in which to set it down. Covering it carefully with a sheet of cheesecloth, she closed the door behind her. There they were to sit burping happily, transforming themselves into the envy of the neighbourhood.

By the evening of the second day my father started to complain about the smell from the pantry, which seemed to intensify by the minute. With the cooler nights of autumn closing in, we were at the mercy of the fetid menace whenever we closed the windows.

"We can't go on like this, Jean. Do something!" was my father's urgent plea from behind his white handkerchief.

"You're right," she agreed. "Help me move it to the shed." In this case, out of sight did not necessarily mean out of mind. In my imagination, the pickles had turned themselves into a witch's brew, crouching in their crock bubbling and belching and casting off gaseous green fumes that probably glowed in the dark. Actually they were quite well behaved, though the odour worsening daily made close inspection difficult.

"I wonder where I went wrong," Mother mumbled to herself, reading and rereading the handwritten page Althea had given her.

After another peek into the cloudy depths, she admitted they would never be safe enough for human consumption. If the smell didn't kill someone, the first bite of pickle surely would. The time had come to give in to the inevitable. The pickles would have to be put down, and the deeper the better.

This time my father moved the crock to the middle of the back garden. Mother followed close behind with the spade, while I carried nothing heavier than curiosity. When the brick, the plate, and the rotting cabbage leaves were removed, the contents were revealed in all their glory. A veritable garden of mould bloomed on top of the brine. It looked almost pretty, in a lethal sort of way.

"I'd never eat anything that smells like that," claimed my father. I wasn't convinced. In my opinion, anyone who could eat blue cheese, smoked kippers, and steak-and-kidney-pie had lost all credibility in the olfactory department.

Trying to remove the mould resulted in distributing it further among the grey-green cucumbers that floated like dead things on top of the cloudy brine. Mother dug a hole in the far corner of the garden, deeper probably than was necessary. Carrying his heavy burden, my father struggled over to the hole, set it down, and tipped it over onto its side.

Into the hole slopped the contents of the crock—the cabbage leaves, the brine, the globs of colourful mould, the dreaded 'dills of death' and a large portion of Mother's confidence. The only creatures remotely interested in the pickles now were the flies, and then only until the soil thumped back into the hole. Once the crock had been washed and aired on newspapers, Mother put it back in its place on the pantry shelf, her first experience at pickling an apparent failure.

Over a cup of tea a few days later, Mother admitted her defeat to Althea. Sadly she relayed the story of the terrible smell and how she had moved the crock to the shed with little improvement, of the horrid mould, the greying cucumbers floating in the cloudy brine, and my father's pleas to put us out of our misery.

"Maybe I misread the recipe. I don't know where I went wrong."

"But that's the way they should be, Jean. The brine draws out the water from the cucumbers so they can absorb the pickling solution," she explained. "That mouldy solution would have been rinsed away with the clear water in the next step. You gave up too soon, that's all."

The time wasted on their preparation was bad enough, but the wasted ingredients proved the most humbling for Mother. With the scarcities of the War years and the Great Depression still painfully vivid in her mind, she tried never to waste anything. For years we had been sleeping on embroidered pillow cases made from bleached sugar bags, under quilts fashioned from the best parts of our worn-out clothing. No one could remember the original owners of the little dresses I wore as a child. Nothing was thrown away if it could be put to further use. Personal and household items were repaired and reused so many times, in the end they simply gave up.

In the years to follow, Mother perfected the dill pickle recipe. With her confidence restored, her successes soon lined the pantry shelves, but not always without mishap.

* * * * *

In a subsequent pickling season, our once white kitchen, warm and steamy and smelling of vinegar and cloves, unexpectedly transformed itself into a Jackson Pollock painting. Left unattended too long, the pressure cooker exploded, propelling pulverized beets onto every surface of the room. It's remarkable how much coverage, in terms of square feet, you can get from an exploding pressure cooker full of beets. Fortunately we were out of the room at the time.

Hearing the explosion from upstairs, Mother realized she had forgotten to release the steam valve, but it was too late now to do anything about it. Someone had to venture into the war zone to assess the damage, and as usual, we went together.

An awesome spectacle greeted us when we opened the kitchen door. For a moment we were shocked into silence, which for us was pretty shocked. It looked like something out of a dream—one that could have been better appreciated if it hadn't been for the inevitable cleanup. Ruby stalactites hung from the ceiling and roseate snails slithered down the walls leaving wide, crimson trails in their wake. The lid from the pressure cooker lay in the middle of the floor in a pool of beet juice, like an armoured warrior mortally wounded in some ancient battle.

I waited for Mother to explode too as soon as reality sunk in, but she surprised me. Whirling around and around she surveyed the carnage, laughing a pitiful, scary little laugh. No other sound could be heard but the slow tick-tock of the cuckoo clock in the hallway and a barely audible reference to the Holy Family, her normal vocabulary overwhelmed by the situation.

When the scrub pail had been filled with soapy water for the first of many times, Mother set to work washing the ceiling first, then the walls and finally the floor. Nonetheless, the stains set immediately. Until she repainted the kitchen several weeks later, it wore the rosy glow of sunrise all day long. On succeeding attempts, Mother paid closer attention to the pressure cooker, and soon jars of pickled beets joined the colourful array of preserves lining the shelves of the pantry.

Scary Kids!

Ranking next to Christmas for anticipatory excitement, the preparations for Hallowe'en kept us busy for months. Elayne and I began designing our costumes in a still-summery September, two aspiring Edith Heads coming up with one outlandish concept after another. At a time when costumes of any kind had to be homemade, our mothers flatly refused to consider any that would cost the equivalent of a week's groceries and take a Hollywood costume designer a week to sew. Out the window went our dreams of being butterflies, or sequinned mermaids for the evening—designs shamelessly copied from the latest Esther Williams extravaganza—replaced by the far less imaginative cowgirl or princess outfits. In any case, these simpler costumes fit better under a winter coat. The fact that we lived in a northern climate, where an unseasonably early blizzard often dampened any Hallowe'en enthusiasm, took years to sink in. During the costume planning stage, snow was the furthest thing from our minds.

The whole idea behind dressing up and wearing a mask was to keep our identities a secret, and goodness knows we tried. But with the weather forcing us most years to wear our winter coats over our costumes, this was not an easy task. Because we lived in a village where no one was a stranger, even with most of our faces covered we could be recognized by our winter coats. It didn't seem fair.

For the first few years Mother dressed me as a ghost, draping part of a worn-out sheet over my coat, with a pair of eye holes to see through. I'd been content with that as long as I found a treat or two in the bottom of my candy bag by the end of a very short evening.

The year I turned five, Mother let out all the stops and made my first real Hallowe'en costume for a competition sponsored by the Lions Club, to be held at the town hall. She worked hard to make the evening one I would long remember, and in that she succeeded beyond her wildest dreams.

As a Hawaiian hula dancer, I wore a skirt of fringed black and orange crêpe paper many layers thick, with leis and anklets made from a mountain of popcorn she popped and strung by hand. My costume was so time-consuming that Doug, at his independent best, had to pull his costume together on his own. This he did without complaint or hesitation. In our family, self-sufficiency, while not exactly mandatory, was strongly encouraged.

Entering the National Costume category, Doug chose to dress as a Turk. He wore a red lampshade as a fez, with a tassel borrowed from the living room drapes dangling down one side, a colourful silk scarf as a cummerbund, and one of our father's white shirts bloused at the wrists by two of Mother's garters. With a handlebar mustache he painted on himself using black shoe polish and his pants tucked into high winter boots, he looked striking if not entirely authentic.

The town hall bustled with every costume I could imagine—hobos, pirates, fairies, cowboys, witches and clowns. Noise and excitement rose in waves as the hall filled to capacity. Soon the lights faded to a single spot on centre stage as a tall, skinny clown skipped out from the wings for a few words of welcome, promising us all a fun-packed evening. With the announcement of the first costume category, the competition began.

Six or seven children shuffled onto the stage in front of the judges, while haunting music floated from the upright piano. One mother, who like mine had been bitten by the theatre bug in a serious way, dressed her courageous little boy as Madame Dubarry. Peeking out from behind a feathered fan, he stood on stage with the others, either oblivious or simply resigned to wearing a white powdered wig, bustled taffeta gown and rows of pearls enhancing a credible looking bust line. With little competition in the 'Famous Persons' category, he won first prize easily. I did not hear if there were any serious repercussions at recess the next day.

Before I had myself prepared, the emcee called my category—whatever that was. Intrigued by the costumes and dazed by all the noise and confusion around me, I forgot for a moment why I had come. When I tried to stand, none of my moving parts would work. I stuck to my chair as if I'd been glued there. Even my eyes wouldn't blink. Mother pleaded with me to go up on stage with the others. She tried to shove me off my seat, first gently, then less so, but I had hooked my toes around the chair legs and was holding on with ten white knuckles. The only way she'd get me up on that stage was if the chair came with me. A hundred pairs of eyes turned to stare at Mother in sympathy, and at me with something that didn't feel a million miles from disgust.

Whether my problem that evening was debilitating shyness or downright stubbornness didn't seem to matter to Mother, who had spent hours working on my costume and wanted to show it off. I clearly exhibited a frailty of spirit which she considered one of the seven deadly sins. Her disappointment in me was obvious.

As I was soon to discover, time waits for no hula dancer. A winner was chosen from the brave little assemblage on stage, and with the announcement of the next category my first moment in the spotlight had come and gone. All those fringes. All that popcorn. All for naught. I can still remember those first feelings of guilt with a twinge in the pit of my stomach.

When Doug's turn came, he strutted across the stage like the confident Turk he pretended to be and won first prize in the national costume category. My despair was total. I hated myself. And at that moment I wasn't particularly fond of him. For some reason known only to the prize committee, first prize in his category was a small covered aluminum roasting pan. I especially hated it. Completely indestructible, the thing lasted for years. Each time I looked at it, I felt the guilt all over again.

After the death of my mother thirty years later, as I struggled with the task of integrating her household items with mine, I came across the little roasting pan. Although it was well-used, it remained as good as the day it was awarded—giving every indication that it planned to outlive me. For just a moment I considered keeping it, as a reminder of what can be accomplished with a little fortitude. Thankfully the moment was fleeting—I threw it out.

* * * * *

As I recall, only the dead or dying missed school on November first. This was the morning we gathered in the hallways to stare in wonder at the pranks masterminded by the high school students during the long preceding night. Climbing through a window left ajar at the end of classes, the boys returned after dark to unlock the double front doors. Through these doors all manner of farm implements, most of them in pieces, were carted to be assembled by flashlight in the hallways. Manure spreaders—as fresh from use as could be found—hay rakes, wagons and buggies lined the corridors both upstairs and down. Most of these students had a keen knowledge of machinery that can only be gained from life on the farm, so the reassembly was all in a day's, or in this case, a night's work. Occasionally a couple of chickens were left to wander through the halls, shedding feathers and whatever else came to mind, adding greatly to the bucolic atmosphere.

Even the teachers found this amusing for the first few minutes, until the principal ordered the older boys to clean up the mess. What had taken an hour to assemble the night before became a complicated and time-consuming business, requiring their attention for most of the day.

* * * * *

Every Hallowe'en, the town bell peeled incessantly. This mysterious occurrence, considered an integral part of the Hallowe'en festivities, could not be completely silenced until the tower was demolished years later. On one particularly tuneful evening, a length of wire was discovered stretching from the tower all the way to the culprit's second-story bedroom, a block away, from where he could ring the bell in relative comfort.

The early 1950's saw the last of the working outhouses in the village. Before that time, every first of November morning saw six or seven privies in assorted styles and colours lining the main street, each with an Eaton's catalogue tied to its door. Those who were merely curious, or quietly desperate, slowed what little traffic there was on Turnberry Street until noon, when the last of them had been claimed and carted away by their embarrassed owners.

Amusing stories circulated about how these stunts were accomplished. One owner, intent on keeping his outhouse safely on his property, sat inside to discourage anyone with bad intentions. This was not the clever plan he envisioned, because he had been spotted entering the privy. When he did not appear in a reasonable amount of time, recognizing his motives the rascals crept up behind the outhouse and slowly tipped it over onto its door, trapping the protesting owner inside. I don't want to think what the poor man had to do to get out. That part of the story was always left to our imaginations.

One repeated victim of these pranks decided to get even one year. Early one Hallowe'en, he moved his outhouse a few feet away from its original spot in the back garden, leaving the half-filled hole exposed but hidden in darkness. Lurking behind the curtains of one of his windows, he waited expectantly for his revenge. He did not have long to wait.

Several young men, up to no good, crept across the garden to claim their prize, and stumbled into the half-filled hole. I don't care to dwell on that either—but I imagine this particular outhouse was safe from pranksters for the rest of its useful life.

I Just Go Nuts
At Christmas

Love and joy come to you
And a joyful Christmas too…

I remember Christmases white with snow, the dining room table laden with special holiday treats, and gifts for all of us under the tree. Not once did I question how this happened or who was responsible for the bounty, though I am certain it must have been difficult for my parents some years. It seemed enough to trust that it would happen, and it always did.

A successful season in our store depended on the local farmers receiving a decent price for their produce and livestock at market. If they did, some of that good fortune trickled down to us. If they did not, we too felt the pinch, and it hurt until May. Declaring bankruptcy would have been a moral as well as a personal failure to my parents—a fate too horrible to contemplate. To avoid this catastrophe in years when sales were low, we depended on my father's skill at watchmaking. There never seemed to be a shortage of repairs at which he worked much more than a forty-hour week.

But on those Christmases when the merry ring of the cash register filled the air, my parents caught a good dose of the holiday spirit that lasted all season. Not many Christmases passed before I learned that it took more than colourful decorations to make our holiday bright. It took a steady flow of satisfied customers. This little insight into the reality of Christmas for my family made me appreciate even the commercial side of the season.

If Christmas was responsible for money flowing into our store, it was equally responsible for it flowing back out again, and I soon discovered it was even more fun flowing in the opposite direction. At the age of six, I experienced my first of many last-minute shopping sprees. With just a bit of coaxing, my father reached into his pants pocket and brought out more than the usual shirt button. This time he handed me a whole quarter. Accustomed to a weekly allowance of ten cents, twenty-five cents represented a considerable windfall.

At any time of year the 5¢ to $1.00 Store attracted me like no other store before or since. At Christmas it was positively magical. The interior, festooned with red and green twisted streamers, tinsel icicles and silver bells, propelled me into the Christmas spirit. I loved the smells, the sounds, the colours, the piles of merchandise displayed on every inch of counter space. Painted fire-engine red, with a shiny brass door handle set low enough for me to feel independent, the 5¢ to $1.00 Store welcomed the smallest shoppers. Once inside, the warm air filled my lungs with a strange blend of gum drops, rubber boots and cheap perfume, the bare wooden floor heaving and creaking with every footstep.

Barely tall enough to see over the counters, I gazed in wonder at the abundance spread out before me. Rows of plaid shirts, piles of striped pajamas, and stacks of colourful socks and ties filled each display area to overflowing—and on one headless figure, a set of fleecy long underwear, its flap charmingly askew. Beside the lace-trimmed lingerie, a mysterious pair of long legs grew out of the counter, reaching toe-first for the ceiling. These were covered by a pair of flesh-coloured stockings of the sheerest nylon with dark seams running up the back, held in place by the clasps of a garter belt, unseen beneath a cloud of tulle.

I spent most of my time admiring at nose level the different shades of red nail polish and sniffing the sweet-scented EVENING IN PARIS toilet water in its famous dark-blue bottle with the image of the Eiffel Tower. All of Mother's perfumes made my father wheeze, so she kept her small supply tucked away in her dresser drawer for visits to her sisters in Niagara Falls. At first I believed toilet water to be just that, water from someone's toilet. Whose, I wondered? I can't tell you how relieved I was to learn the truth.

On another counter there were pretty paper cases of sewing needles and threads in every shade of the rainbow, colourful paper for writing letters, and pens to do the writing. But none of it seemed right for Mother. I had almost given up when I spied a row of pickle dishes prominently displayed on a shelf to one side of the store. How could I have missed them before? Trying to decide between round and square, I spotted one in pink-tinted glass and couldn't reach for my quarter fast enough. We had a shelf at least half-full of pickle dishes in our store, but once I set my mind on that pink one I could think of nothing else. The sales clerk told me I had just enough money to pay for it, and with that bit of good news, my first Christmas shopping spree came to an end.

There is an exceptional but little known fact about the merchants of Brussels at that time. Whether or not we had enough money to cover the purchase of our mothers' Christmas gifts, if we could at least come close, the stores in the village, ours included, took the loss in the spirit of giving. My first purchase may have been a case in point. All I know for sure is that from then on I was a loyal customer of the 5¢ to $1.00 Store. Sometimes I bought Mother a wooden spoon, not that she needed another one. She had a drawer full at home, but she always seemed so delighted to get one more that I couldn't bear to disappoint her.

I was still young and selfish enough to want Mother to love my gift best of all, to stare at it in wonder and praise my superior shopping skills. She never disappointed me.

"How did you guess?" she'd cry in amazement. "It's exactly what I wanted!" And I believed every word for as long as she said them.

In the beginning my budget rarely stretched past Mother. My father's turn would come.

* * * * *

At a time in my life when Christmases seemed five years apart, I found the last week crawling at an excruciatingly slow pace. How could seven days take so long? I was in bed sniffling through an early winter cold, a bad case of pre-Christmas blues and a new obsession with the clock. Mother had errands to run for my father. At Christmas he left the store only to sleep, for fear of missing an important sale. Tiptoeing downstairs to the gloom of an unlit Christmas tree, I knelt to admire the presents—and if the truth be known, to have a good feel around. Luring me onto the rocks of dishonesty, the gayly wrapped presents stripped me of what few principals I may have accumulated in my first seven years of life. I could hardly help noticing one strategically placed Christmas seal had dried out and now lay curled like a potato chip in my hand. Honest.

Before SCOTCH TAPE became a popular household item, only a few tiny glue-backed seals kept the presents a mystery until Christmas morning. For a normal person, this would have been enough. But I was light-years away from normal at Christmas. A whirlwind of rascally thoughts tore through my head. How could it hurt to have a peek at what my aunt and uncle had sent me from the city? It was almost Christmas. Only six more sleeps. Resolving to open this gift and this one only, I squeezed the sides of the box together and it slipped easily out of its tissue paper sleeve. Inside I found a miniature enamelled stove on four sturdy legs, with an oven door that opened and closed, a tiny frying pan, pots with lids that could be removed and a shiny tea kettle to sit on top. I could hardly breathe. It was perfect. If only I could set it up and look at it forever. But I knew I couldn't. Not yet. I squeezed the sides of the box together again and it slipped back into the tissue paper as easily as it had slipped out. A little spit and pressure applied to the curly Christmas seal and the parcel looked as good as new. I placed it under the tree in exactly the same spot—in case Mother had memorized their positions—and stood back to admire my ingenuity.

It had been too easy. More rascally thoughts were queuing up behind that last one. Mother had only been gone ten minutes. It took an hour to walk to the Post Office, pick up the mail, deliver it to my father and walk home again. Little horns began to sprout on my forehead. *Do I have to stop with one gift? No! hahahahaha!!!* I chose another, opening it the same way, then another and another, until I could find no more with my name on them. *Should I stop here? No! hahahahaha!!* I opened my brother's gifts too, rewrapping each one and returning it to its original spot with the others. It did cross my mind that I could have changed a name tag or two if I found he had received gifts obviously meant for me. But Doug's gifts were things only boys would want—a pen knife, a flashlight, a Maple Leafs jersey, a model airplane kit, brown socks. The name tags remained intact. I thought I had taken the moral high ground on that one, so you can see what a frightful mess I had become in one short hour.

I sat down and looked at what had been, until then, a thing of wonder and mystery. I now knew what lay behind every merry snowman and colourful candy cane on the wrapping paper. There were no surprises left for me under the tree. My insatiable curiosity had ruined the suspense that is so much a part of Christmas. The worst part of all was that I could blame no one but myself. I trudged upstairs and fell into bed with a heavy heart.

Christmas did not hold the same excitement for me that year. All my cries of delight had to be faked. Now I know I wasn't the first child to peek at a Christmas gift —or ten—nor would I be the last, but that year I discovered the terrible cost. With the fiasco of my seventh birthday party still uppermost in my mind, and my Christmas now in a self-imposed shambles, my eighth year was off to a less than auspicious beginning.

* * * * *

They arrived like clockwork, every spring and fall, but the one most eagerly awaited, arrived in time to arouse a good case of Christmas greed. When I think of the books that most influenced my childhood, the EATON'S mail-order catalogue ranked as high as *Black Beauty.* No book caused more excitement or offered more hours of fun. Like a whole department store spread out in front of me on the living room rug, I believed that if I wished for something hard enough—I mean really hard enough—it could be mine.

Hours were spent scanning the pages and making lists. At the end of the Christmas season, the catalogue gave us weeks of additional fun as a cut-out book, with clothes and furniture and people for our make-believe stories. After a few months, its pages now dog-eared and torn to pieces, the catalogue took on its final role in the kitchen wood box, helping to start the fire in the morning. It was easily the most useful book in the house.

When I would give up the catalogue long enough for Doug to make his list, he chose a *Meccano* construction kit, or more track for his electric train. Boy stuff. My list usually included another doll or a set of tiny furniture for my doll house. If I'd wanted one, I suppose I could have asked for a baseball glove, but Doug had all the gloves I would ever want, if and when I wanted one, which wasn't often. My natural inclination was for more dolls in a wondrous assortment of sizes, hair colours and life-like abilities.

The year I turned nine, I decided to branch out a little. Content to make do with my existing horde of dolls, it was time to ask for something more adventurous. I thought about it for a long time, poring over the catalogue for clues to possibilities. Downhill skis looked the most appealing. A distant cousin of today's skis, they did not require separate ski boots, but had a simple strap binding that wound tightly around our regular winter boots. Once buckled they were there to stay, through thick or thin, through accident or injury, as long as our legs stayed attached. When we fell, at least we were free from chasing runaway skis, as by this time they was firmly attached to our knees.

I practiced my skiing technique by sliding in my winter boots down the hill at the back door, being sure to keep my knees bent and my head pointing downhill until I reached the bottom. After many attempts and minor spin-outs, I mastered what I imagined to be the proper skiing form. Now I was ready for Adams Hill. With weeks of shopping pleasure still ahead, I told my parents about my decision, then counted the days until Christmas.

On Christmas morning I dashed downstairs to the living room, barely touching a step. There they were, tied back-to-back with a big red ribbon, propped against the wall behind the tree, shining as if under a spotlight. They were magnificent strips of pale varnished wood, sporting red pin-stripes and bright red bindings. I could almost feel the wind on my face as I glided fearlessly to the bottom of Adams Hill. This had been my most brilliant idea yet.

But, what's this? Something had gone wrong with my plan. The tag attached to the binding read: 'TO DOUG, MERRY CHRISTMAS. LOVE, MOM AND DAD.' *How could this be?* I searched around the tree for another pair, but these were the only skis in sight. *They were supposed to be mine.* I read the tag again, but the name remained the same. They were Doug's. *I was the one who asked for them! How could this have happened?* I fought the feelings of disappointment and jealousy that welled up inside me, but I had an uphill battle on my hands. There were other gifts for me under the tree that year, perfectly good gifts too—but much, much smaller—a gold ring, a pair of pink pajamas, white fur-backed mittens, earmuffs...

Doug was delighted with his skis, of course. Who wouldn't be? What a surprise they must have been! He went out to try them on the hill at the back door right after breakfast. I stood and watched with a jaundiced eye from the dining room window. Down the hill he flew, along with any dreams I had of becoming a downhill skier anytime soon.

Even in my existing state of mind, it was hard to blame my parents for the mix-up. They were always so busy at Christmas, and at the family gift buying stage more than a little frazzled. One of us had asked for skis, but because I had never asked for anything remotely like them before, it must have been easy to confuse the request.

I saw Doug become proficient on his skis that winter, following him down Adams Hill on our toboggan, making sure nothing drastic happened to them. I vowed the next year I would make my wish known in July, and follow it up with frequent reminders.

In the bigger scheme of things, this incident served as an important lesson in forgiveness and understanding, probably the best Christmas present they could have given me. Though I must admit the lesson did not sink in until June.

By the next Christmas, the skis had been long forgotten. In the meantime Barbara Ann Scott, Canada's first figure skating champion, had spun her way onto the scene and into every little girl's heart. My earnest wish that Christmas was for a pair of white figure skates. Even my parents had trouble confusing this request, and these were waiting for me under the tree on Christmas morning. My cup was full!

* * * * *

My father, a proper English gentleman, actually owned a pair of pale grey spats. I assumed he kept them at the back of his bottom drawer in the event he wished to impersonate a 1920's gangster, because he wore them at no other time. He doffed his hat to the ladies on the street—which even then was a rare courtesy—never swore, did not raise his voice in anger, and never wore a colour more flamboyant than navy.

A year or two after the skis episode, Mother gave me instructions to shop for a tie to give him for Christmas. Of the opinion that I need not take a back seat to anyone in the proficient shopping department, I could hardly wait to get started. Checking the shallow drawer of his dresser to see what kinds of ties he had on hand, I found about a dozen, all of them old and well-worn but with one thing in common. They were boring, boring, boring. One though, a black bow tie, almost new, was the one he had worn the day he married Mother. I remembered seeing it in their wedding pictures. There was a white bow tie too, for an event even more formal than their wedding. Boy, was that tie in the wrong town! I tried on a few. They smelled like shaving soap, as did everything else in his dresser. No doubt about it, he could certainly use a new tie.

I began my quest in the shop where I felt most comfortable, the 5¢ to $1.00 Store. The ties I saw there were plain, spotted or striped, and he had plenty of those already.

With the tenacity of a seasoned shopper I tried other stores until finally one very special tie caught my eye. Although not exactly what I had seen him wear, I loved it the moment I saw it. Better still, it was within my budget. I bought it, wrapped it lovingly in its long thin box, placed it in a prominent position under the tree, and began dropping none-too-subtle hints to pique his curiosity. By Christmas Eve I had him worked up into such a frenzy of anticipation, I was afraid he wouldn't sleep a wink all night.

According to family custom, my father slept late on Christmas morning, opening his presents last with the rest of us as his audience, insisting that being able to sleep late was the gift he wanted to open first. When he finally did get up, he made me wait until he had opened all his other gifts before turning to mine. I hoped it was because he liked to save the best for last, but he was probably teasing me. I could always tell when he was teasing, because he stuck his tongue in the inside of his cheek to keep from laughing and that tell-tale bump was there when he reached for his last present. He turned it over, squeezed it a few times, then shook it, listening to the soft rustling sounds from inside. Suddenly I wished I hadn't given him so many good hints.

"I know. It's a hat," he exclaimed at last, "I really need one. Have you seen that old…"

"Don't be silly, Daddy," I interrupted. "A hat wouldn't fit into that box." Clearly he was mystified. The tension was unbearable. I changed positions four times until finally I could no longer sit at all.

After such a lengthy build-up, it all happened too fast. First the ribbon fell to the floor, then the wrapping. The top of the box seemed to be stuck, so I had to help him with it. Then the layer of folded tissue paper was removed—by me, because I couldn't stand the suspense a second longer—and there it lay in all its glory, a brown satin beauty with two gaudy orange and yellow roosters fighting each other to the death, splatters of blood and shed feathers raining down all around them. I had forgotten how incredibly beautiful it was—a veritable masterpiece of colour and style! Who could resist it? Not me. And not my father, that's for sure! The astonished look on his face I interpreted as pure joy. I remember he was even speechless for a time.

I recounted endlessly my tireless search for the perfect tie and my discovery of this most amazing specimen, until I had extracted the last drop of wonder and appreciation from him. I just knew he could not have been happier with my choice.

He wore it often, most of the time with a vest that covered one of the bloodied combatants, and the shared giggles with Mother stopped after a few weeks. I bought him many other ties over the years, but I am certain none of them made the same impression as that first one.

* * * * *

Revelling in the constant, tuneful ringing of the cash register one Christmas, my father, at his most magnanimous, gave Mother a hundred-dollar bill in her Christmas card. I had never seen so much money. I didn't think you could hold that much money in one hand. In truth, I didn't know there was such a thing as a hundred-dollar bill. I was thrilled for her. Just think of the possibilities! Whenever Mother and I had some time alone, we discussed what she could buy with that much money.

I thought about a fur coat, like the ones I'd seen on a few women at church—the ones I ached to touch but was told I could not under any circumstance. Mother said it would take a few hundred-dollar bills to buy one of those. A car was out of the question. They cost even more than a fur coat. Days passed and still we thought. This being the dead of winter, and Mother and I being forward-thinking people and all, we decided on a set of matching lawn furniture, maybe wooden, the kind we'd seen on the lawns of the larger homes in the village. We could paint it white. That was it. As soon as we had the garden looking its best in the spring we'd buy wooden lawn furniture—and paint.

Mother had no intention of spending the money on lawn furniture or indeed on anything else. She had seen our store's books at the end of every February since they started the business, and knew there would come a time when the money would find a more urgent use.

After one of those months when my father wondered how he would pay the electric bill, Mother went to her jewellery box to retrieve her Christmas gift. She had planned all along to keep it for a rainy day, and this one was definitely clouding over. By spring I had forgotten all about the lawn furniture, so her noble deed went unnoticed by me. Years later my father reminded me of the story about the hundred-dollar bill. Just planning what to do with the money, and knowing she could spend it when and however she chose, was gift enough for her.

* * * * *

Years later, when I had started working in Toronto, I asked Mother if I could buy her something special for Christmas.

"Yes, you can," she said without hesitation. "I would like a copy of the AMERICAN WOMAN'S COOKBOOK."

Why? She hardly ever referred to a cookbook. Most of the recipes she used were right there in her head. But if that was what she wanted, I promised I'd try to find it. As it turned out, trying was not good enough. I searched every bookstore in my area of the city, but this particular cookbook was years out of print and no longer in stock.

Now what? Finally, a saleswoman at the downtown EATON'S store remembered the bins of old books in the basement, and sent me there. She figured if I could not find that particular book, perhaps I would find something similar. I didn't want similar. I hadn't scoured all those bookstores for similar. But still it wouldn't hurt to take a quick peek. For over an hour I lifted, read and tossed every book in several bins until I came across a heavy one that was wrapped in brown paper and addressed to someone in Australia. That was odd. On closer examination, I discovered that it had been returned from Australia—unclaimed and unopened. This was the Christmas season after all, and the parcel was begging to be opened. So I opened it. There it was—THE AMERICAN WOMAN'S COOKBOOK—published sometime in the late 1930's, all nine hundred pages of it, a great doorstop of a thing, just slightly bashed around the edges from its long journey to and from the other side of the world.

How lucky was that? And it was half-price too, seeing as how it was old and battered. I didn't mention this to anyone, of course, but I would have paid double the price for its history alone. In triumph, I took it to my little apartment, wrapped it especially carefully and counted the days until I would be able to give it to Mother. This being the second week of December, I had a few days to wait.

Finally the time came when I could hand her my special gift, the only thing she had asked for, the one I bought for her with my own money and the ton of luck I can't believe to this day.

Astounded at its weight, she opened it and exclaimed, "Oh, good! You found it! Bill, hand me a pen, will you?"

In her lovely handwriting on the inside cover she wrote: 'To CATHY, MERRY CHRISTMAS 1959, LOVE MOM.'

"I've been looking for this cookbook for you for years. I knew you wouldn't bother searching for it for yourself. So here. I hope you will use it in good health."

I was stunned, and more than a little deflated, but she *was* right, I wouldn't have looked that hard for anything for myself. I did use it in good health though, many times, and still do. You just had to love someone like Mother! What else could you do?

Hogmanay

*... And God bless you and send
You a Happy New Year–
And God send you a Happy New Year.*

–Unknown

Of all the holidays celebrated in our home in a busy year, Mother's favourite was New Year's Eve. In the Scotland of her memory, Christmas was still celebrated as a religious holiday, and had not yet succumbed to the pressures of commercialism. Instead it was a time for innumerable church services and family dinners, when few Scots could be bullied into buying anything frivolous. Mother recalled receiving an orange one Christmas, a rare treat at that time of year in Scotland, savouring its exotic aroma for weeks until it was almost too late to eat it. So it is not surprising that everyone looked forward to the merriment surrounding a holiday like Hogmanay.

Of pagan origin, Hogmanay was the traditional name given to New Year's Eve in Scotland, observing the end of the old and the beginning of the new year. Hogmanay celebrations could be boisterous, though this behaviour was considered acceptable, even encouraged. It was also known as Daft Day for obvious reasons. Not to be outdone by the adults, the children visited from house to house gathering oatcakes as their New Year's treat.

Too preoccupied in the store during December to give the house more than a quick dusting, and too tired to give much thought to celebrating, my parents simply went through the motions at Christmas. New Year's Eve—now that was a different story! With the Christmas rush behind her, Mother's energies were quickly restored with a few days' rest. At last the fall housecleaning and polishing could begin in earnest. Although she tried to observe the yearly house cleaning rituals as set down by generations of Canadian women, her heart was rarely in it. The discipline of housework from morning 'til night several days in a row seemed more than she could bear.

"There is as good in the house as will come into it," she used to say, giving herself the excuse to put away the vacuum cleaner and sit down at the piano for an hour, turning her back on the drudgery that held little interest for her. With the approach of Hogmanay, and the fall cleaning binge already a month overdue, there was no time to waste. Tasks were assigned. These included a full day of silver polishing, and the dusting and waxing of any flat surface within reach. Although we might fail the white glove test at other times of the year, Mother insisted we start off the new year sparkling.

Tom Sawyer's whitewashing strategy worked well for Mother, who allowed me the pleasure of polishing a sink full of silverware, claiming this chore to be the most fun. I believed her. How she could keep a straight face I'll never know. That little ploy worked only once. Which doesn't mean I got out of cleaning the silver on any succeeding New Year's Eve, but simply that I knew I wouldn't have much fun while doing it.

In the meantime, Mother disappeared outside to clear off the front step. A cheerless, late December sun offered little warmth and did not help much in the task. A cleared front step was all important for the traditional 'first footing' ceremony that would take place later in the evening.

"If there's a place for everything, why is something else always in it?" Mother groused, as she attempted to straighten the kitchen cupboards, never satisfied with the amount of space they provided. And it was not just the house that came under scrutiny for the beginning of the new year. Everyone in it had to be in top form too. Doug and I were scrubbed and pressed and ready by the front door to greet guests by eight o'clock.

My parents' parties were always warm, friendly and intimate, usually including our friends as well as theirs. We had the dining room to ourselves, keeping busy with a jigsaw puzzle or a game of Chinese checkers, taking time periodically to crack more nuts or pop more corn. The adults, in suits and fancy dresses, sat in the living room catching up on news they had missed during the busy Christmas season and eating awful smelly grey things like oysters.

As with all get-togethers at our house, these evenings were predictable. At a point where the conversations began to lag and the refreshments to take hold, the party progressed to standing around the piano singing seasonal favourites and the popular tunes of the day. Bobs, my favourite guest of all time, always had the latest sheet music with him and could play any new song I'd heard on the radio. During the War, Bobs was the handsome soldier with the neat mustache who smiled at me from the black-and-white photograph on top of Althea's piano. When he came home after the War, I could hardly believe he was real. He had been just a photograph for so long—like the photos of movie stars included with every picture frame. Just a face. A nice face, but just a face. Now he was home, living, breathing, laughing and playing the piano better than anybody ever did. I was in love.

While I sat quietly beside him on the piano bench, he played request after request, though sometimes he played a wartime favourite just for the adults, one that made them laugh out loud. That was fine with me, as long as he played *Swingin' on a Star* a half-dozen times and let me sing along with him.

Shortly before midnight, Mother disappeared from the party to gather the necessary items for the 'first footing' ritual at midnight. An old Scottish tradition, the custom ensured warmth, nourishment, prosperity, and spiritual growth for the family in the coming year, brought into the home by the first foot over the threshold after midnight. A little luck, if he could swing it, would be more than welcome too.

There were, however, several important stipulations. The first foot must belong to a dark-haired man, and that foot cannot be flat. This custom probably prevented many Scottish men from 'first footing' their own households, if not from enjoying the celebrations to follow. What little hair my father had left, was black, and because his feet were not flat, he first-footed his home each New Year's Eve for as long as he lived. The ceremony could have been performed the next morning, I suppose, but having my father first-foot us at midnight guaranteed a better night's sleep for the more superstitious among us.

At a few minutes to twelve, my father left the house with an armload that included a plate of sliced Christmas cake, enough money to share with all those present, a bottle of sherry saved for the occasion, two or three nuggets of coal, and his Bible. I watched him from one of the bay windows in the living room, standing in the pale yellow glow of the front porch light, huddled against the house for protection from the wind, reading his Bible and checking his wristwatch for the approach of midnight.

As it was vital to his work as a watchmaker, my father always had the correct time. Every day he listened to the Dominion Observatory official time signal at one o'clock, just before the CBL Toronto News. Each time he'd slap his knee and say, "Right on the button again." I thought he must be playing a little game with the man on the radio, and I felt proud he was so good at it.

On the final stroke of the mantel clock, with the village bell peeling, Mother opened the front door to usher in the New Year, a blast of cold January air, and my father in a whirl of fluffy snow. Without a word to anyone he walked to the coal stove in the living room, dropped in the nuggets of coal he had taken outside with him and poked a few times at the glowing embers. Then he turned to kiss Mother who just happened to be standing within reach. The 'first footing' ceremony was complete.

This was the cue for all the hugging and kissing and the wishing of Happy New Year to begin. The boys at the party flatly refused to go along with this aspect of the festivities, not surfacing again until it was time to sing *Auld Lang Syne*, for which Bobs needed no sheet music at all.

I could never understand why, if Hogmanay were a Scottish celebration, did we stand around singing about some old Chinese man? I soon learned the truth. Mother explained that the title of the song was not 'Old Lang Sang' at all, but *Auld Lang Syne,* a song rendered in the

Lowland Scottish dialect. This was all too confusing. *Auld Lang Syne* still sounded Chinese to me. In any case, I preferred my lyrics, and for years continued to sing what I considered to be the Chinese version.

After everyone in the room had been given a share of the money gift and a sliver of Christmas cake, the adults were offered a glass of sherry. Christmas cake and sherry were my father's favourite holiday treats—the snack Doug and I left out for Santa Claus on Christmas Eve. The glass was always empty the next morning, and there were only a few crumbs left on the plate, so we assumed it must be one of Santa's favourites too.

In our home, the Christmas crackers were saved for New Year's Eve. Their loud cracks, wise pronouncements and silly paper hats added liveliness to the party. Mother whipped up a batch of eggnog for the younger guests, topped with a dusting of grated nutmeg. If she were in a particularly festive mood, she might add a drop or two of sherry. For the younger guests, this signalled the end of our New Year's celebrations. We were billeted in cots all over the house, and sent off to bed as soon as the eggnog disappeared. I imagine the adults stayed for tea and sandwiches after we went to bed, though I can't be sure. The eggnog I was in the habit of drinking too quickly removed any desire to eavesdrop.

My father stoically complied with most of Mother's Scottish traditions, Hogmanay being one of his favourites as well. But he drew the line at eating haggis on Robbie Burns Day. Mother forgave him. He was English, after all, and anyway she claimed she couldn't make a decent haggis without a sheep's pluck. Apparently you couldn't find a pluck in Brussels at any price. This was good news for the sheep, but even better news for the rest of us. To be fair, my father's choices of delicacies were not above reproach. His favourite Sunday morning breakfast was smoked kippers—a salty, flat, brown thing that lay on his plate like the sole of a shoe and took an hour to eat around the bones. The house smelled like a fish market for days. Then there were those dreaded winter nights when he insisted on having steak-and-kidney pudding, which to me had the unmistakable essence of barn about it. Surely haggis could be no worse, pluck or no pluck.

New Year's Eve represented a time for fresh starts, clean slates, and for making resolutions, whether or not we had any intention of keeping them past breakfast. With more than a little prompting from my parents, I resolved to fight less often with Doug, and to practise my piano lessons for an hour every day without having to be told—resolutions I found impossible to keep.

Just as it did every year, New Year's Day arrived bittersweet, the first big trial of our New Year's resolutions. Everyone stuck to them somewhat reluctantly for most of the day. This was also the time for hanging up new calendars, proudly replacing the dog-eared ones of the old year. Because they were given away free at Christmas to advertise many of the businesses in the village, every room in our house displayed one. The calendars I remember most fondly had realistic snowy landscapes embossed with salt-like crystals that glittered in the sunlight. Those we hung in the dining room by the telephone. Many idle moments during the coming year were spent talking to friends while flicking off this snow with a fingernail, one grain at a time.

The first of January was also the day we took down the Christmas tree, packed away the old familiar ornaments for another year, and moved the Boston fern back to its rightful place in the bay window. Little by little, life returned to normal. During these first years of peace, the 'Cold War' still meant only one thing—the fierce daily battle we waged against winter. Those hostilities had just begun.

Getting Plastered

It isn't the cough that carries you off,
It's the coffin they carry you off in.

–unknown

To chase away the common cold in the 1940's, many mothers subscribed to the effectiveness of the mustard plaster. Mine was no exception. In fact, they put great store in home remedies of all descriptions, partly out of necessity. With most of today's patent medicines still unavailable and no drug plan for their families, the inevitable doctor's prescriptions became a major expense, resorted to only when all else failed. The 'all else' in this case being the mustard plaster.

To prevent a cold in the first place, Mother gave us cod-liver oil as a vitamin supplement, with a sprinkling of salt on the spoon to make it more palatable. We may have taken this once a day or once a week or whenever she could catch us, I can't remember. Arriving in the world too late for the old-fashioned sulphur and molasses tonic in spring—for which I am eternally grateful—I was just in time for NEO-CHEMICAL FOOD, a thick, brown syrup that looked like chocolate and tasted like motor oil. Packed with vitamins or not, I couldn't get enough of it. Anything that looked that much like chocolate had to be good.

Despite Mother's best efforts to prevent it, I managed to contract a cold at least once each winter. This meant packing me off to bed with a piece of wet silk around my throat and a hot toddy in my hand. I remember that famous Scottish drink as a vile concoction of honey, lemon, hot water and a shot of whatever was left over from New Year's Eve—like a cup of tea that had gone terribly wrong. Just in case I tried to give one of her house plants a little pick-me-up, Mother stood over me until I drank it to the last drop. I remember my bed floating around the room in a fog and the wallpaper melting like water, but little else until morning. By then, if the hot toddy had not killed me, perhaps it had cured me. And if neither had been accomplished, she pulled out all the stops, promising a mustard plaster would do the job. Which job I wondered? Kill or cure? Maybe I wasn't sick at all. Maybe I was just hung over from the hot toddy. All I know is that I'd have opted for the cold, given the chance to opt at all.

I'm not sure which of the mustard plaster's elements I found most disagreeable, but its uncanny ability to burn straight through my chest to the mattress came pretty close to the top of the list. Its pungent odour too remains an unpleasant memory to this day. The ideal age for experiencing this procedure ranged between six and twelve. Few children younger than six would stand for it long enough to work, while most children over twelve were wise enough to avoid the ordeal altogether. I just happened to be smack dab in the middle of the right age group, too inexperienced to think I'd get away with refusing it and too stupid to think I'd live long without it. How I yearned for spring—and not just because Mother would not allow me to roller skate in the house, though I did sometimes anyway.

This then, is what I remember about the procedure. Mother always administered it when I was at my lowest ebb, otherwise it wouldn't have been any fun for her at all. Like some mad scientist in a 'B'-movie, she couldn't wait to get into her lab to begin work on her latest potion. From my bedroom upstairs I could not hear any murmured incantations, though only too distinct was the banging of cupboard doors, the opening and closing of drawers and the final dreaded whamp-whamp of the wooden spoon as the flour, dry mustard and water approached its evil perfection. Anticipation did little to raise my spirits.

Mother used warm water to begin with, but in no time at all any trace of heat had vanished into the cold bowl and utensils. A piece of worn bed sheet was dampened with what had to have been ice water, then placed flat on the kitchen table—the nearest cold surface. Next, the cold, yellow-brown globule was plopped out of the bowl onto the centre of the cloth, where each side was folded over carefully to prevent the mustard mixture from oozing out onto the bed while it worked its magic.

Far too soon, the woman into whose hands I had entrusted my well-being stood at the bedroom door holding the yellow menace and grinning a disturbing little grin.

"It's time to bare all," she instructed. "Now this might feel a little cool at first."

No. A snowball might feel a little cool at first. An icicle might feel a little cool at first. The mustard plaster took the meaning of cool to a new low. It was smacked onto my bare chest like a stone-dead mackerel—in one merciful motion, so as not to prolong the agony, you understand. And with that, every nerve in my body attempted to abandon ship.

"Sometimes we have to be cruel to be kind," she reminded me, buttoning my pajama top over the bulging mustard plaster, giving me an instant and ample bosom I was too sick to appreciate. After piling a mountain of blankets on top of me and tucking them in all around so no heat would escape, she left me alone to stare at the ceiling.

For the first few minutes I focussed my entire being on transferring what little body heat I had left onto that cold wet thing, its pungent and peppery vapours assaulting my nostrils with every movement of the covers. Soon I felt the slightest prickling warmth on my skin beneath the plaster, which was not at all unpleasant and almost a relief from the cold. But it didn't take long for the warm prickles to change to something a whole lot hotter. So hot in fact that sweat began to trickle in little rivulets down my neck and onto my chest, where I visualized it sizzling and dancing like spit on a hot stove. I flipped my pillow endlessly to find a rejuvenating cool spot. Every few minutes Mother appeared in the doorway to make sure I hadn't hurled myself out of the window and into the nearest snowbank, where I'm sure I'd have melted it clear through to the ground, leaving a perfect outline of my body like in a *Woody Woodpecker* cartoon.

"You probably feel better already. Don't you?" Mother asked, trying to raise my confidence in her curative abilities. I concentrated. Yes, I was sure of it. I felt worse. And if worse were not bad enough, I knew I could spontaneously combust if I had a mind to. Once or twice she peeked under the covers, lifting a corner of the plaster to confirm my worst fears. I wasn't done yet.

"Not done yet? I'm dying in here!" I moaned, not shy about raising the emotional ante.

"It's too hot! Get this thing off me!"

"Stop your whingeing! There's many a dead man would envy you." True as that may have been, I was pretty sure her bedside manner needed some work. Where was the sympathy? Where was the humanity? Where was the fire extinguisher?

Whenever I lifted my blankets, I could feel a rush of cool, life-restoring air—just enough to give me the will to go on. Ceilings can be boring when you are forced to stare at them for any length of time. So with nothing better to do, I discovered that by taking as deep a breath as I could and twisting just so, I could shift the plaster from one half of my chest to the other, saving a few more square inches of skin. Exhaling shifted it back again. Applying these tactics sequentially made me look like a pulsating queen bee, but it gave me something to do while I endured the last few minutes of the procedure.

Proclaiming me 'done to a turn', Mother removed the mustard plaster, revealing a bright pink square that felt sore to the touch. She rubbed me with camphorated oil which she had actually warmed first, before covering the area with one of her silk scarves. Getting rid of the mustard plaster was such a relief, I couldn't help admitting I felt a little better.

Does the mustard plaster deserve its elevated status among home remedies? Who knows? Maybe. Or maybe just the threat of it brought on miraculous recoveries. I do know that once experienced, avoidance seemed the sensible solution. Sick indeed was the patient forced to endure a second application.

Poultry in Motion

Spring had arrived, and the call of the chicken hatchery was heard the land. Any time we were not in school, Elayne and I could be found standing at one of the hatchery windows, noses pressed to the glass, keeping watch as baby chicks came popping out of their shells like dandelions, each one a yellow ball of fluff. Occasionally a less than perfect chick hatched along with sixty or seventy of its cousins, and for a day or two lived with all the others on a large metal tray under a red heat lamp.

Because the hatchery was in the business of providing only perfect chick specimens to its customers, these hapless little birds would eventually have to be destroyed. This sad fact of life came as a great shock to us, though the first year we did nothing but agonize over their fates. The next spring, when our interest in the unfortunate babies had not diminished, one of the hatchery workers made us an offer we found difficult to refuse.

"How would you like two chicks of your own? Free!"

Well within our budget, we agreed to take them, with little thought to their future care or quality of life. Our deep thinking started and ended with having two new downy pets to show off to our friends. These were not flawless chicks you understand, but flawless enough for us. Goldie and Fluffy—or something equally inane—had one shrivelled leg and one shrivelled wing respectively. Every other moving part seemed to be present and accounted for and in its rightful place as far as we knew. We carried them carefully in their square, flat box with the holes in the top, stopping every few feet to investigate any sounds coming from within. In spite of these constant interruptions, the chicks survived the two-block journey to what we hoped would be their new home.

Now came the part we had been dreading—the part about persuading Mother to let us keep them in the back yard. She had forbidden me to bring home any more stray, sick or scraggly animals for her to take care of, and since we hadn't had time to soften her up, there was a good chance we might encounter some opposition. Having new pets that day had not been planned. It just sort of happened—the way things always happened with Elayne and me.

After careful deliberation, we decided to promise the moon in exchange for keeping the chicks, but we were relieved to find such drastic measures unnecessary. Instead, Mother seemed almost eager for us to experience animal husbandry first hand, offering us a shaded corner of the garden on which to set up our chicken pen. We did, however, have to agree to do all the nasty bits ourselves. It seemed a small price to pay.

This amazing transformation in Mother was due in large part to the memory of Gersey, who was Mother's pet hen when she was young. As the story goes, Mother and her two younger sisters, Maggie and Cathie, played with Gersey, fed, watered and kept her from harm until she grew into a beautiful hen. One morning she disappeared. The sisters were inconsolable, spending hours in an unsuccessful search for her latest hiding place. But Gersey was not gone forever. She reappeared at dinner, this time on a large china platter surrounded by sage and onion dressing.

The tears the little sisters shed at the sad plight of Gersey ruined dinner. If anyone managed to swallow a mouthful of roast Gersey at that meal, it was certainly not her three protectors. Mother never forgot that experience or her fond attachment to the little hen. But just in case the years had somehow dulled the memory, I made her promise nothing like that would happen to little Skippy and Flippy, as they were now called.

Their new home consisted of an inverted cardboard box with a door cut in one end, placed inside a sagging enclosure of chicken wire. We had been given a small bag of chicken feed by the man at the hatchery, suspecting no doubt that it would last for as long as they would need it. Our pathetic little charges snuggled together into a nest of torn newspaper on the grass underneath their box while we sat back and watched them take a nap. Certain that a sufficient amount of love and attention would heal their contorted appendages, we busied ourselves with the business of satisfying their every need. Along with the chicken feed, we set out saucers of water and hand picked clumps of fresh grass—a child's answer to any and all nutritional needs of birds and animals alike.

We were dutifully attentive for the first few hours. Our friends came over to see Peepy and Sleepy—same chicks, different names—and for a time we were the envy of the neighbourhood. No one dared snicker at our lop-sided pets, at least not within earshot. Supportive but realistic, Mother, like the man at the hatchery, did not see a rosy future for these little chicks. She carefully explained that the first night away from the warmth and safety of their heat lamp would be crucial, and I suppose she secretly hoped the inevitable would serve to simplify her life. Either the chicks would be lying with their three good feet in the air by morning or missing altogether, a tasty midnight snack for a passing skunk.

But with evening drawing in, and the meagre heat of the spring sun disappearing, Mother's affection for babies of all kinds took over. It wasn't long before a heat-supplying light bulb had been set up on an extension cord above a cardboard box in the kitchen, where they could expire in relative comfort. But they did not expire. They thrived. And grew day by day into two slightly tilting adolescents with ever-changing names.

Each night Mother brought them in from their sunny pen in the garden to sleep in their safe warm box until morning.

As much as Elayne and I loved the chicks, we were young and our attention spans were short. Soon they were spending more and more of their days alone in their pen with only occasional visits from us.

One night, a few weeks after their arrival, Mother awakened to a crash she was sure had come from the kitchen. Remembering the bare light bulb and the cardboard box filled with newspaper and feathers, she leapt out of bed and ran to the top of the stairs, expecting to see flames licking at the kitchen door.

Without taking time to put on a light or her slippers, she flew down the steps, tripping halfway and sliding the rest of the way on her back. We heard the terrible noise and the moaning and found her in a crumpled heap, unable to move, on the dining room floor at the foot of the stairs. Hoppy and Floppy continued their slumber in the corner of their box below the light bulb, unaware of the uproar going on right outside the kitchen door.

For the next week Mother lay in bed on a board as motionless as possible, and the thing that went bump in the night remains a mystery to this day. With Mother unable to direct our sporadic care of the chicks, my father did not take long to find someone who promised to give them a good home. At least that was his story and he stuck to it even under cross-examination.

The chicks had enjoyed a longer and fuller life than they would have otherwise. But just the same, we parted with them sadly, afraid their new owners would not be as committed to their welfare as we had been, most of the time—okay, some of the time. At first, at least.

The chicken hatchery did not receive a visit from us the next spring, or in any succeeding spring. Elayne and I had moved on.

* * * *

Despite her years in the city, Mother began to develop the stout heart and firm muscles of a modern pioneer. Steadfastly believing she could do anything she put her mind to, without a backward, or indeed much of a forward glance, she simply went ahead and did it. Her successes usually rewarded her self-confidence. But not always.

When the memory of our two pet chicks had faded sufficiently, Mother decided to give chicken farming another chance. The concept of fresh eggs on demand overshadowed the reality that she had little knowledge of what such an enterprise would entail.

.

A used chicken coop was not hard to find, living as we did on the edge of town, across the road from the farming district. Mother bought one from a neighbouring farmer, scrubbed it inside and out with antiseptic and hot water, and whitewashed it to gleaming perfection. Twenty-four little Leghorn pullets arrived in boxes to be released in a pen surrounded by chicken wire fencing in the garden behind the apple tree.

They crowded into the chicken coop, squabbling and squawking and choosing their favourite places to roost, while Mother ran around in the hen yard scattering mash hoppers and tall metal drinking fountains for their comfort and convenience. They were quite an attraction for a day or two, but since every chicken looked the same as every other, I didn't go through the painstaking process of finding just the right names for each of their personalities. And aren't you relieved?

With a village full of expert advice for the asking, Mother was soon offering her brood diet supplements in their water and chopped oyster shells to promote egg-shell formation. She was told the good layers would have full red combs and well-rounded, low-slung bodies. They would be diligent scratchers in the hen yard, and have a certain lullaby to their voices. The non-producers, on the other hand, would have short pale combs, pointy beaks, and spend most of their time quarreling and taking hissy fits just for the fun of it. Now that Mother was an expert on all things fowl, she knew in no time at all we would be having fresh eggs for breakfast every morning, and angel food cakes from scratch, using a dozen egg whites, every Sunday.

The wait seemed endless. And in truth it was endless. Over time we gathered a few small eggs for our use, but feeding, cleaning and protecting these fussy birds from marauding nocturnal wildlife proved to be an expensive and exhausting business. Mother hadn't had a good night's sleep in weeks—running to the window each time something real or imaginary scared her flock into a squawking, fluttering panic. Occasionally she arrived on the scene to find a hole dug under the chicken wire, a handful of bloodied white feathers near the hole, and a definite hole in the number of hens in the chicken coop. This was clearly not going to be one of Mother's more successful ventures. Not only did she worry night and day about her hens, but her duties in the store, in the gardens, and in the house began to suffer. Soon we were having roast chicken every Sunday. It was during the preparation of one of these dinners that Mother learned another lesson.

She had chopped off the heads of a few chickens in her day, even before she had her own flock, but she did not relish the job. It was simply necessary. A means to an end. You see, she had chickens who refused to commit suicide, and there seemed to be no other way to make them lie quietly in the roasting pan.

"Don't look at me like that," she protested after every execution. "If it were up to your father, we'd all be vegetarians."

She was right about the fact that we would have to be starving to death before my father would attempt to kill a chicken that wasn't actually trying to kill him first. But the entire blame cannot be placed at my father's feet. No one liked to eat more than Mother. She came from a long line of carnivores, claiming her family's coat of arms to be two crossed chicken legs on a field of steak with lamb chops rampant, and I had no reason to doubt her.

An oversized chunk of firewood, too full of knots to be chopped small enough to fit into the kitchen stove, served as the dreaded chopping block. The instrument of execution was a short handled axe used for splitting kindling, but fully capable of chopping off a chicken head if the need arose. When Mother had the chosen neck correctly positioned on the chopping block, one sharp *whack* usually got dinner started. But on this occasion the hen refused to take its fate lying down, and in a state of shock got up and ran around the shed in a bloody headless condition. Nothing could be more alarming to a city slicker like Mother, who stout heart or no stout heart, fainted dead away amid the feathers, the blood and the head.

"You went down like a felled oak," claimed my father, who found her stretched out on the floor boards of the shed, with the chicken—or what was left of it—giving up the ghost on top of the woodpile. I guess without that extra weight it could really fly.

"Some chicken!" he teased.

"Some neck!" she croaked. Then they laughed for days over how well they had captured one of Churchill's best lines.

The remaining birds to sacrifice themselves for dinner were hobbled, so nothing like that could happen again. In time, the hen yard stood quietly empty, the chicken coop was up for sale, and our family was out of the chicken business for good.

The Killer Tent of Doom

OR

30 minutes to a slimmer, trimmer you

Every spring, tents sprung up on lawns all over town like mushrooms after a rain. Our lawn usually had one and sometimes two, though the sophistication of the tent construction depended largely on our ages at the time. With the arrival of warmer days, Doug and I couldn't wait to strike out on our own into the wilds of the back yard. Doug preferred the picnic blanket over the clothesline model, while I leaned heavily toward the old sheet spread over a kitchen chair design. I remember being content just to crawl under the chair and be out of sight for a few minutes—my attention span being about as short as I was.

In later years, when Elayne came over to our house to play, we stretched a broom handle between two chairs, draped an old blanket over it and put a rock on each corner to keep it tent-shaped. Into this private world we disappeared, taking with us our most cherished possessions—our collection of Betsy McCall paper dolls, some tiny dishes, or a passing cat, if one could be persuaded.

Our first and only real tent arrived one June, just in time for Doug's tenth birthday. He found just the right site for it in the far corner of the back yard between the grapevine and the white currant bushes—well within taunting distance of the large family who lived behind us. Younger than my brother by several years, and considered useful for holding things and crawling into confined spaces, I came to most tasks willing to pay any price just to be included in the action.

Mother was no stranger to tents, having been one of the first Scottish Girl Guides ever. She pounded the first tent pole into the ground with a certain authority, holding up the tent at one end. The rest of it lay on the grass, a deflated canvas puddle emitting a tarry odour that smelled to me like adventure. Worn down by my pleadings, but with their usual misgivings as to my reliability, Mother and Doug allowed me to crawl inside the tent to hold the pole in position while they stayed out in the fresh air pulling on the whatsits and hammering in the thingamajigs. Made of sturdy brown canvas and treated with a strong-smelling water repellent, the tent promised to keep Doug dry through anything short of a monsoon. The air inside the tent was much warmer and more humid than outside, but I made up my mind to tolerate it in the hope that once the tent had been erected, I would be allowed to play inside too.

Straining to hold the pole upright with the weight of the canvas pulling in all directions, my discomfort level increased with every degree of temperature. Beads of sweat began forming on my upper lip. I didn't care. What's a little hardship? Besides, I knew if I started complaining too soon I'd never see the inside of the tent again. I wiped off the sweat with my arm, and puffed warm breath in the direction of my streaming forehead. This had little cooling effect, but it did make my bangs stand on end, out of the way of any free-flowing perspiration.

Outside, all was busy activity and encouraging conversation. Some things were adjusted, some were hammered and others were tightened. The work seemed to be progressing well until the quarrel broke out—something about a missing part. Who was responsible for this carelessness they both wanted to know? Boxes were searched. Accusations were made. Bags were shaken. Alibis were given. Papers were checked. And the grumbling from both sides persisted. At one point someone began raking the grass around the tent in a vain attempt to find the missing part. What were they supposed to do now? Nothing was what they decided—absolutely nothing. At least they agreed on something. All the while, I remained at my post inside the tent, holding onto the pole that grew greasier by the second.

After a few more minutes I realized the insinuations and the usual tent-erecting noises had stopped. All was quiet. Too quiet for my liking. I called out. No one answered. Where were they? I called again. Still no answer. Five minutes went by, then ten, with me calling at fifteen second intervals. Not a sound could be heard, except for a neighbour's dog who barked at having his midmorning nap disturbed.

Still holding the pole, I kicked at the canvas in the spot where I figured a front flap should be. My leg wasn't long enough to reach past the folds. If I released the pole, the tent might fall down and smother me before I could find a way out. I'd never been inside a real tent before, so naturally I had never needed to get out of a real tent before, especially one in the middle of construction. A recurring thought began to nag at me. There was a chance I might have to hold that pole until I fell over dead, a pitiful, empty shell of a thing. This was so sad I wanted to cry, but I couldn't spare the moisture. And with that predicament in mind, my half-hearted yells became full-throated screams. Nobody came. Even if the neighbours heard the ruckus, they had long since learned to filter out such irritations.

This sudden wave of self-pity quickly turned to distrust, then slid dangerously toward indignation as my constant cries attracted nothing but mosquitoes. I began to doubt the wisdom of volunteering for any job that involved those two careless meanies.

Fifteen minutes went by, then twenty.

Holding onto the pole with all my strength, I lashed out again with my foot. It still wouldn't reach. In fact I was sure it had reached farther the first time. That's just dandy, I thought—now I'm shrinking. With sweat dripping from my chin, I clung desperately to the consolation that when they did find my shrunken, prune-like body, my father would have a few choice words for you-know-who. Imagining my sweet revenge was not the cooling diversion I expected.

Just as I was losing all hope of ever breathing fresh air again, I heard voices in the distance—vaguely familiar voices that swam around in the slippery fog that had become my brain—first near—then far—then near again. Gathering up what strength I had left, I screamed a most blood-curdling scream that even scared me, and with my last drop of moisture, I squeezed out a single tear. A nice touch if I do say so myself.

With reinforcements on the way, it was easy to drum up the required amount of courage to release the pole and make a flying leap toward the front of the tent. Scratching and clawing I made my way through the folds of canvas until I reached fresh air, emerging from under the pile on my hands and knees, a soaking, sobbing, smelly mess.

Mother's explanation, about going to the store to find a replacement for the missing part and forgetting I was inside the tent, was less than satisfactory. They were sorry, of course, but sorry wasn't good enough. Not this time.

"How could you forget? I could have died in there. What would you do then? Huh? Huh? What would you tell Daddy? Huh? Huh?" But I had pushed them one 'Huh?' too far.

"You could have crawled out the way you crawled in." Doug retaliated.

"Hey wait a minute—You crawled out just now, I saw you. Why didn't you do that twenty minutes ago? What's with you anyway?" Proving once again that there's no better defense than a strong offence. He clearly didn't appreciate my dedication to duty. Neither one of them seemed interested in grovelling, so I had to make do with their less than effusive apologies, vowing to get as much mileage out of the episode as was humanly possible.

In September, when it came time to take down the tent, I was nowhere to be found. A dry, brown rectangle remained on the lawn where the tent had stood, mute evidence that it was determined to kill something. Better the grass than me.

Even after all these years, it comes up in conversation once in a while—you know, for old time's sake.

Blessed Diversions

Life was one big race for Elayne and me. The only thing we liked better than racing was laughing, which made for some interesting races. In winter we raced down Adams Hill on our toboggans, or we raced from one end of the arena to the other on our skates. The rest of the year we raced on our bicycles, our roller skates, or on foot. We simply could not get where we were going fast enough, even though we had nothing special to do once we got there.

Occasionally our competitive natures took over and our races became more serious. We did not warm up before any of these races because we had never heard of warming up for anything, and besides we had hardly cooled down from all our other races. Whenever either of us succumbed to a piercing side stitch, which we did regularly, the rule was to suspend the race while the afflicted runner kissed her knee to relieve the pain. This rule was strictly adhered to by any runner who expected to be speaking to the competition for the rest of the day. That being settled, the race continued. In the races between Elayne and me there could be only one winner. Which also meant there was one loser, and seldom a gracious one. Second place doesn't count in a two-girl race.

After one too many lost races threatened to damage our friendship, we knew something had to be done. An unexpected solution presented itself during another of our races.

"Let's laugh!" panted the trailing runner. And of course we did—immediately and uncontrollably—as if we had both just taken a deep whiff of laughing gas. The fact that we could laugh on cue made it even more hilarious, so we laughed for the sheer joy of having this wonderful talent. We laughed until we had to lie down and curl up on the sidewalk, helpless and teary eyed, attracting a small but appreciative crowd in the process. When the mood passed, we struggled to our feet and continued running, although seldom with the same enthusiasm. This trick rarely worked twice in the same race—though neither of us was above trying.

Sometimes we did walk, but usually only when we were eating something that might spill. It was then that we noticed the aging, broken sidewalks of the village. Aware that one misstep could cause our mothers untold agonies, we avoided stepping on any one of a thousand cracks between our two homes.

"Step on a crack and break your mother's back!" we warned each other, and we almost believed it. Besides, with Mother's recent fall down the stairs still vivid in my mind, I was afraid to test the theory. We must have been a strange sight darting and weaving, staggering and stumbling down the street in an attempt to maintain a forward motion while avoiding every one of the cracks. No one seemed to notice. A few of the men from the village walked that way all weekend, so I suppose it was nothing new. It *did* take us longer to get anywhere, but then we were rarely pressed for time.

* * * * *

New adventures were hard to come by in a small community. Sometimes Elayne and I had to settle for a trip to the public library, a place our parents had encouraged us to visit, with limited success. It was not that we had an aversion to books, far from it, simply that a library visit was the subdued activity we felt we could better appreciate at a more sedate time, like a rainy Sunday afternoon between three-thirty and four o'clock. Walking into the library took a certain initiative. Playing outside the library was what we did on a regular basis.

Alone on a quiet stretch of lawn beside the library, stood the grey granite War Memorial, its long columns of names clear evidence of the tragic sacrifice made by our small community during both World Wars. I knew from an early age that these were the names of servicemen who had not returned to their families after these wars. On Remembrance Day, this place brought Mother to tears, and sometimes it gave me a peculiar feeling in the pit of my stomach.

But our summers were filled to the brim with peace and freedom. Children who had been sheltered all their lives from the brutality of war did not dwell for long on death and memorials. The thought of fallen soldiers would have to wait for a more somber moment, sometime in November when we gathered there as a community, everyone wearing their poppies—the cold wind chilling us to the marrow.

For the time being, we were young and alive and enjoying every precious moment of summer. Whirling out into the middle of the lawn beneath the memorial, Elayne and I twirled with arms outstretched until we fell in a dizzy, tangled heap onto the grass. For a long time we lay there trying to focus on the grey granite slab with its long list of names—names we did not recognize—our calm, secure world spinning around us. There would be a time for tears. We were too young, and we'd been too safe.

Occasionally we twirled next door to watch the blacksmith at work. Not many farmers owned horses by then, but for those still in use, new horseshoes were needed from time to time. That's where Mr. Gibson came in. We cringed when he placed the red-hot horseshoe onto the horse's hoof, listened to it sizzle, watched the smoke as it billowed. Although we never heard a peep out of any of the horses, we couldn't be convinced it didn't hurt them just a little. At the first whiff of seared hoof we dashed back outside into the fresh air with far more urgency than we had twirled in.

Bolted to a cement slab at the front of the library and aimed directly at a busy intersection, the First World War heavy machine gun sat peppered with holes and rusting quietly away. At first I believed these holes were made by enemy bullets during a fierce battle. The truth was less colourful. They were simply holes left over when the bolts rusted and fell out over a period of thirty winters.

Most of the time the gun was surrounded by a crowd of boys intent on a noisy game of war. We girls learned to wait our turn—the way we waited for the swings at the park and the drinking fountain on the corner. In our experience, boys bored easily. Eventually they wandered off to find something else to destroy, leaving Elayne and me in charge of the gun. We took turns sitting with a leg on either side of the metal brace, pretending to pick off cars as they drove through the intersection, earning us more than a few annoyed glances from those caught in our sites.

After five or ten minutes we had exhausted every possible avenue for adventure having to do with a stationary gun. There wasn't much to be done with this instrument of mayhem except aim it at somebody and make those irritating machine gun noises. The time had come to actually enter the library.

Inside it smelled pleasantly of floor wax, glue and old books, much the way it smells today. Making our selections from the two rooms full of children's books did not take much effort, though keeping quiet while doing so required all of our concentration. On the rare occasions when Mrs. Ballantyne, the librarian, accepted our promises to keep quiet, we were allowed to enter the glass-partitioned boardroom. Here stood an imposing display case, filled to capacity with mysterious artifacts donated by people we didn't know, brought back from places we'd never heard of. We never tired of the same twisted grins on the brightly coloured African masks, the fragile remains of the long-dead puffer fish, or the menacing shark's jaw with its rows of jagged teeth, teeth that could rip off a leg without any trouble, and probably had. A poor stranger's fate we imagined, too horrible to contemplate—but contemplate it we did, in great gory detail.

One display case does not take a lot of looking, so with this adventure exhausted, we settled down to read the NATIONAL GEOGRAPHIC magazines spread out on the tops of the long, polished boardroom tables. The result was inevitable. At seven and eight years old, there is nothing in the world funnier than the NATIONAL GEOGRAPHIC, a magazine specializing in articles about all the primitive tribes on earth, some wearing little more than a look of disdain and a ton of jewellery. With tears streaming down our cheeks and our composure now in tatters, we were ushered out of this quiet sanctuary into an environment more in keeping with our unruly behaviour—Brussels on a Saturday night.

* * * * *

On many Saturday evenings during the summer, a wandering contingent of Salvation Army band members came to Brussels to make a joyful noise unto the Lord. Dressed in spotless navy blue uniforms and carrying their polished brass instruments, the band drew a crowd wherever it went. Because it was Saturday night and all the stores were open, most of the families in the community and many from surrounding farms came together on the main street to shop and gossip, swelling the population to double its normal size. Only too aware of this opportunity, the band members set up their music stands beside the bank at the busiest intersection—which also happened to be the location of the only drinking fountain in the village. Forever surrounded by a strangely thirsty bunch of kids, the band had chosen not only the busiest corner—but the wettest.

If being where the action was meant being with the band, we stuck with them as closely as new converts. On the iron railing surrounding the fountain, a dozen kids with nothing better to do sat drinking gallons of water as if it were lemonade, humming along whenever the band played a familiar hymn. Soon after the fountain had been installed, the boys discovered that if they turned on the water full blast and held a finger over the spout, they could direct a stream of cold water with amazing accuracy at anyone within a fifteen foot radius. Now I can't be certain the boys meant to aim directly at the band members, but I do know the oversplash had a mind of its own.

At any rate, a half hour into the concert, the band, their instruments dripping, their sheet music soggy, but with their senses of humour miraculously intact, formed a line and marched down the street to the tune of *Oh, We'll Gather at the River*. The intersection they chose, a stone's throw from the Maitland River and a safe distance from the drinking fountain, promised to provide a much drier environment, river or no river. I'm sure the band members dried off over time. As for the instruments? Brass doesn't rust, does it?

The show over, Elayne and I wandered up one side of the main street and down the other in tiresome loops, looking in all the shop windows, hoping to find something that hadn't been there the last time around. If the windows always looked the same, the village did not. The rough spots—paint jobs five years overdue and brickwork crumbling in spots—were forgiven, hidden for the moment in deep shadow. Even the broken sidewalks, so familiar to us in daylight, seemed less noticeable. On a busy Saturday night Brussels looked almost prosperous and in much better shape than usual. Let's face it, there's nothing like a little incandescent lighting to bring out the best in a village.

Scaredy-Cat

As brave by day as any other kid, when it came time for me to turn off the bedroom light my secure world dissolved into a darker, more sinister place. Despite this irrational fear of the dark, I asked to be put to bed every night, a habit that never ceased to amaze my brother.

But first, one or the other of my parents had to search every inch of my bedroom before I would enter it, thoroughly convinced as I was that something terrifying, though admittedly rather flat, lived under the bed. No amount of searching ever set my mind at ease. While it was true there were few hiding places for a monster in an eight-by-eight foot bedroom, that was small consolation to someone with my particular problem.

The moment I closed my eyes I could feel something sneaking up on me. I could even feel the air move—though all that moving air may have been caused by the hair on my head snapping to attention. I lay still, eyes wide, covers up to my nose, listening. Not a sound could be heard but the sleepy chirping of a robin in the tree outside my window, the occasional snippet of conversation from the safe world of grown-ups downstairs, and the continuous pounding of my heart. For the first fifteen minutes, any attempt at peaceful slumber was hopeless. My eyes flew open every five seconds. By that time I had enough adrenalin pumping through my system to outrun any monster who *did* show up. Although why take a chance? AAIIIEEE! always brought one of my parents on the run.

Grappling with a situation they had not encountered with my older brother, my parents resorted to leaving a light on. For the first five minutes this seemed workable, but in the end I couldn't relax with the light shining through my eyelids. Next they suggested a night light. I knew that wouldn't work either unless it came attached to a lighthouse. It wasn't, and it didn't. The only route to sweet oblivion for me seemed to be total exhaustion.

My fear of the dark did not diminish with age. One night I decided to take a shortcut home from a friend's house, a distance of no more than a hundred yards across a small field and our own back yard. This signalled a departure from my usual cautious behaviour where darkness was concerned, but the experiment proved to be no breakthrough. I thought maybe, just maybe, I could face my fears and overcome them once and for all. Okay—I'm lying. I was just too lazy to walk home the long way around.

It is 9:45 p.m. one dark night during summer holidays. A reasonably brave nine-year-old is leaving the comfort of her friend's porch light, heading into the field between their two houses, eyes wide, ears alert to every sound...

There is a faint rustling noise off to my left. A field mouse has scurried into the long grass to avoid being trampled. It's a familiar sound and a familiar animal. Nothing to worry about there. I take another few steps into the dark when something cold and hard strikes my bare leg.

AAIIEE! What was that? A toad? A snake? A disembodied hand clutching at me from beyond the grave? What grave?? This departure into the macabre is never a good sign for me. I know if I don't get thoughts like these out of my head in a hurry, what happens next will have a lot to do with running and screaming, and that is never good. Especially in the dark.

A neighbourhood dog hears my yelp and barks an inquiry, but that too is familiar, and almost a relief from the sound of my heart pounding in my ears. I try talking out loud to fill the darkness with safe daytime noises.

"What a friendly place this is, even in the d-d-dar... " This works for about ten feet, before my fear, fed by a hair-raising imagination, starts screaming at me.

You call this a friendly place? Are you nuts? Bogeymen love these places! In fact—Welcome to Boooo-geyland!!

Now every kid knows the Bogeyman, like a horse, can smell fear. It's important to look cool and indifferent, even in the dark. I force myself to slow down, to stroll, arms swinging, giving the appearance of total nonchalance, just in case someone, or heaven forbid, some *thing*, is watching.

But who's kidding who? By this time even my eyebrows are standing on end. Darkness to the right of me. Darkness to the left of me. Behind me. In front of me. On top of me. I can hardly breathe with the weight of it pressing in on all sides.

Unconcerned during daylight hours with such trivial matters as a fear of the dark, I had allowed myself the luxury of imagining this part of the garden to be stalked by creeping unseen beasts with fierce eyes and ripping jaws who watch and wait for the unwary traveller. I may even have mentioned it to one or two of my younger friends. *Uh oh! I'm the unwary traveller now. I wish I hadn't thought of that.*

Did you see those eyes glowing in the dark back there? Blood red they were!! shrieks the scaredy-cat inside me. *Don't look now, stupid!*

The warning is hardly necessary. My eyes are glued to the lighted windows of our house fifty yards away beyond the trees. Afraid to search the shadows to either left or right, my imagination seethes. Every wind-stirred leaf causes me to whip around expecting to see a bony hand reaching for my throat.

Okay. That's it. Cool was a dumb idea. Stark terror makes a lot more sense. And soon I'm strolling at a brisk thirty miles an hour across the last expanse of darkened lawn, fear screeching accusations at me.

You had to take the shortcut, didn't you! You wouldn't listen, would you? Not you! Now you've done it! RUUUUN!! I take off like a startled gazelle, each leg a coiled spring. Now every nerve in my body is screaming HEEEEELP!! The rest of me—the noisier bits—are screaming AAAIIIEEE!! I am just about to will myself to fly, when suddenly...

Gggaaahhkk!!—WHUUUMP!! My feet shoot out level with the ground and every part of me makes contact with the lawn at the same time.

I lie there for a moment, trying to remember where I am, but the slate is blank. I have to wait until my brain stops ricocheting around inside my skull before I can complete even the most primitive thought. When the fog does clear, I realize I've run into the clothesline, strung across the back lawn, neck high and taut as a guitar string. I can't move. I can't breathe.

Hey! Wait a minute. I'm not breathing. This is different. Maybe I'm dead. No, I can't be dead with this throbbing headache. Well, that's good news at least. No it's not. It isn't good at all. I can't breath. I can't move. I'm defenseless—against the BOOOOGEYMAN!! AAAIIIEEE!!

I scream a scream now that would shatter glass if only I could make a sound. Nothing comes out of my mouth but a lot of dry hhhhhhh's. I try again. Hhhhhhh! My worst fears are realized. I can't scream. I can't breath, I can't move. I stare into the darkness with the eyes of a terrified rabbit.

Wait! What's that? Thump!-thump!-thump! *Footsteps. Oooh no—they're coming this way. Real footsteps. It's the Bogeyman. I'm not making this up.* Closer and closer he comes—faster and faster...

So this is it—I'm a goner for sure! AAAIIIEEE! But the only sound I can make is a pitiful little *gaaaaaack!* I close my eyes as tightly as I can and concentrate on being invisible. Thump! Thump! THUMP! *gaaaaaack!*

"What are you doing out here in the dark, trying to trip me?" yells the Bogeyman. Or could that be...?

Ah, there's nothing like the kind, honest concern of an older brother. *Hey, wait a minute! A brother! Brothers have* to save you from the Bogeyman, right? They have to, right? Or so I think for a split second before he jumps over me, lifts the clothesline and runs on toward the house. I turn my head and watch in quiet desperation as he disappears into the shadows, leaving me alone again in the dark. *Bogeyman bait!* One big, hot tear rolls down the side of my cheek and puddles in my ear.

Nothing for it now but to lie here and wait to die. Life was so good...

As soon as Doug realizes I haven't made a move to follow him, he returns to where I'm stretched out on the lawn praying for a merciful death.

"Aren't you coming? Hurry up."

"Ggaaack!"

He helps me to my feet, and I start to feel warm again, beginning with a burning sensation across my throat and ending with a blast furnace inside my chest. After a few painful breaths, I grab my throat with both hands and croak out the shortened version of my tale about the Bogeyman and the clothesline.

"There's no such thing as a Bogeyman. You ran into the clothesline and knocked the wind out of yourself, that's all. You should have been watching where you were going." It felt good to be safe at last, so good I didn't even feel like having the last word, at least not out loud.

Looking back on the episode, I suppose the worst thing to happen to me that night was to be left alone in the dark with my overactive imagination. Though just to be on the safe side, I made a vow never to take another shortcut through any dark place at any time. It hasn't been a difficult vow to keep.

The Little Dog Laughed

...to see such sport,
And the dish ran away with the spoon.

Nursery Rhyme

*C**anis yukitupatus* was a dog pound adoptee whose pedigree would not have been recognized by even the most nonchalant kennel club. We believed him to be a Welsh Corgie cross, but what that Corgie had been crossed with was anyone's guess—a stand-up comedian maybe. One thing for sure, for a dog he had a well-developed sense of humour.

I had been on vacation with my aunt and uncle in Niagara Falls, and away from home long enough for my parents to forget what sometimes happened to my best intentions. It was during one of my weekly mercy calls back to Mother that I asked if I could bring home a dog, and found her trust in me had been somehow miraculously restored by a two week absence. After a minimum of pleading she gave her consent, but with the following stipulations: "It must come from the local dog pound. It must not be too old or too young, too big or too small. It must be a good family dog with short hair that won't shed too much. Remember, your father has asthma."

What could be easier? Since my uncle had agreed to drive us home at the end of the week, I still had a few more days to stew over those instructions.

When Saturday arrived, I found the responsibility of choosing another member of the family intimidating, though not intimidating enough to forego the whole thing. Knowing the dog could not be returned under any circumstances, and realizing I had another life to consider, merely added a certain edge to the excitement. I love stress.

The dogs at the local pound were creating such a din I could hardly think. There were about ten of them from which to make the first important choice in my life. Right away I could see some were too big for transporting easily in a car that was bound to be overloaded with luggage, picnic baskets, a cousin, and two or three aunts. Some of the dogs were still young and probably not housebroken. Beside the fact that I had my orders, even I could not do that to my aunt, who never had any animal in her house. No, I was looking for something else in a dog. A special undefined something that would become clear to me once I saw it. I couldn't tell if any of them were too old, but age would not have mattered in any case if I found the one I was looking for.

One particular dog sat upright on his haunches, his front paws dangling in front of him. He appeared to be laughing his head off at my dilemma. Of course he wasn't really laughing, I knew that, but he looked as if he were, and that was good enough for me. A long pink tongue lolled out the corner of the biggest grin I'd ever seen on a dog. He wasn't too big or too small. He didn't look too old or too young, and he didn't seem the least bit aggressive—more amusedly self-assured, I'd say. That one wasn't even on the list. He had a short wiry coat the colour of pale honey, stubby legs with slightly splayed feet, and an unmistakably dogged demeanor. All the requirements had been met, plus a few extras I added to the list just so I could check them off.

Given the choice of four people to run to, when the attendant opened the door of his cage he dashed straight to me. So he was perceptive too. How else could he have known I would be the one to make the decision on his somewhat uncertain future? The attendant did not have a record of his former name, so I gave him one I thought suited him best. *Dash*. The sad set of circumstances that brought him to the pound in the first place were never revealed. It seemed enough that I had a *dog*, and it didn't matter to either of us that he was second-hand. Besides, second-hand was a state not unfamiliar to me.

For the long drive home to Brussels, Dash sported a neon chartreuse ribbon which I bought for him at WOOLWORTH'S, it being my favourite colour in the whole world that week. It captured perfectly his effervescent personality. Dash sat on the back seat beside me with his nose out the window, biting off chunks of air and chewing them thoughtfully, happy to be on his way to anywhere.

Forever anxious about the interior of his car, my uncle pulled over to the side of the road every time Dash stopped grinning. Six feet of clothesline threaded through his chartreuse ribbon kept him safely in my grasp on these numerous occasions, some of which were more productive than others.

At the end of our journey, Dash bounded out of the car to meet Doug—who was probably wondering what kind of mutt I would bring home to the family. But I had done my shopping well. They bonded quickly and easily. Even before my parents had a chance to succumb to Dash's charms, I had an ally in Doug. My parents, weary of my habit of bringing home any animal I considered to be a stray, were relieved that this time they would not have to scour the neighbourhood for the rightful owner after I had gone to bed.

It did not take long for the little dog with the mysterious past to become a valued member of the family. Within five minutes he had every smell in the yard indelibly stamped on his doggy memory. As he patrolled the perimeter of the property, tail in the air and nose to the ground, cats of every colour and stripe could be seen scrambling for the safety of their front porches. Without a moment's hesitation, he assigned himself the job of keeping our yard safe from creatures of the feline persuasion. Those of the squirrel persuasion were not destined to lead uneventful lives either.

To make up for any yearning he may have felt for his former owner, we tried to fill his days with love and happy activity. This naturally brought him into contact with our friends' dogs, who for some strange reason all seemed to be female. Dash was in heaven, and quickly gaining notoriety as the canine Casanova of the village. Unaccustomed to this kind of notoriety, our parents instructed us to keep him under closer supervision. Many an unscheduled change of direction had to be taken to avoid an embarrassing encounter. This entailed dragging behind us one very disgruntled suitor. But it was inevitable that sooner or later Dash would run into a good looking, leggy female who would set his ardent mind spinning. Fortunately for all concerned, Dash was long on enthusiasm but short on stature, so he seldom lived up to his reputation.

Whenever we felt like showing off to our friends, we had only to ask. Sometimes we didn't even have to ask. Dash often seemed to sense when the time was right for showing off. Sitting up on his haunches he would roll back his head and wrinkle his face into a grin, as if convulsed by some inner joke. Of course we accepted any and all praise that came our way, keeping secret the fact that he came with this special talent intact.

Aside from his ability to laugh on cue, in every other respect Dash was a normal dog. He chased everything that looked at him sideways—squirrels, cats, groundhogs, and the occasional skunk. Touted as the only antidote for skunk spray, large tins of tomato juice were a staple on our kitchen shelves. Even after this messy bathing procedure, he continued to wear the musky odour for weeks—but with a decided blush of pink. Now not every male dog can wear pink, but Dash could pull it off, thoroughly confident in his masculinity. Incidentally, the only effective antidote for skunk spray is time.

One day Mother discovered he could talk, though only when he had something important to say. Whenever she spoke to him in an earnest, animated fashion, he'd knead the floor with his front paws, cock his head from side to side, ears erect, looking extremely alert, and then he'd grumble out some tale of woe. At first she took this to mean he was analyzing their conversation with his ultra-keen canine senses, absorbing every nuance at lightning speed, or at least agreeing with her. But I'm pretty sure all Dash meant was, "Huh?" It didn't matter that they didn't understand each other's language. They simply enjoyed conversing.

Preferring the company of cheerful humans, Dash could not bear to see anyone sad. While we seldom exchanged thoughts and ideas or anything else of a cerebral nature, I could get a response from him by pretending to cry. Burying my face in my hands I'd let out wails of anguish, and each time he would whine and paw furiously at my hands, leaving behind angry red welts in his attempt to change my mood. If this failed, he barked in my ear at the same decibel level as a train wreck. At this point it was wise to drop the charade or risk serious hearing loss.

Like most dogs, Dash loved nothing better than a car ride. Anybody's car. At any time. We did not yet own one of our own—waiting as we were for our ship to come in. But unlike the rest of us, Dash had no intention of letting life pass him by. Taking advantage of any open unattended car door, he thought nothing of hopping in and making himself at home. Dash was always returned to us after his stowaway adventures, but we engraved our phone number on his collar anyway, in the hope that he would choose only scrupulous drivers.

Right up there with his love for cars and the females of his species was his fondness for the older generation of the village, perhaps because of their slower movements and unthreatening manner. Whenever he met one, he stopped to be petted. Most of them knew him by name. Once while exploring the neighbourhood for the more disreputable of the local canines, Dash spotted Mrs. Ballantyne, the elderly village librarian. She was about to be driven home by a friend after a pleasant afternoon bridge party at the home of the Downing sisters. Getting settled into their seats took the older ladies several minutes, and in the meantime one of the car doors had been left open. Not one to miss an opportunity, Dash jumped in uninvited and unseen, making himself comfortable on the back seat. As she adjusted her rear view mirror before starting the car, the driver spotted him sitting there and proclaimed with some surprise:

"Mrs. Ballantyne! There's a dog in the car—and he's laughing at me!"

Mrs. Ballantyne turned around to see Dash sitting up and smiling happily, well-pleased at this unexpected stroke of luck.

"Oh yes, so there is," replied Mrs. Ballantyne. "That's Dash. He laughs, you know. And he loves cars. Let's give him a ride home." It had worked again. Dash had insinuated himself into not just another car, but into a car with one of his special friends.

Life for Dash was one big adventure. Every morning he had his routines. Our property line had to be well sniffed to make sure it remained secure from the night before. Every shrub in the yard needed a thorough watering. Squirrels had to be chased. And since no one could do this better than he, a great deal of barking needed to be done. The earlier the hour, the more barking was involved. Invisible trails that only Dash could follow crisscrossed the lawn in every direction. Who had made them? They weren't there last night. Things were clearly out of control. It's a good thing we had him to protect us.

Sooner or later, one of the trails led him to his bowl of dogfood at the back door, which seemed to take his mind off his worries for a minute or two. After breakfast, his responsibilities could take a back seat to some serious wagging and grinning. And then it was time for a nap. It had been a fraught morning, and the day had just begun.

In the five years he lived with us, Dash taught us many lessons, the most important of which is the value of greeting each day with a smile. The little dog with all the right stuff is buried in one of our flower gardens, beneath a carpet of forget-me-nots. The reminder has never been necessary.

Fun and Games

We played outdoors in all kinds of weather, but most often in summer and always with as many friends as we could gather together. At a time and in a place where it was still possible to trespass on neighbourhood properties with impunity, we played 'Hoist Your Sails', a game that took 'Hide and Seek' a step further. I called it 'Oyster Shells' at first, but then I was still singing 'Old Lang Sang'.

Every child could play this game regardless of age as long as they could follow instructions, though the younger players were never called upon to mastermind the strategies. They followed orders, and the first order given was always, "Shut up and listen!"

This is how we played it...

Separate all the players into two teams of equal numbers, assigning a captain to each team. Decide which team is going to hide and which team is going to hunt. The hunting team stays at home base—usually someone's front step, while the other team and its captain finds a place to hide. The hiding place could be somewhere on the property, in a neighbour's yard, or time permitting, somewhere far from home base.

The object of the game for the 'hunting team' is to find the other team's hiding place by following a map and to get back home first. The object of the game for the 'hiding team' is to avoid detection by following a set of vocal signals until the time is right to try to get home before the 'hunting team'.

The 'hiding team' captain hides his team and selects a set of code words to represent different instructions. Colours, numbers, or letters of the alphabet could be used as code words as long as his team is familiar with what each word represents. For instance, the colour blue could signal 'danger, be quiet, they're close' and the colour red could mean 'run home, they're looking the other way'. The code words should be changed at the beginning of each game because cracking the other team's instruction code is a high priority.

As soon as the hidden team has memorized the new code words, their captain returns alone to home base to draw a map for the hunting team to follow. The directions given on the map should be as correct as possible, even if the map is not drawn to scale. No specific landmarks have to be named, making it difficult to determine whether the team is hidden around the corner or blocks away. For map-making tools you may use chalk on a sidewalk or a sharp stick on a bare spot on the lawn, as we did—since there was never a shortage of bare spots—but there is no rule against using paper and pencil.

Meanwhile, the hidden team remains quiet enough to hear their captain yelling his coded instructions, making 'shut up and listen' an integral part of the game. The hunting team runs off in the general direction shown on the map, its captain confident in his map reading abilities and the rest of his team, if not sure, at least pretending they know where they're going. The captain from the hiding team, in full cry, yells his coded instructions to his hidden team. Listening for the volume used in the delivery of the code words might be a clue to the distance involved, but not always. Most of us lived at the top of our lungs anyway, so this could simply be the normal mode of communication, *or* a clever ruse.

If even one person from the hidden team, hearing the code word to run home, arrives at home base first, they win the game for their team. They may hide again. If they are beaten to home base by one of the hunting team, it's the hunting team's turn to hide. Remember, whoever arrives at home base first yells 'Hoist Your Sails!'—or if you like—'Oyster Shells!'

* * * * *

Whenever Elayne and I found a white daisy, we pulled off its petals one at a time to see if our boyfriends loved us. The fact that neither of us had ever had a boyfriend didn't enter into it. Every little girl liked someone, and whether or not they were admired in return made no difference to the game, or to us come to think of it. We spent many a self-absorbed afternoon sitting in a field pulling one petal off with each line of the poem until there were no petals left. The last petal told the tale.

> *He loves me,*
> *He don't.*
> *He'll have me,*
> *He won't,*
> *He would*
> *If he could,*
> *But he can't*
> *So he won't.*

The result of this research was not taken seriously unless the last petal revealed that our mystery someone did love us. Then we considered it to be an exact science. Millions of daisies have been sacrificed in this way. That's why they have petals, doncha' know.

Bored or temporarily out of daisies, we counted each other's buttons to determine in what line of work our future husbands would be gainfully employed. It was amazing to see how many places we could find buttons if we happened to land on one of the less popular occupations.

> *Tinker, tailor, soldier, sailor,*
> *Poor man, rich man, beggar man, thief,*
> *Doctor, lawyer, Indian Chief.*

Indian Chief was the most popular occupation. As far as we knew they were all movie stars. They appeared on their pinto ponies at most Saturday matinées, riding across the screen wearing buckskins and war bonnets. Frankly it is difficult to imagine anything more romantic to a nine-year-old girl. Sailor was a close second. The rest of the occupations were well-represented in the village, and therefore lacked a certain fascination.

* * * * *

We did not always play in a large group, but we always found something to amuse whatever size group we had. Doug's pinto rocking horse, Dobbin, somewhat mangy after being well-loved through several childhoods, often appeared on the back lawn as the brave steed of our favourite movie cowboy. One day he was Trigger, another day Scout, Buttermilk or Silver, depending on what movie we had seen most recently. We took turns riding him while we rounded up strays, or made daring escapes from the sheriff's posse. This gave us the opportunity to use the cap guns and cowboy hats lying around the shed, and a perfect excuse—as if we needed one—to whoop and holler and make plenty of noise.

In the rare quieter moments, Dobbin was transformed into the milkman's horse, with clothesline reins to keep him under control while he plodded along on his daily rounds. Of course, he delivered only chocolate milk, a skillfully conceived concoction of mud and water poured into jars and handed out at every imaginary door. If we could talk one of our more gullible friends into tasting it, so much the better. But this usually meant the end of the game, since our victims were seldom good sports about it. And their mothers could be downright hostile.

The large lawn surrounding our house received little attention outside of an occasional once-over with the lawn mower and a meagre sprinkling of water during a dry spell. Whenever the sprinkler appeared, so did a crowd of squealing kids suitably attired in bathing suits, ready to trample the lawn into an oozing quagmire.

We grew in abundance every grass-destroying weed known to man, adding texture and interest to an otherwise boring landscape. Because most of these weeds were green, getting rid of them seemed counter-productive. They were left in peace to multiply or not as they saw fit.

Almost everyone we knew had a lucky four-leaf clover pressed between the pages of a favourite book. All of them came from the grounds of Saint Ambrose Catholic Church. Why they seldom grew anywhere else in the village became the great religious mystery of my childhood. After pondering the question for some time, I decided that by concentrating the four-leaf-clovers on the lawn of Saint Ambrose Church, God was evening the odds by giving extra luck to the smallest of the four village congregations. I've never found a better answer.

For most of the summer dandelion blossoms gilded every lawn, public or private, and were highly prized for another of our games. Holding the golden heads under each other's chins we addressed that age-old question: Do you like butter? The yellow reflection—which always appeared unless we were posing the question in a darkened closet—indicated that we did indeed like butter. It never failed to delight us to discover we all belonged to the same secret butter-liking society. Our hands were stained with dandelion juice all season long, though we never found out why a substance so white could turn hands so brown. We merely accepted it as fact and got on with life. Deep thinking took time, and meanwhile we had a field full of daisies to pull apart.

Owning a lawn usually meant owning a croquet set. These were cheap and entertaining and were intended to lend an air of refined gentility to the summer scene.

Sometimes it worked. The croquet games Doug and I played with our parents began as sedate Sunday afternoon activities, accompanied by lemonade on the lawn, quiet conversation and escalating boredom. However, left to play the game on our own, any gentility quickly dissolved into a dog-eat-dog, outright civil war. As with most siblings close in age, my brother and I were arch rivals whenever we played together. Not only was he two years older, he was also five years smarter and six years stronger. This stumbling block did not dampen my enthusiasm for the fray. I was, after all, many years sneakier, and usually the cause of the ruckus that ensued. Balls were smacked into the vegetable garden or disappeared altogether. Wickets were shifted mysteriously or bent to impossible angles. When Doug continued to win in spite of my devious efforts, a smart *whack* on the ankle with my mallet seemed the only recourse. This, not surprisingly, had the same effect as digging around in a wasp's nest with a sharp stick.

When the game ended with a minimum of bloodshed, the job of putting away the equipment fell to the two of us. It was difficult to keep track of all the wickets, they had been moved so often. Almost every time, one escaped detection, leaning drunkenly against a clump of plantain. Of course it was found later by one of our parents taking an evening stroll across the lawn. The discovery resulted in a painful tumble, a twisted ankle, and a lecture at breakfast about everything from poor sportsmanship to our total disregard for the safety of others. Naturally I shared the blame with Doug. I am nothing if not an equal-opportunity sister.

One afternoon when we had nothing better to do, three close friends and I decided to play a game of tennis across the clothesline—incidentally the same clothesline that nearly decapitated me the year before. Mother saw no reason to give up her clothesline just so this couldn't happen again. She had a pretty good idea I'd remember its location for all time, making unnecessary any sacrifice on her part. Parents in my day rarely adjusted their lives to accommodate their kids. We learned our lessons, often painfully, then adjusted our lives to accommodate them. It was the natural order of things, and we accepted it as such. Meanwhile, back to the game...

We didn't know anything about the rules of tennis. We didn't have a court, a tennis ball, or even a proper net. There were also two more players than the available racquets, so I guess we couldn't really call it tennis at all, could we? The remainder of our equipment was rudimentary but serviceable, consisting of two of Mother's long-handled rug beaters and an India rubber ball. The control of the ball was the same whether a player used a racquet or a rug beater, that is to say, no control whatsoever. We knew we should bat the ball back and forth over the clothesline, but knowing this and doing this were two different things. Most serves were delivered at blistering speed under the clothesline and straight to the solar plexus, signalling a delay in the game while the unfortunate opponent regained her composure. Only a few serves were correctly delivered and returned, though several rug beaters were kept in play for over a minute.

The only organized team sports in town consisted of boys' hockey in winter, and boys' and girls' softball teams in summer. If you were a girl who didn't excel at softball, there was no alternative. I belonged to this group. Most boys seemed to be good at either hockey or softball and sometimes both, and were seldom left to their own devices. Lawn bowling under the lights was exclusively for the blue rinse set and that was fine with us. The one and only tennis court, constructed too close to the river, often lay under two feet of water for a month after the last snow disappeared from its cracked concrete surface, keeping well watered the waist-high weeds that erupted in mid-court. Nobody had a net for it anyway, so it hardly mattered. This was a good place to roller skate if you didn't mind jumping over the weeds. Any other games were left to our creative imaginations. Just the way we liked it.

It's Simply Not Cricket

If cricket had ever been played in Brussels, by the time we arrived it had long since been replaced by the more popular North American game of softball. In an attempt to remedy the situation one Sunday afternoon during a particularly severe bout of homesickness, my father decided to teach the game to Doug and me and as many of our friends as came within pleading distance.

Familiar with the rules from growing up in England, my father turned our side lawn into the site of the strangest games of cricket ever played. As if having a completely inexperienced team were not bad enough, he was forced to teach the game using equipment from an entirely different sport. A cricket ball or bat could not be found for fifty miles in any direction, so we used conventional softball equipment, adding an element of the bizarre to the game.

Not yet well-known in North America, cricket is often unfairly criticized by the uninitiated for its curious terminology. When you consider some of its terms, the reason, if nothing else, may become clear. Here are just a few: batsman, wicket-keeper, slips, cover, square-leg, leg-break, mid-off and mid-on, not to mention silly-mid-off and silly-mid-on. I know just enough about the game to know I know nothing about the game. And if that is not confusing enough, and your knowledge of the game is no better than mine, I can say with some authority you will be little wiser by the end of this chapter.

There are eleven players to a side—about half of what we had on that day. The sides are called ons. There are two home plates called wickets and two batsmen. Both are up at once. Well, not up exactly—more in. Batsmen are always in, not up. There are also two pitchers called bowlers who bowl six balls from either end. When one of the batsmen hits the ball in any direction he can run or not as he chooses. He is out if the ball is caught, or if he lets the ball hit his wicket. A wicket is three sticks stuck in the ground with another two smaller ones, called bails, laid across the top. The batsman is also out if he blocks the wicket with any part of his body. If the batsman hits the ball away from a fielder, he runs down the pitch to the other end—the pitch being the playing field between the two wickets. While this batsman is running, another batsman runs to the opposite end.

If there is time, they can run twice or three times, each time counting one run. If he hits the ball over the boundary on the ground, he scores four runs. If he hits it over in the air—an automatic six runs. There is usually only one innings to a match—and 'innings' is correct in this case, not inning—but there could be two if the match lasts more than a day. Follow me so far?

A good batsman can make a hundred runs. This is called a century, for obvious reasons. The best batsmen can stay in until the end of the game and are never out. One game can last for days. Imagine!

Now cricketers do not slog along all day without food. They're a civilized lot indeed, breaking for lunch at noon, maybe for a few cucumber sandwiches and fancy cakes, and again for tea and strawberries with cream in the middle of the afternoon. Everyone wears white and no one gets dirty unless they spill the strawberries.

Here is a little about the scoring. When the bowler bowls six balls, it is called an 'over'. With no runs it is called a 'maiden over'. That's right, the bowler can bowl a maiden over and this is considered a good thing—even by the maiden. I haven't mentioned a 'googlie'. That's a naughty bowl that is both difficult to execute and all but impossible to hit, and it can make you very unpopular with the opposing team. Back to our side lawn on that Sunday morning so long ago…

Remember now, none of us except my father knows anything about cricket. Up to this point our ignorance of the game is complete. We had never even seen a picture of a cricket match, far less an actual game in play.

"Where does the batter stand, Daddy?" I inquired in all innocence.

"Right here—but he's not a batter," he corrects me with more of an English accent than I remembered him having.

"In cricket, he's a batsman. Right. Now where was I?"

"Bats-man? Bats-man, batsman," I practised.

"Now, I can't explain the rules with all this chatter."

"Chats-man?" I murmured, with too much cheek.

"That's not funny! Do you want to learn this game or not?" Without waiting for an answer, he continued his instructions.

"Now watch me closely, this part is tricky."

My father proclaimed himself to be the bowler and went on to demonstrate the correct form used by both the batsman and the bowler.

"The bowler bowls the ball to the batsman, and the batsman tries to hit it—like this," he explained, scooping a softball bat full of air.

"Remember, it's not baseball. Here now, let me bowl you a practice one so you get the idea."

It was a well-known fact, at least to Mother, that my father had some skill as a bowler. I'm sure she meant a cricket bowler and not a ten-pin bowler. Anyway, I had to take her word for it, because this is how it looked to me:

After a long, loping run from the other end of the lawn, my father skipped a few times with a fancy hop at the end, flung the ball unexpectedly from behind his back, over his shoulder and above his head, to bounce once then hit the broom handle wicket he had stuck in the ground behind the batter—I mean batsman.

"There! That's how it's done," he gasped, once he had stopped running, hopping, skipping, twirling and flinging. His team was speechless. I was mortified. What if someone laughed? I'd have to beat them up right there in front of him. I tightened my jaw and inspected every face. No one even smiled. They were too stunned. My father remained sweetly unaware of how absurd he looked to Canadian kids who had, until that moment, believed cricket to be a little black insect that chirps.

"Now, here are a few rules to remember. Try to concentrate," he instructed. Cricket rules make little sense to the uninitiated, especially to those of us who have grown up with softball.

"Each man on the 'in' side goes 'out', and when he's out he comes back in and the next man goes in until he's out. Got it?"

We nodded our heads in agreement, but goodness knows what any of us got out of that.

"When they are all out, the 'out' side comes in and the 'in' side goes out to try to get the side that's in, out." My eyes glazed over at this point.

"Now don't look at me like that. It's not hard. Children in England play this game all the time. Let's just do it. You'll catch on."

Whoo-boy! He didn't know who he was talking to. I had no idea what was going on. Even the boys found it difficult to hit the ball when it was thrown at them that way.

The bat eventually made contact with the ball and was driven, softball fashion, into the currant bushes at the far end of the lawn.

"Yaaaay! Run! Run!" we encouraged.

"No, no, no. Not that way! You have to run over there! Now get back here. Yes. You."

"Why can't I run around the bases? Where are the bases anyway?"

"We aren't playing softball, remember? There is the base! You run from here to there and then you run back again. Now you try it. It's not hard. It's a little different, that's all!"

We tried to remember the differences, making mistake after mistake, forgetting cricket rules and substituting softball rules in an attempt to keep the game progressing. Surrounded by incompetence, my father's voice became louder and his accent more pronounced as his wacky team raised hopelessness to new heights. After a few more futile attempts, he gave up and let us try to teach him how to play softball. That was easier—for us at least.

Back in familiar territory at last, it wasn't long before we had the game and the side lawn to ourselves. With his newspaper and a cool glass of lemonade, my father retired to the tranquillity of his lawn chair, no doubt to enjoy the memories of real cricket matches from his childhood.

In the years to follow, I drove with him to Stratford, Ontario where he watched more proficient teams playing in front of the Shakespearean Festival Tent. Never again did he attempt to teach us the intricacies of the game. It is our loss.

God's in His Heaven

The lark's on the wing;
The snail's on the thorn;
God's in His Heaven—
All's right with the world!

Robert Browning

Brussels was diversely religious. A large part of our social life centred around the four busy village churches—Saint John's Anglican, Melville Presbyterian, Saint Ambrose Catholic and Brussels United. Members of one church could and often did attend the services of another when something out-of-the-ordinary was on offer.

Although there were many of these special services during the year, our congregation especially looked forward to Flower Sunday, when the sanctuary of our church burst into bloom. Baskets of spring flowers decorated all window sills and garlands of blossoms entwined every railing, making sneezes from the congregation as frequent on Flower Sunday as in any flu epidemic in February.

The various women's groups kept themselves busy and the community well-fed all year. One such occasion was the annual turkey supper before Thanksgiving in October, when the aroma of roasting turkey and homemade pies attracted hungry customers from miles around. Shrove Tuesday pancake suppers before Lent in the Anglican church and strawberry socials at the United church in June were two more events on everyone's social calendar. During the weeks leading up to Christmas, we attended Sunday school Christmas concerts at as many churches as we could squeeze into an already crowded schedule.

While I was still quite young, I accompanied my parents to adult services in our church, spending most of my time examining at close range the sunburned necks of the farmers who sat in the pews in front of us—necks deeply lined and darkened from years of field work in the blazing sun.

Noticing right away that our church had its particular smell, I decided it must smell like God. Every house had its own smell, and this was God's house after all. My parents said so. Some houses smelled like bread baking or toast burning and some like line-dried laundry, while still others wore the honest, earthy smells of boiled cabbage or cats. God's house smelled like furniture polish, as if He had just finished His weekly cleaning chores—this mingled with the smells of musty hymn books, starched shirts, and last night's coffee. God's house had a comfortable, lived-in sort of smell.

But it was the windows of His house that fascinated me beyond imagining. When the morning sun slanted through the stained glass at just the right angle, coloured shards of the richest intensity spattered the congregation. The absence of those bright colours on cloudy Sundays made a big difference to my attention span, which meant I had to find some other way to amuse myself. Sometimes I managed to sit quietly between my parents for forty or fifty seconds at a stretch.

The pews in our church were not reserved, though everybody knew where they were to sit each Sunday, and few changes were made to the seating plan over the years. I could close my eyes, turn my head, and know who would be sitting there when I opened them again. The same applied to the pews behind ours and the ones in front. I ached to shake them up in my hand, the way I shook my jacks, then let them fall into different pews for a change. Wouldn't they be surprised?

If a stranger arrived, he was seated by an usher in whatever part of a pew no one had claimed as their own. Squeezing into a pew unushered could result in an distinct aloofness on the part of the longtime occupant, or at least a momentary fluster, as hymnal racks were cleared of everything from gloves to lace handkerchiefs, orders of service and bags of mints—brought to stem a bout of coughing. Then everyone in the pew would slide over one place.

It was during a Sunday church service that I discovered my father had an English accent. Whenever he sang his favourite hymns, which I thought he did rather too loudly, his voice did not sound like those I heard around me. I grew to love listening to him sing, as though I were glimpsing a page from my history with each hymn. He snored with an English accent too, as I recall—though never in church—forming his mouth into a perfect oval and emitting rich, plummy tones.

One Sunday morning, when I began to think I'd seen enough colours and examined an adequate number of necks for one lifetime, I was spared the sermon I could not yet understand. Those of us who were still too young to sit quietly through the last half hour of church were taken downstairs into an enchanting world of music and stories.

It seemed to take forever to wend our way through the choir loft, across a small back room, and down a narrow twisting stairway to the basement, but eventually we assembled in a large Sunday school room where we were told to sit on tiny chairs facing the piano. Taking up the collection was the first thing on the agenda, a wise enough decision, before our nickels rolled under the piano or found their way down our throats. It didn't take long for me to realize I had spent most of my time twisting my nickel inside my handkerchief until it resembled a long, white spike. This took an agonizing amount of time to unwrap as the collection basket moved ever closer. For holding up the process, I had to endure impatient stares from everyone else in my row. Hurrying resulted in my wrapping it even tighter, and finally some kind soul had to help me separate the two or we'd still be there.

Sometime during the following year, Mother enrolled me in regular Sunday school, where I began more serious Bible study, beginning with the same children's stories and hymns that had been taught for the past hundred years. Making this experience even more intriguing was the fact that our Sunday school had a real orchestra—a small one, but real just the same—a piano, a trombone and sometimes two violins to accompany the hymns we were learning.

To a child in the days before television, a slide projector was still an instrument of mystery. Whenever we saw a picture in living colour flashed onto the wall beside the words to our hymns we paid particular attention. I learned to identify the tunes, picking up the lyrics from the others, who tended as most children do to substitute familiar for unfamiliar words. As I listened carefully to the jumble of sounds sweeping over me, I tried to memorize those words I recognized. At the reciting of the Lord's Prayer by the fifty voices in the room, I made a discovery. God's name was Harold. *Our Father who art in Heaven, Harold be thy name.* I had always imagined God having a fancier name like Elephelehu or Obadiah. But Harold? What a relief.

I recited His name with confidence the next Sunday. None of our teachers ever listened closely enough to detect any incorrect pronunciation, so Harold it was for an embarrassing amount of time. The question of a last name never came up.

In the weeks preceding Christmas, I developed a particular problem with *King Wenceslas,* referring to him instead as King Wetshispants, having heard that name sung by the boys in the back row behind the furnace. I imagined him to be one of the 'Weeing Three Kings of Orientar' I had been hearing so much about. At least that would account for his damp state. He remained King Wetshispants to me until after my first Christmas concert. Walking home between my parents in the crisp winter air, thoroughly caught up in the spirit of Christmas, I could not help singing, *Good King Wetshispants look out, on the feets of Stephen!* This revised version of the beloved carol did not go unnoticed or unreprimanded.

"I don't care where you heard it," lectured Mother, "it's wrong. And anyway, nothing good ever came from boys hiding behind a furnace." A sweeping generality to be sure, but one I've kept in mind all the same.

On a subsequent Sunday morning, a disturbing picture of Daniel in the lion's den was flashed onto the screen to gasps of horror from me. The lion, wearing a homicidal grin and a particularly murderous glint in his eye, made me fearful for the safety of poor Daniel. I could not imagine such an alarming scenario inspiring a song. The piano began to play and the older children in a variety of keys began to sing, *O to be a Daniel! O to stand alone...*

My eyes were glued to the lion. Everyone but me sang with increasing joy, as if being torn to pieces by some great hulking beast was something to look forward to. I thought I might reconsider being a Christian. It was beginning to look dangerous. And all this was before I heard that David slew Goliath with a rock, and before people were getting smote right, left and centre. And when Harold smote you, boy—you knew you'd been smitten. This Bible was no Goldilocks and the Three Bears, that's for sure. I was a nervous wreck.

My parents knew their Bible well, answering all childish questions with total honesty and correcting any misconceptions to the best of their abilities. Another glaring inaccuracy presented itself as the years wore on. While trying to explain a recent lesson to my father, I referred to the members of a leper colony as leperchauns. The reality, when explained to me in greater detail than I thought necessary, proved to be less charming than what I had envisioned. Ruined was the picture I had in my head of little red-haired men in green suits, guarding pots o' gold at the end of rainbows. What a sobering experience real life can be.

Our family had no fewer than six Bibles of various sizes and ages in bookcases around the house, many of which I have inherited. One little battered, leather-bound Bible has the following inscription inside its front cover: *Awarded to Willie from the Queens Road Wesleyan Sunday School, for good conduct and regular attendance during 1913.* This one belonged to my father, who brought it with him when he emigrated from England in 1923. He would have been eleven when it was awarded. On a blank page near the front, in a child's scrawl, there is the following warning:

> *Steal not this book for fear of shame,*
> *For in it stands the owner's name.*
> *For if you do, the Lord will say*
> *Where's that book you stole away?*

The warning seems to have worked for only part of this Bible. When I discovered it years later, all the pages were missing after Isaiah, Chapter XXVI, probably misplaced during one of our oh-so-solemn roadkill funerals. What's left of it remains as precious to me as it was to my father on the day it was awarded.

Another Bible I have in my possession from that time belonged to my Uncle William, the youngest of Mother's three brothers who died while serving in the Great War. This was the Bible that Mother read to herself every Remembrance Day, November 11th, at eleven o'clock in the morning, for as long as I can remember.

* * * * *

As children, we played church almost as often as we played house. I borrowed a white shirt from my father's closet, put it on backwards, slipped into one of his suit jackets, and PRESTO! I was ordained. The rule—thought up by me, so naturally to my benefit—stated that whoever owned the minister's costume officiated at the religious ceremony of the day. Of course *that* would be me.

In a village where everyone knew everyone else, most families attended a wedding or a funeral every year, sometimes both and occasionally more than one of each. Because Brussels was largely a community of retirees, funerals were more common, though weddings were by far our favourite functions. Elayne and I rarely missed one if we could help it.

As I had recently been given a long, pale green tafffeta dress with a pink satin sash, two local brides, Shirley and Evelyn, asked me to be their train bearer, while the dress still fit. On other occasions when my presence was not requested, I refused to take the hint, and went to all the weddings anyway. Elayne and I stood outside the church doors for what seemed like hours waiting for the bride and groom to appear after the service. But seeing their radiant faces was not why we had come. We had come for the confetti—stick-to-your-face, hair-tangling, out-of-this-world confetti. Drifts of it decorated the sidewalks and more of it blew into the gutter. And still they threw it until everyone was covered with it and wading through it, and digging it out of their mouths, their ears and their eyes. Passing cars sent clouds of the stuff billowing away behind them. The minute the wedding party left the church, in a blaring of car horns and rattling of tin cans, we dove in headfirst, scooped up as much as our pockets would hold and ran for home leaving a colourful trail in our wake.

Mother donated one of her old nightgowns, with a little lace trim still intact, to use as a wedding dress. It was far too long for any of us, but that was part of the fun. An old discarded lace curtain from the rag bag served as a trailing bridal veil. All the flowers any make-believe wedding would ever need we found in the garden. Strangely enough, grooms were not that hard to find. Confetti—now that was the hardest thing to come by and the commodity most coveted. If we had real confetti to throw at our pretend bride and groom, our weddings were something special. I don't remember anything of note happening after the ceremony—no banquet, no speeches, no honeymoon. I suppose once we ran out of confetti we soon tired of the whole business.

* * * * *

At a time when many families were comprised of three generations living together under one roof, Brussels had not yet developed an aversion to death—death that is confined to hospital beds and funeral homes. A natural part of life, death touched most of the families we knew, and like the family doctor, it still made house calls.

Many of us accompanied our parents to funerals and visitations in the homes of friends and neighbours, where to symbolize their bereavement, a wreath of the darkest burgundy velvet was hung on the front door. Colours have always had a strange attraction for me, especially dark reds, and I loved this particular shade so much I tagged along whenever my parents went to pay their respects to the grieving family, just so I could see it again. Out of all the people who came to the house during the customary visitation period, I imagine I was the only one who came to visit the wreath.

The coffin took up most of the living room of the home, banked with baskets of flowers and surrounded by the family on wobbly metal folding chairs. Although I can recall attending one visitation where the coffin sat on the bed in the bedroom of the deceased, this was exceptional and probably meant that no room in the house was big enough to accommodate the coffin, the flowers, a large extended family and friends all at the same time.

The day I discovered my passion for that burgundy wreath, Mother instructed me outside the front door of our neighbour's house to shake the hands of the grieving family members, and to tell them I was sorry. Sorry for what, I wondered? But I knew if I hoped to see that wreath again, I'd better say it with some conviction. As it turned out, I must have sounded sufficiently contrite because no one held me in any way responsible for their grief. Or at least they weren't holding a grudge. Mother led me over to the coffin so I could see our old neighbour lying there in his Sunday best. I had never seen him looking so peaceful. Or clean. Or orange.

"He looks so natural. Just like he's asleep. Don't you think?" Mother asked. Asleep nothing. He looked dead as a doornail to me. Dead and decidedly orange. Is that what happens when you die, I thought? You become a human Cheezie? Everyone in the room spoke in whispers. Maybe they thought he *was* asleep. I could smell chrysanthemums. That, and moth balls from suits too seldom worn, and salmon sandwiches. A weird combination, but somehow comforting.

There had not yet been time in my life to mull over the intricacies of death, with its unthinkable finality. But of this I was certain. For the loved ones left behind, there was nothing like a death in the family to perk up an appetite. What followed the funeral can only be described as a potluck feast. Mother baked an angel food cake—which I considered fitting under the circumstances—though the kitchen bulged with everything from plates heaped with sandwiches to casseroles, hams and fancy cup cakes—all donated by friends and neighbours. The smaller the community, the bigger the spread. This must have been the origin of comfort food.

Before freezers were a fixture in most homes, it was understood that the mountains of food showing up at the door would have to be eaten within a day or two, or be given away. As a result, some of what entered the house before the funeral left by the same door. Funerals were attended not only out of friendship and sympathy, but sometimes out of need. One or two of the older women in the village—widows of long standing on severely limited incomes—arrived to extend their condolences with empty wicker shopping baskets over their arms. They had no intention of going shopping, or at least not in the usual way. Their need was a well known fact and the women of the village did what they could to help them. They had only to show up in the kitchen, drop their baskets in a corner and leave the room to pay their respects to the grieving family. The women helping in the kitchen, well aware of their circumstances, simply took their baskets, filled them with assorted sandwiches and cakes and returned them to their original spots, considerably heavier. Now the older women were able to leave the house with their pride intact and enough food to last until their pensions came in, or until the next funeral, whichever came first.

* * * * *

With a few more funerals behind us, my friends and I began to understand the concept of death, to treat all manner of dead things with the utmost respect. We knew we could not have a funeral without a minister in his back-to-front shirt, a Bible, a coffin with a body inside, a number of mourners, and of course flowers. Lots and lots of flowers. In fact I had everything we needed to hold a funeral service right there in the back yard. Even bodies were not hard to find. Birds and small animals were always giving up the ghost somewhere in the neighbourhood, and if all else failed, we could wait until Googy-Buzzy brought home an offering for Mother, head him off at the back door and relieve him of his prize.

A box. Now finding just the right box for a coffin could be a problem. We had been known to eat as much as a half-box of chocolates just so we would have a proper coffin for a funeral. It seemed a small price to pay.

Depending on the size of the body to be buried, we sometimes needed to make a few cursory folds and bends to make everything fit right, but we hardly ever had to discard any parts. Tails, wings, ears and legs always fit, given the right twist.

One day when Elayne and I were in a particularly funereal mood, we found a flat and very dead frog on the road, one we hoped had died a quick and painless death. I dug a hole for the grave in the garden. We harvested as many of Mother's flowers as we dared, to brighten the occasion, then spread the word that mourners were required. Borrowing a Bible from the bookcase in the living room, I rooted through it for a suitable passage. This was made more difficult by the fact that I had never paid particular attention to what the minister had to say during real funerals, busy as I was trying to catch the faintest twitch of an eyelid from the dear departed. Elayne, a year younger, remembered even less. So faced with this decision on my own, the easiest solution was to close my eyes and choose a passage at random. Neither of us knew what the words meant, but we were satisfied that a sufficient number of 'thees' and 'thines' made it sound authentic. In any case, the mourners were no more proficient at the language than we were, and they would be the last to argue about semantics.

By promising lunch after the service, we gathered together as many mourners as we could find, guaranteeing a small crowd who hoped the lunch, if nothing else, would be worth the time commitment. As the minister of the day, I looked suitably clerical in a back-to-front shirt, despite two large brown scabs on each of my bare knees, the results of a roller-skating accident earlier in the week. Carrying the Bible, I took my place in the garden at the far end of the grave facing my little congregation of mourners.

The coffin, lined with peony petals and wrapped for the occasion in bright birthday paper, contained the tiny body of Benjamin Moore, so named because of the name printed on the paint stick we planned to use to mark his grave after the service. I don't remember burying anything female, though none of us ever checked. We wouldn't have known where or what to check in any case, so every body we buried was automatically male.

Wracked with sobs and dabbing at an imaginary tear, Elayne carried the box holding poor flat Ben to his final hop, as it were. I think that was an imaginary tear. You could never tell with Elayne. She was a sensitive child. Anyway, real or contrived, I considered the tear to be a sympathetic touch, setting an appropriate mood for this sad affair. After the box had been placed gently into the grave, the mourners in a moment of common grief, threw their wilting sweet peas in the general direction of the hole. Most of them missed the mark and landed on my feet in a tangle of pink blossoms. Taking this as a tribute of sorts, I began the service with a hymn.

God Sees the Little Sparrow Fall seemed suitable even if it didn't mention a dead frog. Besides, with the exception of our favourite, *Jesus Loves Me*, this was the only hymn for which we knew the approximate tune and at least some of the words. Pretend hymnals cut from old newspapers and strung together with yarn, were passed around and the hymn from memory sung—more or less in unison—by those voices present.

We began in a certain discord, sliding headlong into a total demolition of tune and tempo, though even this began to take on a harmony of its own as the hymn progressed. Everything seemed to be going well until two of the more combative members of my congregation took a stab at a differing set of lyrics, and the altercation that followed can only be described as dueling hymnals. Being the minister and all and therefore the boss, I condoned no fighting in the ranks and threatened all dissenters with expulsion, or worse, no lunch.

One of the boy mourners, when asked to say a few words, waxed poetic about poor Ben being struck down in the prime of life.

"Squashed flatter than a pancake in mid-hop. Guts all over the road," was how he put it—followed by sympathetic nods of agreement all around. I considered these words to be a trifle graphic for a eulogy, but I was in the minority. Clearly I should have invited a more refined bunch of mourners.

Reading only the recognizable words from pages near the back of the Bible, I liberally sprinkling my sentences with blesseds, verilys, and thou shalts where and whenever I saw fit. The congregation stood in rapt attention—or as rapt as eight-year-olds ever get—waiting for me to finish rambling and bring on the feast. Sighs of relief accompanied the sound of earth hitting cardboard, as the soil was shovelled back into the hole. Someone stuck in the paint stick that read: BENJAMIN MOORE, R.I.P. 1948. That last part had been printed in black crayon.

The congregation, out of patience by this time, lost their tenuous hold on dignity and galloped as one to the back stoop where lunch sat waiting—a handful of white currants and a fresh unwashed carrot straight from the garden. Those who complained about the grit were reminded that they had to eat a peck of dirt before they died, so they may as well get started.

Wandering off in two's and three's, the mourners seemed satisfied with the afternoon's entertainment, if less so with the repast that followed. We were convinced Benjamin would hop directly to Heaven after such a fitting service, where it would be warm and sunny every day and there would be no cars.

Dangerous Attractions

Across James Street behind the softball diamond, about a hundred yards from first base, the dam at Logan's Mill sat tantalizing those who could swim and even those who couldn't. By necessity, swimming here had to be done early in the summer before the water level dropped, leaving what was left behind dangerously polluted. It took the spring runoff to bring the river back to normal levels, though what was considered normal was usually preceded by extensive flooding. For most of the spring and early summer, the continuous flow of water over the dam kept the area around the flume clear of scum, if not of leeches and snapping turtles—the dam's appeal being less for its esthetic qualities and more for its decided dangers. Neither I nor any of my friends had any real permission to go near the dam—by that I mean we knew better than to ask—so the attraction was overwhelming. Lying on the sun-warmed cement abutment in our bathing suits on a warm spring afternoon gave a welcome intimation of the freedom of summer still to come.

My introduction to deep water came one afternoon when Allan, a classmate in grade five, pushed me into the flume, either as a token of his high esteem or simply to demonstrate his lack of common sense. It was hard to tell with boys of that age. Now I had two alternatives. I could sink to the bottom—and Heaven only knew what horrors lay down there, besides death—or I could learn to swim, and fast. The choice was easy. My natural inclination was to dog paddle, keeping my mouth shut and my face as far out of the murky water as possible. It seemed to take forever to paddle the twenty feet around the cement abutment and through the leech-infested reeds, but as you will have deduced from the existence of this book, I managed to keep all my moving parts churning until I felt solid ground beneath my feet.

Needless to say, this impromptu swimming lesson did not endear Allan to me. At home later in the day, I took our brand-new grade five class picture, and with a straight pin and greater relish than I'd care to admit, poked a few strategic holes in his image. To my knowledge, he felt nothing. I still had a lot to learn about voodoo.

With no diving board at their disposal, the boys took a running leap off the corrugated tin roof of the grist mill to land cannon-ball fashion in the little flume, an area surrounded on three sides by cement walls and the wood and metal mill gates. To our amazement and their extreme good fortune, none of them ever missed the target.

Here in this dangerously intriguing place, Elayne and I smoked our first cigarette. Because I had always been wary of fire, no matter what size, lighting the match had to be done by Elayne, who took this task in her stride. We did not inhale, despised the taste, and repeated the experiment whenever the opportunity arose, which wasn't often. This was the extent of our research into adulthood at the dam, though we knew of a few others who took advantage of the seclusion of the bushes on the far side of the river to solve a few mysteries of their own.

In summer when the tea-coloured water below the dam lay warm and motionless, we waded in the shallow water, startling minnows and tiny crayfish from their afternoon naps. Long hairy moss grew on the rocks littering the riverbed, drifting freely with every movement of the water. We hopped from one rock to the next, screeching when our toes became entangling in the moss. By shifting some smaller rocks we managed to corral a few crayfish and offered them hand-picked grass to eat. They pushed away our offerings with claws like tiny oven mitts, showing little interest in changing their diets. As we had caught them for no other reason than to feed them, we set them free to scuttle under the first rock they could find. Electric-blue damsel flies skimmed the water in search of smaller prey, and dozens of water-striders on long slender legs skated dizzy circles on the surface without ever getting wet.

Closer to the mill wall, in the shadow of the water-blackened boards, flashes of silver darted back and forth between darkness and light. Here, close to the deeper water, the boys fished for sunfish and suckers. We were more interested in the fishermen than in the fish, but it took no time to discover that boys intent on an afternoon of solitary fishing make poor conversationalists. Once every avenue of adventure had been investigated and found wanting, Elayne and I rode off on our bicycles to find more stimulating diversions.

* * * * *

Before I owned a bicycle, I used to sneak rides on my brother's whenever I found it unattended. Still too short to swing my leg over the seat, I stood on the pedals with one leg under the cross bar, my body forming a perfect letter 'C'. When pedalled furiously, the bicycle stayed more or less upright and moving in a straight line. When not, both of us fell to the sidewalk, where I did my best to protect it from damage by hitting the cement first. Despite the occasional scrape, being able to proceed under my own steam was empowering.

I counted the days until I could own a bicycle of my own—even promising to do extra arithmetic homework. This seemed to work the charm. After school one day I found it standing against the shed, a little beat up, but all mine and completely beautiful. It was third hand. I painted it burgundy, my favourite colour until I discovered chartreuse. On the handlebars a rusty bell gurgled more than it rang. A loose rear reflector shook and rattled whenever we hit a bump. I washed both of them. Washing was the extent of my mechanical knowledge—my solution for anything that needed fixing. The reflector continued to rattle and the bell kept its watery gurgle for as long as I owned the bicycle, but at least I was satisfied that everything humanly possible had been done to restore them.

As soon as the burgundy paint dried, I set off to explore a rapidly shrinking world. But without Elayne, cycling wasn't as much fun as I had imagined. Within days she had her own bicycle, a SCHWINN CRUISER with white-walled balloon tires. It may even have been new. Imagine! But that didn't matter, we both had wheels and we were on the move at last.

Few places drew Elayne and me more reliably than the CNR train station. On many lazy summer afternoons we found ourselves on the wooden platform waiting for the afternoon mail train. Sometimes we came early so we could have a look around, and sometimes we came on time but the train was late, which amounted to the same thing. Either way, there always seemed to be enough time to wander into the station to play a game of 'let's pretend we're going somewhere'.

Dominating the waiting room, a black potbellied coal stove cast off the unmistakable odour of coal gas even when stone cold. The hard wooden surfaces of the little room echoed to the clacking of the telegraph machine, whose inscrutable messages were received by Mr. Kerr the Station Agent, wearing his familiar dark green visor. He clacked something back at it, with a little black lever he manoeuvred between his thumb and forefinger. And sometimes he just let it clack away incessantly without getting involved.

Sliding from one end to the other along the smooth wooden benches lining the walls, we viewed the waiting room from every possible angle. A big map on one wall showed all the railroad lines on earth converging on Toronto, the home of EATON'S and SIMPSON'S and the real

Santa Claus. It didn't matter that several rail lines continued beyond Toronto. For me, Toronto was the end of the line—the Emerald City—where all the trains stopped and all the roads ended. I couldn't imagine being farther from home than that.

I placed a penny on the track, if I happened to have one, in the hope that the train would flatten it when it passed by. I would carry it around in my pocket, like the one my father kept with his collection of loose shirt buttons. His coin, reputed to be especially lucky, had been flattened by the train bringing King George VI and Queen Elizabeth to Windsor on their 1939 tour of Canada. My father told me I was born the next year because he owned that lucky coin. He also told me that was our little secret, and I haven't told anyone until now.

With few sounds around the station other than the monotonous clacking of the telegraph machine and the sparrows bickering over weed seeds between the rails, we dug up the courage to put our ears to the track listening for the clatter of approaching wheels. When that first, faint, mournful wail was heard, we bolted back to the platform for fear of losing our heads. The black locomotive, wearing a cowcatcher apron and a smokestack like a top hat, puffed into the station hissing clouds of warm steam onto our bare legs. The conductor swung down from the caboose, checked his pocket watch, and settled down to the serious business of discussing baseball scores with Mr. Kerr. After the incoming mail and freight had been loaded onto a steel-wheeled freight wagon, the conductor jumped back onto the steps of the caboose, and in his special train voice, yelled "BOARD!" Hardly anyone ever did. Maybe he was really yelling, "BORED!" In any case, he waved to us from the veranda of the caboose until he was out of sight. He was bored all right. Flattened or otherwise, I was never able to find my penny again when the train had gone, so after several of these futile attempts I decided that bubble gum was a more reliable investment.

Elayne and I had been warned not to go near the tracks, but like the warnings about the dam, this seemed to make the place all the more attractive. With no trestle bridges and few bends in the track, we felt confident a train could not sneak up on us even if one wanted to. There were long hours between trains and there were new skills to learn. As the caboose disappeared in the distance, we stepped up onto the tracks to practise our circus act, balancing on the rails pretending they were tight-ropes strung far above a cheering crowd. In time, we were able to run on the rails without falling off—very often. David, a friend from my class, could ride his bicycle right on top of the rails. I tried it too, but my back wheel didn't seem to know what my front wheel was doing and it kept slipping off. Maybe you had to be a boy to be able to do that.

After fifteen minutes of this, we too were bored. Nothing left to do now but toot around on our bicycles. Everybody tooted around. If you asked any of us what we planned to do on any given day, we'd say, "Toot around." I don't know where the expression came from, since bicyles don't toot, but that explanation even satisfied our parents. To us, tootin' around meant wandering aimlessly, waiting for something exciting to happen to us or to somebody else within tootin' distance. To our parents it meant riding our bicycles up and down the streets of the village, obeying every traffic rule and remembering every warning we had ever been given about every hazard that ever existed. The reality lay somewhere in between, but probably closer to our version.

The local cemetery, about a mile outside Brussels heading south, wasn't necessarily our last choice for tootin' to. I have always felt curiously peaceful in a cemetery, even as a child. Having had no personal experience with death, I was fascinated by the whole idea and intrigued by the mystery of what, if anything, followed the burial. If we knew of anyone who had been buried recently, we tried to visualize how they must look after a couple of weeks underground. Mostly I just wondered if they were still orange.

The oldest tombstones held the most fascination for us, those whose names had all but disappeared from exposure to all kinds of weather through a hundred winters. Many of them were children's graves. Why had so many died so young? We did not come up with an answer at the time, though I realize now the majority died from diseases for which there were no vaccines or medicines. Living life as a child a hundred and fifty years ago must have been a risky business.

Elayne found a log-shaped grave stone that the two of us could ride like a horse, and here we sat to eat the remainder of our toffee bars. Adrian, the cemetery custodian, cut the grass regularly, dug the new graves, and never tired of our questions. If he was too busy to talk to us, he took the time to show us how to fill the watering can from the rusty hand pump and instructed us to water all the plants growing around the tombstones. Since anything green was a plant to us, the job kept us busy and out of his way for quite some time, until we got bored and went home.

The Brussels Cemetery in its rural setting lay far enough from town to allow us a feeling of independence, but not so far that we couldn't rush home whenever our imaginations got the better of us. Because death has never been an exclusively adult condition, it is fitting to mix together the vigorously living with the peacefully dead. I think all cemeteries should have children playing in them from time to time.

Skating On Thin Ice

Every season brought its particular pleasures, but it was winters I remember best because ours were especially long. I might have lived quite happily without eating all those rust embedded icicles, without freezing my cheeks for one more slide down Adams Hill, or without sticking my tongue to the metal pump handle behind the house, but I could not have survived those endless winters without skates. We skated on natural ice then, either in the village arena or on any flooded, low-lying field that froze solid during the night. Every kid who owned a pair of skates grabbed them when the weather turned cold and headed for the nearest patch of ice.

If that patch happened to be a mile away, we had to get there somehow. With our skates tied together and slung over our shoulders, Elayne and I started walking. It could take a half hour to reach the field, unless we were fortunate enough to catch a ride with a farmer heading in the right direction with his horse and cutter. When he didn't have a load of groceries or a passenger with him, he let us ride up front. But most often we had to hold onto the back of the sleigh, as he pulled us all the way to our destination sliding on the soles of our winter boots.

It was no wonder we wore our boots through to our socks as often as we did.

When we arrived at the patch of ice we had to climb a rusty barbed wire fence in our snow pants, which invariably got caught on the top strand, then wade to the ice patch through snow up past our knees. Only then could we sit on the ice to pull our skates onto feet already numb with cold. We rarely found an ice surface large enough or free enough of debris to skate very far in any direction, but what we did find more than made up for these obstacles.

Unlike artificial ice, natural ice rarely freezes evenly. Skating over those bumps added a touch of excitement to the sport. Sometimes the bumps had been formed by the wind while the water was freezing, and sometimes by a long-lost pitchfork lying tines up just below the surface. A variety of objects lay close enough to be examined as if under glass—fallen tree branches, clods of dirt, clumps of last year's alfalfa, ribbons of dead grass, frozen cow patties, and yes, even a pitchfork.

Field ponds were typically not more than a foot deep, so we would have had great difficulty drowning, but if we *did* fall through we could at least expect soaked feet, and the water was frigid. Whenever we skated onto thin ice, we could hear a faint hissing sound before an explosion of frozen stars burst just beneath the surface. Ignoring these warnings meant a long walk home with cold, wet feet—the spectre of the mustard plaster ever present in the back of our minds.

Most children had skates of one kind or another. Some were new, but most were passed down from older siblings or neighbourhood children, regardless of colour, style, or condition. If we were lucky they fit right away. If not, we wore as many pairs of socks as it took to make them feel snug. It could take a whole year for our feet to grow a size or two, but sooner or later they would fit, hopefully sometime during winter.

* * * * *

By early January all attention centred on the Elizabeth Street arena. Like so many arenas built in the 1930's, ours had a corrugated metal exterior and an interior of tinder-dry wood. The whole thing could have easily transformed itself into an incinerator with a carelessly tossed cigarette or an unattended stove.

Such natural ice surfaces relied on weather being sufficiently cold to freeze water sprayed onto a sawdust base, layer after layer, day after day. In a matter of weeks, if the weather stayed cold, an ice crust formed, thick enough to withstand most January thaws. One particular person was paid to do this cold, lonely work—Watty the rink manager, wearing his navy blue duffle coat and a red-and-black hunting cap with the ear flaps down. He rarely did it cheerfully.

Twice on Saturday and several nights during the week, the young people of the district met at the arena for public skating. We came to see and to be seen, fearing that to miss even one session could mean social extinction. The ice was often so packed with skaters that falling down flat was difficult if not impossible. Tripping, and dragging down those in front of us, was the most likely scenario and the best way to meet visiting skaters.

The admission charge for two hours of evening skating was twenty-five cents, a whole week's allowance for many of us. Quibbling about the entrance fee made little difference to Watty, who offered no credit and quelled his conscience with the notion that a drop in attendance would make his life easier.

The girls' and boys' dressing rooms, wisely separated by the front entrance and ticket office, were each heated by a pot-bellied Quebec heater, continually fed with wood by the irascible Watty. Assuming he ever had a fondness for kids—and I *have* heard stories of sudden, unexplained acts of kindness—by the time I was old enough to recognize it he had learned to keep it a secret. Watty's demeanour seldom changed, no doubt the direct result of having the coldest, most thankless job imaginable. I'm positive he was not paid very much for his labours. We should have thanked him for those long hours spent in the mind-numbing cold—but I don't know of anyone who did. Alone with a hundred noisy kids several nights a week and all day on Saturday, he must have thought a gruff exterior necessary to keep some semblance of order. He was probably right.

An ever-increasing, non-negotiable list of rules was posted at the front entrance:

No mixing of sexes in either dressing room.
No fighting on the ice.
No fighting in the dressing rooms.
No jumping off the boards.
No tossing of hats while on the ice.
No games of Crack-the-Whip—Ever.
Use your heads for Pete's sake. How many times do I have to tell you?
Anyone caught doing anything at all will be killed.

Okay, maybe he didn't post that last part, but I'll bet he wanted to. He meant every word he *did* say, and we knew it. Whenever someone—usually one of the boys—dared to transgress, Watty came charging out of his office and onto the ice, open galoshes flapping and ear-flaps flopping. Pointing an accusing finger at the guilty party, he yelled himself hoarse and purple in the face. With his anger spent and decorum temporarily restored, he disappeared back to his office, slammed the door and waited—ever vigilant—for the next offence.

In all the years I knew him, I never once saw him smile, though the tell-tale laugh lines around his eyes told another story. Maybe he just looked miserable on the outside while he was laughing his head off on the inside—sort of an inside-out Pagliacci.

Watty had definite ideas about the music he chose for public skating. If the record wasn't a waltz with 'blue' somewhere in the title, it wasn't played on his turntable. As a result, we heard the same three or four scratchy waltz recordings every skating night for as long as I can remember. Even now, the first few bars of *Alice Blue Gown, The Blue Skirt Waltz,* or *The Blue Danube Waltz* will immediately transport any Brussels expatriate back to the arena of the 1940's and 50's.

As a rule, girls skated with other girls. The boys stood by the boards in sullen knots or skated by themselves in the centre of the ice under the lights. This was the pattern until the middle of the eighth grade, when something strange happened to all of us at once. In two's and three's the boys drifted over to the boards where the girls had congregated. We did not know why. Nothing like this had ever happened before. The more confident country boys came first.

"D'ya wanna skate or what?" they asked. We did. The local boys, no doubt feeling some pressure from the competition, followed shortly afterward. Fortunately there were enough of us to go around, freeing Watty from having to run out with his ice-scraper to break up the brawl.

Few if any words were exchanged while we held hands through two pairs of thick mittens and skated to one and only one of Watty's 'blue' tunes. When it was over, we were dropped back at the boards without a by-your-leave and the boys glided off as if they'd never been there. It took us an hour to stop grinning.

There were times in late winter when the weather was not cold enough to freeze the ice completely, leaving water hazards scattered here and there over the ice surface. The boys took turns skidding to a stop in the middle of these puddles, sending sheets of icy water over any girl who caught their eye. By early spring, we had developed a high tolerance for skating under water.

One Saturday afternoon during one of these thaws, after Watty had cancelled skating due to poor ice conditions, a group of us waited just long enough for him to drive away in his Model A Ford, before sneaking in the back door to skate through the water in total darkness. We could see a faint outline of the double doors at the end of the arena, but little else. Before long, the surface of the ice became littered with the bodies of the fallen, as skaters running into mushy spots, stumbled, and piled up in sodden mounds.

Our protesting shrieks aroused neighbourhood suspicion and were reported, no doubt with a certain relish. It did not take long for Watty to storm back to the arena—if storming is possible in a Model A Ford—flick on the overhead lights, and threaten us with everything from lifetime expulsion to physically impossible deeds having to do with his ice scraper. Evidently not a man to mince words, he surpassed even himself that day. Trusting we wouldn't be recognized if we didn't hang around, most of us escaped out the back doors the way we'd come in, still wearing our skates. A few of the foolish, for goodness knows what reason, stayed behind to sputter out an apology and were identified. They had to hang up their skates for a whole week. Deep down we knew Watty's anger was justified, so we didn't do it again. Skating in the dark had lost its fascination.

* * * * *

The boards surrounding the ice surface—scarred by decades of skate blades, hockey pucks and dime store jack-knives—served as the only barrier between the fans and the hockey players on the ice, all of whom could be obnoxious at times. Some truly great hockey games were played in the Brussels arena—minor league in calibre maybe, but always major league in enthusiasm. From behind the boards the home town fans stood yelling encouragement, while dodging pucks and sticks that hurtled off the ice with disconcerting frequency. Sometimes there was as much action in the penalty box as on the ice, as opposing team members sitting out penalties waged private battles with overeager fans. This unsportsmanlike behaviour brought swift justice from the referee, and occasionally from the whole opposing team. Free-for-alls were frequent and bloody during championship play, ensuring a standing-room-only audience for every game. In an arena cold enough to freeze ice, standing was the only comfortable position in any case.

Throughout the summer months the arena remained dark, empty and locked. From early April until late December Watty kept busy hanging wallpaper and painting for those who had not acquired the skills for themselves—his rink duties a distant memory.

Today, whenever I hear one of Watty's waltz tunes—and mercifully that isn't often—I can still see him standing at his box office window, his head wreathed in pipe smoke, glowering out at us as we skate in the same tired circles, to the same tired music, week after week, winter after winter. Not one of us would have missed it for the world.

On With the Show

Early March brought the last blast of winter to Brussels and the first stirrings of excitement surrounding the annual Variety Revue. Anyone with a desire to be in the spotlight heeded the call to audition—never letting a lack of talent stand in their way. That was just as well. If our director had depended solely on those with genuine talent, no doubt she would have been directing a much shorter revue.

Staged in the town hall auditorium each year, the Revue was scheduled for four evenings in April, with opening night six weeks from audition. One year a three-act musical of the children's fairy tale Cinderella appeared on stage, but most often the Revue involved a series of song and dance numbers loosely based on a theme.

Evelyn, a woman with insight and superhuman patience, came up with the master plan, the script and the cast of characters, though assigning roles to match individual personalities and degrees of talent must have been a fearsome task. I am sure there were times at the beginning of rehearsals when our hopelessness caused her blood pressure to rise, but I never once saw her lose her temper.

Volunteer committees met on a weekly basis to prepare the props, and to design and sew the dozens of costumes needed. Others offered their time for dressing room duty, applying makeup, helping the younger cast members with their costume changes, and generally making sure we were ready for the spotlight when it was ready for us. The volunteer musical directors displayed commendable spirit, working their way through countless pieces of music with unflagging dedication on the old upright piano, freshly tuned for the occasion.

On the night of auditions we were drawn to the town hall by some irresistible force. One or two performers took to centre stage as if they'd been born there. The rest of us, suffering untold agonies, had to be coaxed from the safety of the wings. For most of us, these moments in the spotlight every year would be the only ones we would ever know. But for a few, the Revue represented an important start to a lifetime of performing. Those with genuine talent worked alongside those with little or none, and the results were always delightful.

Successfully performing an audition piece proved us worthy of a role, though anything short of throwing up and fainting dead away assured us a part somewhere in the Revue. If she had any misgivings, Evelyn gave us the benefit of the doubt, trusting that we'd grow into our parts as rehearsals progressed. From years of experience, she knew who would be right for each role, and there were always enough roles to go around, even if she had to invent some. Although not exactly a cast of thousands, the list of performers approached and often exceeded a hundred, one-eighth of the total population of the village—almost everyone between the ages of five and eighteen.

For those who were shy, the security of the chorus was the best solution. Here the words to a song could be mouthed or a few easy dance steps stumbled through in relative obscurity until the curtain closed. Some years the choruses were large and numerous, not always reflecting a lack of talent but rather a lack of confidence. As with Dr. Johnson's performing dog, the wonder was not that we did it well, but that we did it at all.

For the younger girls, half the fun of performing was being able to wear the makeup we were not permitted to wear at any other time. Despite the fact that rouge had been applied with a certain abandon to every cast member, most of us blanched in terror as soon as we stepped into the spotlight.

Draped in gold-fringed royal maroon velour, the stage looked almost grand, though slightly incongruous considering the straight-backed wooden chairs that seated our audience. Off-stage, a series of pulleys opened and closed these curtains as if by magic.

From a walkway behind the scenes, three doorways hung in the same maroon velour opened onto the stage, allowing for dramatic entrances, exits and the occasional practical joke. From experience we learned to stay clear of these areas during performances or risk serious interference.

At one performance of Cinderella, a bashful Prince Charming, already feeling vulnerable in his lumpy tights, was tripped during his entrance and somersaulted onto centre stage, where he lay spreadeagled, staring up the hoop skirt of one of the ugly sisters. It was a novel position from which to try on the glass slipper, you must admit. After this incident, even the shyest performers preferred centre stage to the great unknown of the darkened doorways.

*****

One year, after my mother and another volunteer agreed to sew the costumes for two of the musical numbers in the Revue, the second volunteer promptly left for an extended Florida vacation with her family. It would take more than a setback like this to discourage someone as stage-struck as Mother. Without a moment to lose, she threw her considerable energies into the job, planning and buying and cutting material until all hours. But the budget would not stretch far enough to cover the cost of making costumes envisioned by a woman who had seen too many Broadway shows during her time in New York. Suddenly her housekeeping money found a new and more pressing need, and as I recall, we ate homemade soup for weeks.

The calendar had become her enemy. Mother turned our living room into a sweat shop with herself the sole exploited worker. Yards of black satin were transformed into five can-can dancer costumes for the Moulin Rouge number, with frilly lace petticoats caught up at one side to reveal a shapely young thigh. The teenage cast members for whom they were made admitted to feeling a little naughty in them, and had to be coaxed into removing them after the initial fitting.

By now the costume budget had been ravaged, and nothing remained but a few yards of trim and Mother's boundless imagination. Representing just the first of her triumphs, the Moulin Rouge costumes seemed only to whet her appetite for the challenges ahead.

When she began to design the costumes for the harem number, in which I had a role, she was penniless and out of supplies. Enormous amounts of translucent material were needed to fashion the harem pants and skirts, and she dared not think about the sheer, sequinned veils she had planned to complement the costumes. The limited budget and the donated supplies were not going to be enough.

Mother worked long into the night trying to design a costume around the bits of material she had left over, but it was no use. There would have been a scandal. She had run out of everything but ideas. Now this was not the first obstacle she had encountered in her life, and she had never been stopped before. Slowed down, maybe. But stopped, never. If anything could get my mother's juices flowing, it was adversity. So it wasn't surprising that an ingenious idea soon presented itself.

The next morning, my father came downstairs to a brighter than usual living room, with Mother still hard at work at her sewing machine, and several harem costumes in varying degrees of completion draped over all available furniture. In the great tradition of Scarlet O'Hara, she had removed the curtains from the living room windows and stayed up all night making five harem costumes from the sheer material. Admiring her hard work with exaggerated enthusiasm seemed the safest road, and one my father had been down before. Nothing could be done with her once the adrenalin started pumping, and he knew it. The Revue was a hit that year. When it was all over you could say the curtain came down on our act in more ways than one.

* * * * *

Some years, if the Revue was successful enough to pack the town hall for all four performances, we were invited to take the show 'on the road' to one or two of the surrounding communities, who were apparently starved for entertainment. For us these were intoxicating evenings, when totally unfamiliar audiences brought out the best and sometimes the worst in our performances. Springtime also brought its share of seasonal illnesses, making necessary more than a few last minute cast changes, where a new and inexperienced cast could turn a well-rehearsed number into a series of pratfalls.

I encountered this situation the year I was chosen to be the knobby-kneed Sugar Plum Fairy—singing *Pretend* in front of a chorus of six tiny fairies in short white tutus with little gauzy wings. Although I was only eleven, the even younger fairies, ranging in age from four to six, were at the perfect age to underscore any gawkiness I may have had. Unfortunately, I had not yet heard W.C. Field's warning about never sharing the stage with dogs or small children, so I stumbled blindly into chaos.

All went well the week we played to a home town audience, or at least as well as it ever did with an amateur cast. Everybody knew their places and stayed, for the most part, in them. However, the five day lay-off between performances allowed sufficient time for my fairies to contract everything from chicken pox to tonsillitis. The director called for four replacements—a second string, if you will—who represented the tiny daughters of parents who were confident their darlings could do it better if only they had the chance. Their chance had come. Since time constraints did not allow for new costume fittings, they simply had to muddle through with whatever was available.

My new set of fairies included one so tall she wore her borrowed tutu as a belt that came nowhere near what it had been designed to cover. The chubbiest of the fairies filled her tutu to bursting, appearing at first glance like a well-fed butterfly emerging from its chrysalis. The scruffiest fairy, unable to find a pair of clean white socks for the evening, opted for bare feet, which by show-time looked as if they too had been dry since Prohibition. And still another arrived with a chip on her shoulder, ready to pick a fight with any fairy foolish enough to look in her direction.

With a sinking feeling, I led my fairies onto the stage that night to the usual outpouring of love and affection from every mother in the audience. Twirling to my spot at centre stage behind the microphone, I prepared myself for the worst. The pianist gave me my cue and I began to sing, trying with all my might to sound as if I'd taken at least one singing lesson in my life, which I had not. This would be stressful enough when things were going well—but when the fist fight broke out behind me and the lyrics brought nothing but laughter from the audience, it took all my self-control not to run screaming from the stage. Suddenly I was in a skit with the *Six Stooges*.

When ignoring this melée didn't work, a strange desperation took over. I waded in among the warring factions, rapping the dissenters on the head with my wand in a vain attempt to distract them, all the while singing what I hoped were the correct words. *"Pretend you're happy when you're blue..."* I sang, bending over to separate two feisty fairies tumbling about the stage in a no-holds-barred brawl. *"...it isn't very hard to do..."* I continued, or whatever words I could remember as I pulled one fairy's tiny hand from another's tiny curls. My unrehearsed ballet routine of three twirling steps—Bop! Two graceful leaps—Bonk! And a quick twirl—Whack! kept the fairies off balance, if not completely under control. I couldn't appreciate it at the time, but this unrehearsed mayhem took our routine in a whole new direction. The audience went wild. Who would have thought? And their laughter confirmed my suspicion. We were now doing slap-stick.

With my tiara askew and my makeup in desperate need of repair, I waded through the clashing hordes to the microphone, where I ended my song a good six bars ahead of the pianist—such was my superior musical ability. The crowd loved us. Unbelievable. At the end of the number I made a deep bow of gratitude to the audience for not throwing tomatoes, and exited the stage as gracefully as I could behind my little band of hooligans.

The applause went on and on. The audience wanted more. Were they mad? I for one had no intention of ever being seen in public again. However, someone in the darkened wings had other ideas and shoved me back onto the stage. Six bedraggled fairies followed me, tripping and crashing into one another in a frantic attempt to wave to their mothers over the blinding footlights. More applause. This uncritical, and to my mind unjustified, adoration was an eye-opener. I guess you can't really lose when you share the stage with six little girls. You can lose control, certainly. And you'll lose the spotlight every time. But if you roll with the punches, so to speak, you might be surprised at the outcome.

We left them laughing that night, and because this was the last performance of the Revue, we didn't have to prove to anyone we could do it again. Next year we would have a new show, with a new cast of characters and probably a whole new set of calamities. I could hardly wait to audition.

Changes in Attitude

While my father offered indiscriminate credit to his customers in the community, he considered it unacceptable to incur any debt of his own. Most of the profits from the store were channelled back into the business as a defence against leaner times, which arrived like clockwork every February. My parents limped along through this quiet period taking inventory and making plans to branch out into other more profitable lines of merchandise which they hoped would carry them further than February. Nothing ever did.

Rarely clearing more than a hundred dollars in sales for a six-day work week, my father relied heavily on his watch repairing skills. If his customers were going through a similar slump, he had been known to accept anything from a gallon of maple syrup to a jute bag of potatoes or a few limp chickens, as payment for his hours of watch repairing. Together my parents struggled through the hard times, tightening their belts when they had to and putting a little aside whenever they could.

Our store, like the business itself, was a small one. My father could stand anywhere in his store and see every piece of merchandise he owned, which he did whenever he needed a psychological boost. He lost very little to theft in the thirty-four years he was in business, though that may say more for the good citizens of the community than for his eagle-eye. Two women with tendencies toward kleptomania lived in the village, but both were brought to my parents' attention by their husbands. Their weaknesses were not of a moral nature as both were honourable women who lived exemplary lives apart from their conditions. Not often, but once in a while, they had an uncontrollable urge to take something. Both had a special fondness for things shiny, so our store was particularly appealing to them. They were allowed to take whatever caught their eye that day without anyone doing or saying anything to stop them. Their husbands brought everything back the next day, as prearranged.

My father had only two shoplifters worth remembering. One returned later the same week to try to sell the stolen goods back to him while the items were still hot, as the saying goes, price tags intact. The other also returned a stolen watch with the request that it be engraved with his full name. Now when your weekly sales total around the one hundred dollar mark, you have pretty well memorized every sale you've made. It was not difficult to spot the stolen merchandise. The hard part was doing anything about it. In both cases my father settled for having his merchandise back, and the culprits were kept under closer scrutiny whenever they entered our store. Only in a village where everyone knew everyone else, plus most of their extended families, would something like this happen. Other than these few occasions, things were pretty mundane by city standards.

The sale of a diamond ring, that harbinger of another spring wedding with its associated bridal showers and trousseau teas, always put new zip in my father's step. His customers needed gifts for these occasions, and he was counting on some of the sales coming his way. They usually did. Once again young love would keep my father in business for another year.

A cardboard sign hanging behind my father's workbench read: "Work hard eight hours a day and don't worry. Some day you'll become the boss, work twenty-four hours a day and have all the worry." That particular maxim, as much as anything else, has kept me out of the retail business.

My father suffered from asthma for most of his life, though his health deteriorated notably in the spring of 1950 when a local chicken farmer, in an effort to expand his business, set up five thousand chickens in the cow pasture closely bordering two sides of our house. Opening the windows in the heat of summer was no longer an option. If the noise did not drive us crazy, the smell surely would. The dust alone brought on severe asthma attacks for my father whenever he ventured outdoors. Allergies were not taken as seriously then as they are today. Explaining his plight to the farmer got him nowhere. He was a prisoner in his own home, or so it seemed to him. One summer went by and then another, with no relief in sight. The chickens were thriving in their new quarters, but at home my father was not. By early 1952, it was obvious he could not live in such close proximity to an open chicken farm, nor could he continue to walk the six blocks to work and back in winter when the frosty air caused him to gasp for every breath. Nothing short of moving would eliminate the chicken problem, but a car might have been the logical solution for his winter woes. I was beginning to think our ship had sunk.

"We've walked this far. We can walk the rest of the way," was my father's response to any and all arguments to the contrary. Debt of any kind caused him sleepless nights—paying cash the only solution worth considering.

Out of the blue, my parents decided to sell our house and move to the apartment above the store. Doing so would spare my father the cold walks home in winter and the daily bouts of asthma at any time of year. This made sense to everyone but me, whose self-absorbed teenage years had burst onto the scene in a somewhat typical manner—with whoops of joy one minute and moans of despair the next. Chickens or no chickens, the thought of moving back to the main street brought me more despair than I could ever remember feeling. I liked living in a quiet house well removed from the main street. Where could I go to get away from it all? Not that I knew of anything I needed to get away *from*. Still, how could they expect me to accept this move without question? My parents were ruining a perfectly good life. Mine.

All the moans I moaned, all the tears I shed made little difference to the final outcome. After all, my parents were the same two people who had lived through two world wars, the misery of the Great Depression and enough personal loss to last three lifetimes. They were not about to have a perfectly sound plan sidetracked by a little misplaced teenage angst. We owned the entire building on the main street and we were moving to the apartment above the store, and that was the end of it.

And so in June 1952, in a dismal mood even for a twelve-year-old girl, I moved with my family out of our beloved house, away from the gardens and my 'thinking tree', back downtown to yet another cramped apartment above yet another store. We had come full circle, and this to me did not spell progress.

My parents tried to ease me into this new situation by allowing me to decorate my bedroom any way I chose, which I did, with debatable results. It seemed it would take more than a few rolls of gaudy wallpaper to make me feel at home. My tiny bedroom sat next to our tiny kitchen. Next door to the kitchen would not have been an accurate description in this case, since initially my bedroom did not have a door—one that I could shut or lock or slam, or anything else I would gladly have done had one been in place. Such a complete lack of privacy added another dimension to my torment.

To compound my misery, none of our house-sized furniture fit any of the long, narrow rooms. Mother, in an attempt to turn the apartment into our old home, flatly refused to get rid of anything. Suddenly every stick of furniture she had ever owned became more precious than gold. When distributed evenly throughout the eight large rooms of our house, the feeling had been one of airy comfort. But with the same furniture crammed into every square inch of space within five rooms of unsuitable dimensions, it was a horror show! None of us could walk across any room in a straight line. The living room was a labyrinth. Bruised shins were common. We were trapped again, this time in a used-furniture warehouse. I wanted to move back to the house immediately. My family ignored me.

"She'll come out of it the way she went into it," was Mother's matter-of-fact take on things. Mine was slightly less optimistic. "I can't live like this," I whined. "My life will never be the same again." Looking back on the situation, I can see that I considered life never being the same again to be a bad thing.

Given a little time and the necessary changes of space and attitude, even I had to admit life was improving. It had certainly become more interesting. Without any official police presence in the village, certain young men held impromptu car races on the main street late every Saturday night while my parents were trying to sleep. During a brief pause in this dangerous entertainment, while the racers were preparing for a pass in the opposite direction, a parade of revelers as merry as crickets stumbled out of the Legion Hall across the street, to a hail of abuse from their wives who waited none too patiently in the cars lining the street below. Suddenly I had a box seat to a view of life unfamiliar to me. My parents found this less charming, and secretly renamed the village Dodge City, which all things considered, seemed appropriate. Can you imagine if Brussels had had a town crier? There he'd be, roaming the main street every night in his tri-cornered hat, ringing his hand bell as he dodged speeding cars, irate housewives, and tipsy husbands, all the while crying: "Twelve o'clock and all's as well as can be expected under the circumstances!"

In any event, I was beginning to feel more in tune with my community and its pastimes, warts and all. What *had* I been missing stuck out on the edge of town, where nothing ever happened, and the loudest noise was made by a chorus of bullfrogs? There could be little doubt my life had changed—for the better.

* * * * *

With the Fabulous Fifties now in full swing, vacations were no longer the rare occurrences they had been in the 1940's. As money became more available, almost every family we knew owned a car of some kind. But with our garage still empty, we stayed home all year unless we travelled by taxi, train, friend or relative. Every trip we made had to be planned days and sometimes weeks in advance, depriving our lives of any semblance of spontaneity. At least that's how Mother expressed it, and she expressed it often.

After one exceptionally weddingy June, while my father was in Toronto restocking the store, our long-awaited ship sailed close enough for Mother to drag it to shore single-handed. Tired of the years of slogging along on foot, on an impulse she bought a car. It wasn't brand new of course, nor did she know how to drive it, but that was a minor impediment. Doug was old enough and willing to learn in a hurry. A man from the local car dealer drove it to the back door of our store, where the three of us stood admiring it from every angle.

It was into a vastly different world that my father stepped down from the ten o'clock train five nights later. All four of us were there to meet him—Mother, my brother, myself, and Gladys, as the car was now affectionately known. I thought saving my father from the long walk home in the night air to be a stroke of genius on Mother's part.

Stunned into silence, my father decided to reserve judgement until all the facts were in. Fearful of a lull in the conversation, Mother continued to rattle on about regaining our independence, about the car's long list of superior qualities that would soon become evident, and about the great deal she claimed to have made.

Gladys was a turquoise semi-automatic 1952 DeSoto Grandiose, or some such name—as with Googy-Buzzy, more a feeling than a name really. She had something called Fluid Drive Ultramatic Transmission, if I remember correctly, and seats of dove-grey plush as soft as butter. Long before power anything had been invented, Gladys had power nothing. Her steering, her brakes and her windows took so much effort to operate you could actually see your muscles bulging whenever you turned a corner. She sported nearly as much chrome as paint, and to at least three of us, simply oozed possibilities.

My parents rarely discussed money, or the lack thereof, in front of Doug and me, but on this occasion they made an exception. It had been a rather sudden and sizable purchase to make without my father's consideration. Even we had to admit that. But we were confident the advantages far outweighed the risks, and anyway we did not dare show a sign of weakness at this point.

Looking back on the event from a safe distance of fifty years, I think my father's main objection to suddenly owning a car was that his teenage son knew how to drive it, and he at fifty, did not. Never having owned a car, there had been no reason for him to learn. Gladys was about to give him reason.

Professional driving instructors were miles away in the city, so in order to protect a sound father-and-son relationship, a neighbour offered to teach my father to drive. He learned to steer without much trouble, but having been given only two feet to work with, it took longer to master the subtleties of the clutch, brake and accelerator, not to mention the levers and buttons for which this semi-automatic was famous. Because my father started driving so late in life, he had difficulty feeling totally comfortable behind the wheel. Each time he stepped on any of the pedals, it was as though he were touching them for the first time. The various foot pressures required for each pedal also took some time to become instinctive. In the meantime Gladys could be seen hopping down the lane behind the store like some enormous, turquoise jack rabbit.

One of my father's most endearing characteristics was his total lack of direction—in the driving department I mean—a trait he lovingly passed on to me, if somewhat watered down. Doug taught him the routes to three towns close enough to visit on his Wednesday half-day closings, each with a fellow jeweller at the other end. One route took him to Wingham, the other two to Seaforth and Listowel. Although he knew all the routes well, in the beginning he could never quite remember which town lay at the end of which road, and sometimes he became disoriented at finding a town that turned out not to be in the same place twice. I was with him on one such magical mystery tour which began as a predetermined trip to Wingham. On this occasion he turned left onto Turnberry Street headed south in the opposite direction.

"Daddy, we're going the wrong way. I thought we were going to Wingham."

"What makes you think that?" he inquired, with the tone of mild irritation he used when discussing directions. "Anyway, we went to Wingham last time."

"Where are we going then?"

"You'll see. It's a surprise." It was a surprise to both of us, if the truth be known.

One of us always tried to accompany him on these little adventures, afraid that if he were left on his own he might get lost and have to drive around for days before he found a familiar landmark. Like so many of his gender, my father refused to ask for directions.

It has been my experience that some, okay, most men will ask for directions only when touring in a foreign country whose language they do not entirely comprehend. And then only if they are dying of thirst.

That way it's more of a challenge. Christopher Columbus refused to ask for directions to India, and look where that got him. I think it's a biological thing.

Even though owning the car had not been his idea, in time my father learned to appreciate what it could do for him. He was now able to meet other jewellers he had heard about through the travelling salesmen who visited our store. And soon he acquired a new set of friends with the same work and worries he had been struggling against for years.

Cars, delivery trucks, fire engines, even the hearse from the funeral home used the back lane behind our store, across which sat our garage. One Wednesday afternoon early in his driving career, my father prepared to back out unguided onto the laneway, with me in the passenger seat. He pressed a little too hard on the gas pedal and we exited the garage going thirty miles an hour backwards. Lucky for us we were stopped by the woodshed behind the drug store. While adjusting my body speed from 0 to 30 mph in two seconds flat without benefit of seatbelt, I tested the flexibility of the metal dashboard with my forehead. It is not something I care to repeat. What might have happened had a gasoline truck been passing the garage at that moment? Or the hearse for that matter?

I learned a valuable lesson that day, though I had to sit in a dark room for a while to remember what that lesson was. With my father behind the wheel and the open road uppermost in his mind, if I did not guide him onto the laneway, there was a good chance we'd both be killed before we cleared the garage. When the dust settled, we found the shed the worse for wear, but Gladys completely unscathed. A mere woodshed was no match for all that chrome.

Over the years my father continued his battle to feel comfortable behind the wheel, with varying degrees of success. He drove Gladys the way he played table tennis—though not nearly so well—attacking the task side-on with quick, jerky movements, as if he had been welded into one rigid block from his waist up. If this position made him feel confident, it did not have a similar effect on me.

"Loosen up, Daddy." I suggested, as kindly as a teenager can suggest anything. "Don't hold the wheel so tight. It looks ridiculous."

"It's a big car," he argued, glaring at the road ahead. "I have to show it who's boss."

He might have been a natural driving a horse and buggy, but as luck would have it, he missed that era. For years he continued to drive with no further mishaps—more than I can say for my brother and myself, who drove poor Gladys into objects both moving and stationary with alarming regularity. A few years later my father sold the DESOTO, positive it would kill one of us if he didn't.

Our next car, a nearly new, multi-toned, 1957 hardtop CHEVROLET EXTRAORDINAIRE with Triple-Turbo Glide or something, had far fewer levers and pedals, but sported two fabulous fins that went on forever. Best of all, it had not as much chrome to polish. If it is possible to love a car, I loved Gladys II more than any car before or since. My parents owned her for seven years, but I was at home to enjoy her for only two of them.

At the end of the seventh year, Mother, now a recent widow and still without her driver's licence, sold the car to a young man from the village—who immediately flipped her into a farmer's field. Gladys II, unlike Gladys I, lacked the durability of a Sherman tank. The last time I saw her she had four wheels in the air and a very disgruntled look on her grill. Such an undignified end to an otherwise elegant life! There would never be a Gladys III.

TV or Not TV

Life hummed along much as it had always done, until one day in 1953 when a sudden change came in the form of a large wooden box named PHILCO. Two delivery men carried it up the stairs to our second story apartment and placed it on the floor in one corner of the living room, where it sat displaying two large plastic knobs beneath a blank 17-inch glass screen. Mother and I stood staring at the screen until one of the delivery men took pity on us and plugged it in. Never before or since have so few shades of grey brought so much joy.

PHILCO was of course a television set, forever after known as TV, and it made an even greater difference in our lives than Gladys. Suddenly the sophistication of faraway places sprang to life right there in our living room. Concealed under a hinged plastic flap we found two smaller knobs that would prove to be indispensable—the vertical and horizontal hold knobs. In the beginning of this wondrous technology, the picture had a nasty habit of flipping head over heels, or getting the heebee-jeebees and bending to impossible angles, usually in the middle of the most exciting part of the program. Nothing could be done about it unless someone spent five minutes standing in front of the screen twiddling these little knobs while everyone else in the room offered useless advice. By this time we had lost the thread of the story anyway, so it didn't really matter.

The furniture in the living room, whose former arrangement we had only recently memorized, was repositioned to face the new Mecca, resulting in yet more bruised shins. On those lucky mornings when conditions were perfect—that is to say if there were no storm clouds in the area and no idling trucks on the main street below—we could pull in a distant Detroit signal. This meant we could eat breakfast watching Dave Garroway, and watch live street scenes from New York City. On these occasions Mother sighed a lot and looked strangely wistful. After all, there was her beloved New York, just across the breakfast table, but still worlds away.

Before long, nearly every roof in Brussels sprouted a spindly metal antenna, poised to grab any unwary television wave that floated by. These antennae attracted more than television waves—they also attracted a good many lightning bolts and every ice particle ever formed in the atmosphere. After one of our early spring ice storms, buckled and twisted aerials hung like dead insects from gabled roofs or lay in tangled heaps above the apartments along the main street.

The orientation of the antenna determined which station we could watch through the least amount of snow. Adjusting the direction was accomplished by twisting the dial on a brown plastic rotor box, which sat on top of every television set next to the all-important TV light. And any family who cared a whit about their eyesight was advised to have a TV light. This advice took a while to sink in though, as many people still confused television with the movies—sitting in living rooms like darkened caves, but for the ghostly blue flicker from the screen. A bat would have felt right at home.

Our TV light was a square glass beauty, filled with tacky pink and yellow plastic roses set over a blue ceramic base which held a small light bulb. The whole contraption lit up when we turned it on, the roses glowing as if endowed with some supernatural power. There it sat, as quietly as was possible given its wild combination of colours, saving us, we believed, from a lifetime of blindness that would surely result from watching television in any room close to being dark. Some TV lights were made entirely of seashells. Others stretched the imagination to impossible lengths—plaster of Paris being one of the more popular mediums, with plastic running a close second—each one a work of art. In truth, it was a toss-up whether we were in more danger of losing our eyesight or what remained of our good taste. I know I still have my eyesight.

The stations we were able to watch, whose signals could find Brussels, would broadcast for only five or six hours a day. But like true converts, whenever those stations were on, we kids were watching. Hypnotized behind drawn drapes in the pale glow of the TV light, we watched anything that moved—or didn't move.

On Saturday afternoons before my family owned a television set, Elayne and I sat ready, cross-legged in front of her parents' set, well before the station signed on. From our places on the living room rug, we stared at the test pattern, featuring the Indian Chief resplendent in war bonnet, with feathers in every glorious shade from grey to black. The test pattern was commonly used by the repairman when he needed to adjust the set for picture quality during an actual house call. Unaware of that fact, Elayne and I assumed the test pattern was a vital part of the daily programming schedule, and as such, gave it our undivided attention. Whenever a car with bad spark plugs drove by, the picture flickered and the Indian Chief jumped, looking for all the world like he'd stuck his finger in a light socket. Signal interference or not, that was movement enough for us.

"He moved," shouted Elayne. "I saw him move. Didn't you see him move?"

If he moved at all, he didn't move far, and never once did he change that stony expression. We kept a close eye on him anyway, just in case he got the urge to do it again.

We were hooked, no doubt about it, and the addiction spread quickly from one home to another and far out into the countryside. Assuming they ever had it, many families lost the ability to carry on a conversation within the viewing area. To make matters worse, portable sets were soon brought into the kitchen for viewing at mealtime, and into the bedroom at night to watch THE LATE, LATE SHOW. Meaningful conversation, once the mainstay of a civilized society, was now not only unnecessary, but unwanted. TV had taken control.

Before the 1950's we had managed to live reasonably normal lives without a regular movie theatre in the village. Now our appetite for visual entertainment was insatiable. And far from the only appetite to be satisfied—snacking while watching television became virtually mandatory. The sales of cookbooks full of delicacies to be consumed while watching television reached immense proportions—as did many of the TV viewers.

One of the gastronomic delights enjoyed in our home at the time consisted of a slice of day-glo orange processed cheese on white bread, topped with a few strips of well-marbled bacon, and the whole mess broiled to greasy perfection. Mother served this with a blob of ketchup and our pickle of choice. Incredible. I can feel my arteries snapping shut at the thought. Besides being thoroughly devoid of nutrition, every snack had to be fast. Nobody wanted to waste one minute of valuable time in the kitchen cooking when they could be watching their favourite TV program? JIFFY POPCORN in its fascinating expandable, throw-away pan appeared shortly afterward. I don't believe it was legal to watch a TV movie without JIFFY POPCORN. The era of 'fast food' had arrived.

Like zombies from some Japanese monster movie, the moment the television screen lit up we felt an uncontrollable urge to stuff our mouths with food—any kind, as long as it was sugary, salty, or greasy. A dangerous habit had been formed and we seemed powerless to stop it. A constant bombardment of 30-second food advertisements did not help. We drank copious amounts of milk, but most of the time we added heaping spoonfuls of chocolate powder. My favourite TV commercial for QUICK featured a wooden dog puppet named Farfel: "N-E-S-T-L-E-S—NESTLE'S makes the very best ... cho-o-o-o-clate," he sang in a tone-deaf baritone, snapping his jaws shut like an alligator at the end of the familiar jingle. With that final snap still ringing in our ears, we took off running to the nearest refrigerator. Primitive advertising, perhaps, but it worked well enough for NESTLE'S.

The enormous Baby Boomer generation that came along shortly after the War was old enough now to make its wants known, and if the TV commercials were any indication, what it wanted more than anything else in the world was breakfast cereal—preferably pre-coated with sugar. Advertisements for sugar-coated this, sugar-frosted that, and honey-smacked everything else ate up much of our viewing time. No one complained. The commercials were every bit as entertaining as the programs.

While few mothers were as obsessed with nutrition as they are today, the preponderance of sweetened foods may have had more to do with the times. With the memory of the Great Depression and the scarcities of wartime and the rationing system still vivid in most mothers' minds, they were happy just seeing us eat anything we wanted to eat, at any time of the day or night. The stores were full of food, and it was cheap. But why stop with food? The TV commercials told us what to buy next. "Buy stuff," they demanded. "Fill your house with stuff. Fill your life with stuff. And when you're tired of it, throw it away and buy bigger, better stuff." Consumerism was rampant—instant gratification the hallmark of the Fabulous Fifties.

When larger refrigerators with separate freezer compartments began to appear in every kitchen, frozen foods had to be invented to fill them—foods that would make daily shopping a thing of the past. BIRD'S EYE and SWANSON had been waiting for just such an opportunity, and within months they flooded the market with waxed cardboard cartons full of frozen vegetables and fruits, orange juice, and even entire meals on individual aluminum trays, precooked and ready to pop into the oven. Every self-respecting freezer hid a few foil-wrapped TV dinners—for emergencies you understand. TV dinners did not taste the same eaten from a regular table in the kitchen, nor would we have contemplated eating them in a room without television.

Each dinner included two or three slices of rainbow-glazed roast beef, or some other kind of batter-covered mystery meat, all accompanied by a dollup of overcooked potatoes, a spoonful of wrinkled peas, and up in the top left-hand corner, a tiny serving of soggy apple cobbler. Every item on the tray tasted much the same as every other, though to kids my age, this was not considered a bad thing. Better still were the evenings when Mother was so busy with one of her club functions she couldn't be home in time to prepare supper. A choice of TV dinners waiting in the freezer kept us from falling over in a dead faint, choice being the essential factor. We ate them from rickety metal TV trays—forever awash in spilled milk—their long spindly legs attracted passing feet like magnets.

As you might expect, anything that brought such a drastic change to our lives was not universally accepted. Some of the older members of the community were skeptical at first, refusing to buy this new-fangled gadget, convinced it was nothing more than a passing fad, or worse, a Communist plot, cleverly designed to undermine their frugal way of life. As if the Communists could dream up Little Richard, with his mile-high hairdo and incomparable singing style. Or for that matter, Gorgeous George, the blonde, bejeweled wrestler in the ermine-trimmed cape, who carried an out-sized perfume atomizer with which to spray his adoring fans. Nobody could put the blame for either of these characters on anyone but their God-fearing American promoters. Bless them.

Unrestricted television viewing can be an incredible time waster, but it can also be an ever-present, uncritical friend when one has nothing but time to waste. It wasn't long before the seniors of the village discovered television's special attraction for themselves, and soon they too were hooked.

My friends and I grasped this innovation with all the enthusiasm of youth. Experts on the subject claimed that if the current level of mindless programming continued, before long we would become a generation of antisocial morons. Now I am no expert, but I do know the baby boomers went on to become the most highly educated generation in history—with only a few antisocial morons among them.

To our everlasting gratitude and to our parents' revulsion—which seemed only fitting—Elvis, the smouldering sensation from Tupelo, Mississippi wriggled his way onto the small screen, courtesy of the

Ed Sullivan variety show. With his signature duck-tail haircut and bad-boy pout, Elvis gyrated behind the microphone to the sheer delight of every girl old enough to stay up past eight o'clock. Although the cameramen were instructed to film him only from his waist up—to preserve our virginities or something—every girl found him far more captivating than squeeky-clean Pat Boone, if he'd been televised stark-naked.

As with most innovations, the novelty of TV began to wear thin after the first few years, and most of us, now teenagers, returned to our former passion—the radio. Song writers of the time were losing their minds altogether, coming up with song after song about such uplifting subjects as airplane crashes and fatal car accidents. Not to be outdone, many of the musicians went right out and had actual plane crashes and car accidents, taking one-upmanship a bit too far and denying the world decades of their best music. Those who were not depressing all of us or getting themselves killed were busy writing songs with movements built in. New dances had to be learned on a weekly basis so we could dance to the songs that were written about those dances. For a deadly dull decade, the Fifties at least kept us moving in sync.

Around this time, the Russians launched the first Earth orbiting satellite named *Sputnik*—which naturally was not visible from Brussels—and the space race with the

United States was on. Something called the Cold War raged unabated in Europe—which was also not visible from Brussels—and nervous nellies all over North America began building bomb shelters and instructing school children to dive under their desks at the first sign of trouble. Lucky for us, the Russians didn't want to be vapourized any more than we did, and the whole thing fizzled out after nearly half a century of nail-biting near catastrophes.

Miles away in the city, newly constructed indoor shopping malls began to attract their first generation of teenagers. Brussels didn't have a mall. We were stuck in an age of all-weather shopping with everything that this entailed—steamy sidewalks and umbrellas in summer, overcoats and snowboots in winter. New things were happening every day, but all of them were happening somewhere else. It was obvious the world wasn't coming to Brussels anytime soon. I had endured eighteen long seemingly uneventful years. It was time to go.

* * * * *

Mine had been a safe and happy childhood. With the exception of the dark, I had never really been afraid of anything, and I did not fear what lay ahead now. Growing up with love and trust had enabled me to develop an independent spirit that exhausted all but a few childhood experiences. Now I longed for something different—something I hoped was waiting for me in the Emerald City.

"Union Station!" announced the conductor, rocking his way through the passenger car, "This way out!"

I stood up, swept what remained of the memories from my winter coat, swung my suitcase down from the overhead rack, and following the conductor out of the train and into my future.

He who has once been happy, is for aye
Out of destruction's reach.

–Wilfred Blunt

No animals were harmed in the writing of this book.

ISBN 141201120-5